The Psychology of Physical Attraction

D0583739

People have long been interested in the complexities of human beauty, but until recently the science of attractiveness was largely left to poets, playwrights, philosophers, and artists. This book begins the task of providing a scientific look at physical attraction, by presenting an overview of scholarly work on physical beauty, culture, evolution and other aspects of human attractiveness.

The Psychology of Physical Attraction begins by discussing the role of evolution in the development of what it means to be 'attractive' in contemporary society. It provides a general overview of evolutionary psychology and mate choice, as well as an in-depth focus on physical characteristics such as physical symmetry, body weight and ratios, and youthfulness. The book goes on to explore the role of societal and cultural ideals of beauty through a discussion of the social psychology of human beauty. Finally, the 'morality' of physical attractiveness is examined, looking at issues such as discrimination on the basis of looks, body image and eating disorders, and cosmetic surgery.

Combining both evolutionary and social perspectives, this book offers a unique and comprehensive overview of the many debates involved in the science of physical attraction which ultimately allows for a better understanding of human beauty. It will be of interest to students and researchers in psychology, as well as anyone interested in the science of physical attractiveness.

Viren Swami is an evolutionary and social psychologist. He is the author of academic papers on, among other things, interpersonal attraction, gender roles and cross-cultural differences. He is also the author of *The Missing Arms of Vénus de Milo*, and has translated works of literature by George Orwell, Jorge Luis Borges and Franz Kafka into Malay.

Adrian Furnham is an organisational and applied psychologist, management expert and Professor of Psychology at University College London. In addition to his academic roles, he is a consultant on organisational behaviour and management, writer and broadcaster. He is a prolific writer for both the popular and academic press, and one of the most quoted contemporary experts in his field.

The Psychology of Physical Attraction

Viren Swami and Adrian Furnham

Routledge
Taylor & Francis Group

LONDON AND NEW YORK

First published 2008 by Routledge
27 Church Road, Hove, East Sussex, BN3 2FA

Simultaneously published in the USA and Canada
by Routledge
270 Madison Avenue, New York, NY 10016

*Routledge is an imprint of the Taylor & Francis Group, an informa
business*

© 2008 Routledge

Typeset in Times by RefineCatch Limited, Bungay, Suffolk
Printed and bound in Great Britain by
TJ International Ltd, Padstow, Cornwall
Paperback cover design by Design Deluxe Ltd

The publication has been produced with paper manufactured to strict
environmental standards and with pulp derived from sustainable
forests.

British Library Cataloguing in Publication Data
A catalogue record for this book is available from the British Library

Library of Congress Cataloging-in-Publication Data
Swami, Viren, 1980–
   The psychology of physical attraction / Viren Swami and Adrian
Furnham.
        p. cm.
   Includes bibliographical references and index.
   ISBN 978-0-415-42250-5 – ISBN 978-0-415-42251-2
1. Interpersonal attraction.   I. Furnham, Adrian.   II. Title.
   HM1151.S83 2007
   302′.12–dc22
                                                       2007018537

ISBN: 978-0-415-42250-5 (hbk)
ISBN: 978-0-415-42251-2 (pbk)

For my mother and father, Mira and Mohan Swami

VS

For my exceptionally attractive wife Alison, and son Benedict

AF

Contents

Figures

Plates

1 In many species of animal, males have evolved elaborate 'ornaments' to seduce members of the opposite sex. For Darwin, males tend to court, while females tend to choose.

2 Due to their exaggerated nature, mate-attracting signals – such as the large tails of peacocks, deer antlers, the bright colouration of some species of fish, or the horns of a stag beetle – can prove to be a hindrance to an organism. Why, then, do such ornaments evolve?

3 Hair colour and style is an important individual marker and treated fetishistically in many cultures.

4 In almost all cultures, men and women differ in their complexions: in general, women are fairer, while men tend to be darker.

5 Many European paintings of the eighteenth and nineteenth centuries, including Édouard Manet's *Olympia*, show a white woman with one or more black servants who are often depicted holding out pearls, coral, or other valuables to their mistresses. Both the servants and their offerings are signs in the social construction that marked the women as fair and beautiful.

6 The women in paintings by Pieter Pauwel Rubens often depict stylised plump figures that defined exuberant sensuality in Renaissance Europe. But Rubens was not idiosyncratic in his taste: the 'ideal' woman in seventeenth- and eighteenth-century Europe was plump, even overweight, by today's standards.

Tables

Preface

The perception of the beautiful is gradual, and not a lightning revelation; it requires not only time, but some study.

Giovanni Ruffini, Italian novelist (1807–1881)

The tale of the scientist interested in physical attraction

In 1961 Jürgen Habermas described how the coffee houses of eighteenth-century London and Paris had gradually become centres of political, artistic and literary criticism, where 'opinion became emancipated from the bonds of economic dependence'. The coffee houses – where any new work, book or musical composition worth its salt had to get its legitimacy – became a forum for self-expression, for airing opinions and agendas for public discussion. In the twenty-first century, it sometimes seems as though the coffee house has been replaced by the blogosphere, a realm where the major burden is not actually in writing but in reading.

Traipsing through the blogosphere, the bored scientist strikes upon a seemingly novel idea: she or he begins to seek out bloggers' discussions of her or his research. After all, to know that your research has reached the blogosphere is to know that your work is being discussed by the people who really matter. And sure enough, the scientist finds what she or he is looking for – discussion of their work is intense, vocal, even contentious – and the scientist is happy. But for the scientist interested in physical attraction, this episode in self-aggrandisement can be quite trying. For this scientist, his or her work is all-important, perhaps even a little earth shattering; for the blogger, a common riposte is whether scientists should be spending their time agonising over physical attraction. Surely there must be more important things to worry about than whether the 'eyes have it' or whether you really should not judge a book by its cover?

Given the cold reception afforded to the scientist-interested-in-physical-attraction, in cyberspace at least, one might ask why we have chosen to write an entire book on the topic. Well, for one thing, the transmission of scientific knowledge from one end to the other is often akin to the whispering game, where a line of people is given a message at one end, which is whispered to the next person down the line, until it gets to the other end. The final recipient then announces the phrase that he or she has heard, usually much distorted from its original. For the scientist-interested-in-physical-attraction, the whispering game can be particularly infuriating: when her or his research reaches the end of the line, it has usually been detached from any semblance of context. Rather, their research is used to suggest that one celebrity is more attractive than another, or that the average person is not attractive because he or she 'has not got the right (fill in body part as appropriate)'. One reason for this book, then, is to add a little context back to research on physical attraction.

A second, and equally important, reason for this book is that physical attraction is far from trivial. We may like to *believe* that it is, that we are sophisticated beings capable of transcending mere physical appearance, but a great deal of psychological research suggests that – in short – beauty matters. Of course, this does not rule out the possibility that future generations may come to view the perception of others based on their appearance as a particularly repulsive phenomenon of earlier generations. But in order to arrive at that goal, it will first be necessary to understand *why* human beings are so fascinated by physical beauty. After all, human beauty has occupied the minds of artists and poets and philosophers for centuries, which makes it a legitimate topic of discussion (if nothing else, scientists should also be allowed their say, even if belatedly in comparison with their more artistically minded cousins).

Finally, scientists are human beings too, and as such we sometimes succumb to human frailties: we are just as capable as anyone else of admiration, appreciation, wonder and awe in the face of beauty; some of us may even fall victim to vanity, narcissism and of course infatuation. All of which makes the topic of human beauty particularly interesting for scientists. Of course, there is no reason why science should only be about finding a cure for cancer, or seeking out distant galaxies or inventing the next supercomputer. Unravelling the riddles of the human mind – including what makes a person attractive to others – is no less daunting a task. And if scientists can have some fun while working towards unravelling those riddles, so much the better.

Alas, these reasons alone may not be sufficient to placate the more loquacious blogger. In which case, we would direct their enmity at our editors, Lucy Kennedy, Tara Stebnicky and Dawn Harris, whose idea it was for this book and whose support has been unceasing. Many others have also helped along the way: Martin Tovée, David Frederick, Dorothy Einon and Chris McManus are all fellow scientists-interested-in-physical-attraction (among other things), and have greatly influenced our ideas. Henry Plotkin, Debbi Stanistreet, Don McCreary, Malgorzata Rozmus-Wrzesinska, Martin Voracek and John Cartwright have (often unknowingly) shaped the way we think about these issues more generally. As always, any errors and omissions herein are ours alone. Countless others – too many to name individually – have assisted us with data collection around the world, as others have with statistical analyses (Alaistair McClelland deserves special praise). Many hundreds of participants have taken part in our experiments, and the scientific fruits of that labour are as much theirs as ours. And, of course, there are the bloggers – perhaps this short book might give them pause to contemplate.

Viren Swami and Adrian Furnham
London, 2007

1 What Pythagoras unleashed upon the world

There is certainly no absolute standard of beauty. That precisely is what makes its pursuit so interesting.

John Kenneth Galbraith, author and economist (1908–2006)

Is beauty beautiful, or is it only our eyes that make it so?

William Makepeace Thackeray, author (*The Virginians: A Tale of the Last Century*, 1859)

Pythagoras, a Greek mathematician and philosopher of the sixth century BC, is often credited with attempting the first systematic investigation of physical attractiveness (Armstrong 2004; Swami 2007). For Pythagoras and the ancient Greeks, beauty was a matter of having the right proportions, or 'golden ratios', and the same principles that governed the beauty of the human face or body also dictated what was beautiful in architecture, music and art (Gaut and Lopes 2001; Horn and Gurel 1981). Perhaps the most famous example of the application of Pythagoras' principles is Leonardo da Vinci's *Vitruvian Man*, which relates Pythagorean proportions to human anatomy. But so consumed are we with attractiveness that there are many countless more examples of the incessant quest for the 'secrets' of beauty (see Figure 1.1).

Although the Pythagorean view of beauty remains much debated today, what it aspired to was an overarching explanatory framework for understanding one of the most urgent questions for psychologists and philosophers. Attempting to understand every aspect of physical attraction is today one of the most vibrant avenues of research within the psychological sciences, and – like its Pythagorean predecessor – continues to be debated vociferously by academics and lay persons alike (Swami and Furnham 2006, 2007). This book, then, is an attempt to review, appraise and summarise this research, and articulate just what makes the science of physical attractiveness so interesting, even if contested. It provides an assessment of the structure of motivations and processes that lead to the consequences associated with physical attractiveness.

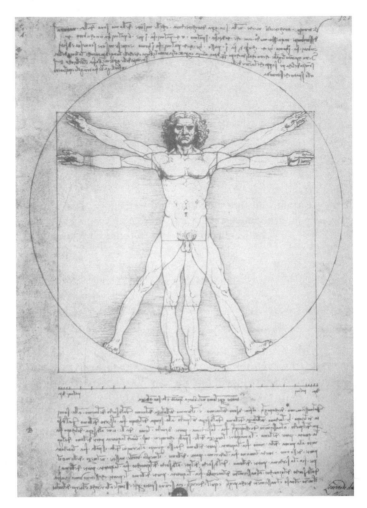

Figure 1.1 Leonardo da Vinci's *Vitruvian Man* (c. 1492), which epitomises the pursuit of objective standards of beauty. The idea that that are mathematical proportions of the human body that define human beauty – an idea borrowed from the ancient Greeks – was considered one of the great achievements leading to the Italian Renaissance. Leonardo da Vinci's drawings, including the *Vitruvian Man*, combine a careful reading of ancient texts with his own meticulous observations of actual human bodies. Copyright © Bettmann/CORBIS.

More specifically, this book is about the evolutionary, social and cross-cultural psychology of physical attractiveness. It draws upon a wide range of disciplines, which is perhaps inevitable given the nature of the topic, to examine what is often an overlooked subject matter. Of course, anthropologists and zoologists, biologists and cosmetic surgeons, sociologists and psychologists, philosophers and artists have all attempted to address the question of physical attractiveness from their respective points of view. But rarely has there been a readiness to combine perspectives under an overarching theoretical framework, an aspiration not unknown to the ancient Greeks.

This reluctance stems from a number of different causes. At a fundamental level, different disciplines invariably ask different questions. Thus, social psychologists find it difficult to separate physical attractiveness from interpersonal interactions (Hogg and Vaughan 2005), suggesting that the two are clearly linked (see Figure 1.2). For such researchers, individuals are attracted to others for a host of reasons, only some of which concern physical appearance. In addition, social psychologists tend to view physical attractiveness as a *gestalt*, and are interested in when, how and why people find others attractive. Often, they attempt to trace the instant of initial attraction through time, from friendship formation to falling in love, being in intimate relationships to marriage. Attraction is thus understood within, and cannot be separated from, the social context in which it takes place (Hogg and Vaughan 2005).

Evolutionary psychologists, on the other hand, are more interested in physical attractiveness per se rather than the process of attraction (Symons 1979). More than any other field of psychology, save perhaps psychoanalysis, evolutionary psychology attracts considerable ire and passion. There are the believers in the original doctrine of evolutionary psychology; then there are those who have attempted to update, revise or even reverse the original doctrine while remaining 'believers' in some sense; and, of course, there are the non-believers. There appear to be no agnostics here, and although this fact

Figure 1.2 For social psychologists, attraction cannot be separated from the social context in which interpersonal relationships take place.

alone does not always make for good science, it can be an excellent catalyst for debate. What evolutionary psychology offers the science of physical attractiveness, then, is a parsimonious and powerful theoretical account of why certain human features are more attractive than others. While not everyone may be in agreement with such a perspective, it is nevertheless undeniable that evolutionary psychology has driven forward the science of physical attractiveness in recent years.

Evolutionary psychological theories are adaptationist and stress a common, or universal, 'human nature'. While it is, in principle, possible to envision an evolutionary psychology that takes into account ecological and environmental variation, in practice most evolutionary psychologists have sought to describe universal psychological mechanisms that govern a variety of behaviours. Moreover, the time frame of evolutionary psychology, stretching as it does over many thousands of years, sometimes implies that we are all captives of our ancestral past, not least when it comes to physical attraction. In this sense, most evolutionary psychological theories of physical attractiveness do not emphasise transnational or cross-cultural differences in standards of attractiveness. Paradoxically, there has been immense interest in cross-cultural and historical studies of physical beauty, often driven by evolutionary psychological theories. Specifically, many anthropologists and cross-cultural psychologists have challenged the notion of a universal and uniform human nature, suggesting instead that patterns of attraction are variable and malleable.

To be sure, there are numerous fascinating accounts of cultural practices designed to enhance a person's physical attractiveness (Darwin 1871; see also Swami 2007: 38–39). Whether it is the facial scarring once popular in Europe (scarring sustained during duels were a sign of courage) or the adornments and behaviours of various tribes still in existence (such as lower lip disks or neck elongation), to pluck but two examples, men and women have clearly sought to enhance their physical attractiveness throughout the ages (see Figure 1.3). These and many other examples serve to demonstrate the lengths to which individuals will go to enhance their physical appearance. Moreover, some researchers have argued that modern-day practices, like dieting to achieve a certain body weight or cosmetic surgery, are no different to the tribal or historical practices of appearance enhancement (Jeffreys 2005).

At a more basic level, it seems obvious that standards of attractiveness vary across the globe. As any international traveller will profess, just as different cultures have different etiquettes and societal rules of behaviour, so what is beautiful in one country or culture may not be considered quite so beautiful in another. What cross-cultural psychologists and anthropologists have done is systematically to test physical attractiveness judgements in different cultures. Thus, they have shown that the socioeconomics, ecology or culture of a country or region can have a powerful influence on who we find attractive, and why.

Figure 1.3 Throughout the ages, disparate cultures have used a variety of practices and adornment to enhance an individual's physical attractiveness.

Consequential, not trivial

In short, then, there is a rich, lively and growing body of literature on physical attractiveness, which forms the basis of this book. While we have interpreted this corpus of research and knowledge as an objective documentation of the physical attractiveness phenomenon, some who read this book may be uncomfortable with such an approach. Some people might object that the topic of physical attractiveness is trivial; it is the substance of glamour and fashion magazines, armchair psychology or conversation fillers, and not real science. Scientists should get on, they might argue, with studying real topics of importance, like intelligence or mental illness, and not physical appearance.

Yet a wealth of psychological and sociological studies on what is now recognised as 'lookism' have documented that a person's physical appearance can have an immediate and profound impact both on the way they are treated by others and how they view themselves (Patzer 2002). Indeed, a poll by the *Observer* newspaper in 2003 found that both women and men have an above average interest in their physical looks, suggesting that physical appearance is an important part of their everyday lives (Mann 2003). It is quite possible that, of the many individual characteristics people have (emotional intelligence, morality, personality traits and so on), it is physical attractiveness that has the largest impact on their life course. Quite clearly, then, such issues are far from trivial (see Chapter 2).

While some people refuse to acknowledge or downplay such a role for physical appearance, others react to evidence of discrimination based on appearance with indifference, disagreement or even anger (Patzer 2002). Yet others might assert that physical attractiveness is in the proverbial eye of the beholder. Certainly we acknowledge this possibility: at some level, all judgements of beauty are in the eye of the beholder. But alongside this, too, decades of research and experience suggest that individuals tend to agree, accept and identify with the physical attractiveness phenomenon.

Our point, of course, is not to condone or even legitimise what can sometimes seem a contemporary infatuation with physical attractiveness. Rather, it is important to acknowledge that, whatever one's opinions about its legitimacy, an individual's physical appearance does have an enormous impact on his or her psychological well-being, at least in most of the cultures in existence today. This does not rule out the possibility that future societies may come to view the physical attractiveness phenomenon as an aberration or other such triviality. But, insofar as such an ideal is both alluring and achievable, it is necessary first to understand why most contemporary societies place such an emphasis on physical attractiveness.

The psychology of physical attractiveness

This book, then, attempts to answer two related questions: *why* do we find certain others physically attractive, and *what* is it about them that we find attractive? While different viewpoints are raised and emphasised, the primary concern of the book is with the evolutionary psychology of physical attractiveness. The simple reason for this is that, in recent years, there has been an explosion of research deriving from evolutionary psychological thinking. There are now numerous studies that provide an evolutionary explanation for why we find certain characteristics on certain individuals physically attractive.

To understand the evolutionary psychology of physical attractiveness, however, it is first important to understand a number of general principles concerning an evolutionary approach to psychology, and this is the focus of Chapter 3. In Chapter 4, we provide a summary of research inspired by evolutionary psychology, focusing on such aspects of the human form that are considered attractive, including symmetry, certain facial features, leg length and hair colour. But to provide a more in-depth analysis of an evolutionary approach to physical attractiveness, we consider preferences for body weight and shape in Chapter 5. Indeed, we have carried out a number of these studies ourselves, but the point of a detailed examination of one aspect of evolutionary psychological thinking is to introduce a critical analysis.

While we have been inspired by the breadth of evolutionary psychological thinking, we remain unconvinced that evolutionary psychology will be able to explain all facets of human behaviour. In particular, we think it unlikely that evolutionary psychology will be able to provide the best explanation for cross-cultural variation in preferences of attractiveness (Chapter 6). Moreover, while there have been numerous studies on physical attractiveness inspired by evolutionary psychology, critical analyses of these have been lacking. We present a preliminary attempt at such an analysis in Chapter 7.

What is needed, in our view, are more considered theories that make use of an evolutionary framework, but which nevertheless view human beings as the social creatures that we no doubt are. In other words, an evolutionary approach to psychology is necessary, but not sufficient, in explaining why physical attractiveness matters. Hence, we return to some of the key concepts introduced by a generation of social psychologists studying physical attractiveness in Chapter 8. This chapter focuses more on the process of physical attraction, which we feel is vital for any understanding of how we come to view other individuals based on their physical appearance.

The pursuit of physical attractiveness, whatever its causes, can have profound implications for individuals, governmental policies and society at large. For example, the physical attractiveness phenomenon asks us to confront important questions concerning the nature of our respective societies, and the value that we place on an individual's appearance. Might not such an emphasis lead, in some cases, to the incessant pursuit of an ideal of attractiveness that remains out of reach? Moreover, is – or should – the pursuit of beauty ideals be a legitimate and meaningful goal for individuals in the twenty-first century? These and other questions are considered in conclusion in Chapter 9.

Not so very long ago, any scientific attempt to understand physical attractiveness would have been met with disdain: human beauty, it was widely believed, should be left to those who truly recognise it, namely artists and possibly philosophers. For others, any attempt to define physical beauty rendered the concept meaningless; beauty, for them, is a quality not easily reduced to scientific analyses. Yet, it seems intuitive that there is something we can recognise as physical beauty, something with the power to influence many different aspects of our lives. The attempt to understand this object of desire is the theme of this book. But, as we set off on this quest, a brief warning from Francis Quarles seems in order (cited in Gilman 1980):

> Gaze not on beauty too much, lest it blast thee; nor too long, lest it blind thee; nor too near, lest it burn thee. If thou like it, it deceives thee; if thou love it, it disturbs thee; if thou hunt after it, it destroys thee. If virtue accompany it, it is the heart's paradise; if vice associate it, it is the soul's purgatory. It is the wise man's bonfire, and the fool's furnace.

2   What is beautiful is good

The good is always beautiful, the beautiful is good!
John Greenleaf Whittier, poet ('Garden', 1882)

Beauty is truth, truth beauty – that is all
Ye know on earth, and all ye need to know.
    John Keats, poet ('Ode on a Grecian Urn, 1820)

It is amazing how complete is the delusion that beauty is goodness.
Leo Tolstoy, author (*The Kreutzer Sonata*, 1889)

Two common and age-old axioms of beauty are that 'beauty is in the eye of the beholder' and that we should 'never judge a book by its cover' (Langlois *et al.* 2000). The idea that beauty is in the beholder's estimation, for example, proposes that physical attractiveness is idiosyncratic or specific to each individual, and consequently a poor criterion on which to evaluate others. And even if there were agreement about who is attractive, received wisdom urges us not to 'judge by externals'. We should endeavour to look for a person's real, inner beauty, and not treat them solely on the basis of their appearance, a fleeting measure, if any. As Shakespeare put it in *The Passionate Pilgrim* (1598/2003):

Beauty is but a vain and doubtful good;
A shining gloss that vadeth suddenly;
A flower that dies when first it 'gins to bud;
A brittle glass that's broken presently;
A doubtful good, a gloss, a glass, a flower,
Lost, vaded, broken, dead within an hour.

And goods lost are seld or never found,
As vaded gloss no rubbing will refresh,
As flowers dead lie wither'd on the ground,
As broken glass no cement can redress,
So beauty blemish'd once 's for ever lost,
In spite of physic, painting, pain, and cost.

Yet a great deal of psychological research suggests that physical appearance is perhaps the most accessible trait of an individual, and plays a powerful, dramatic and sometimes surreptitious role in our everyday lives (Langlois *et al.* 2000; Patzer 2002). When meeting someone for the first time, for example, we form instant judgements, 'putting together' an impression of that person from all the information we perceive. We form a mental image of her or him, integrating all our biases and knowledge into a consistent picture of how we expect that individual to behave (see Figure 2.1). This 'first impression' can persist and strongly influences our interactions with that person (Schneider *et al.* 1979).

The formation of first impressions occur instantly (Baron *et al.* 2006) and, as the name suggests, they are heavily biased in terms of what people initially notice in others. Specifically, they are based almost entirely on non-verbal cues, particularly physical appearance (Park 1986), which can have up to four times the impact of verbal cues on initial impressions. Part of this is down to the fact that we focus on cues that we believe will provide information about another's personality, values and principles – what Asch (1946) termed 'central traits'. This process of impression formation tends to follow the simplest and easiest route (Baron *et al.* 2006), which means placing individuals into social categories based on their physical appearance. Of course,

Figure 2.1 When we meet someone for the first time, their physical appearance plays an important role in the judgements that we form about them. By integrating all our biases and knowledge about others, we form first impressions that persist and strongly influence our interactions with others.

first impressions can, and often do, change; the point is, however, that physical appearance influences how people interact with others and feel about themselves.

What is beautiful is good

Over the years, numerous studies and reviews of the literature have shown that physical attractiveness and appearance do indeed have an important and predictable effect on the judgements that people make about others (Dion 1974; Eagly *et al.*, 1991; Langlois *et al.* 1995; Snyder *et al.* 1977). Nor does this merely involve strangers we encounter in our everyday lives. Rather, our interactions with people we know well, including friends, family and colleagues, often involve attributions made on the basis of their physical appearance (Cook 1971) – which may be as much of a surprise to them as it is to us. But what exactly is the effect and content of such biases of perception?

In their meta-analysis of over 900 studies, Langlois *et al.* (2000) reported that individuals were treated differently based on the extent to which they were perceived as being physically attractive. Specifically, attractive people were judged more positively than less attractive people, even by those who knew them. Langlois *et al.* (2000) concluded, therefore, that despite the proclamations of received wisdom, physical attractiveness does have an enormous influence on our everyday lives. Whether enacted consciously or otherwise, we treat people we perceive as attractive more positively than we do people we perceive as less attractive.

In a now classic study of this effect, Dion *et al.* (1972) had participants rate, on a range of different measures, facial photographs that differed in physical attractiveness. They found that physically attractive individuals were rated more positively on different personality traits and probable life outcomes, such as marital happiness and career success. This led Dion and her colleagues (1972: 285) to claim that, in people's perceptions of others, 'what is beautiful is good'. This effect has since come to be known as the physical attractiveness, or beautiful is good, bias (Alley and Hildebrandt 1988; Berscheid and Walster 1974; Dion 1981, 1986; Hatfield and Sprecher 1986).

The original study was not without its limitations, but the fundamental finding has been replicated many times over the years. For instance, attractive individuals are judged as more honest (Yarmouk 2000), less maladjusted and disturbed (Cash *et al.* 1977; Dion 1972), happier, more successful and more sociable than less attractive individuals (Dion *et al.* 1972). Attractive people are also reported to be afforded more personal space, more likely to win arguments, more trusted with secrets and generally considered better at everything in comparison with less attractive individuals (Cash and Soloway 1975; Horai *et al.* 1974; Patzer 1985).

Nor are these inferences only directed at adults (Corter *et al.* 1978; Hildebrandt and Fitzgerald 1981): the available evidence suggests that attractiveness biases can also be directed at infants. Stephan and Langlois (1984), for instance, asked North American undergraduates for their first impressions of infants from different ethnic groups. Their findings indicated that the most physically attractive infants were regarded more favourably than the least attractive babies, regardless of ethnicity. Moreover, people we expect to be 'fair' often succumb to the same pressures: studies have reported that teachers assume attractive students are more likely to be academically successful than less attractive students (Adams 1978; Clifford and Hatfield 1973).

In another early study, Landy and Sigall (1974) had male students grade one of two essays of different quality, to which were attached a photograph of the supposed writer, a female student. In one condition, the 'good' essay was paired with an attractive photograph and then with a relatively unattractive photograph; in a second condition, the 'poor' essays were paired with

Figure 2.2 Attractive individuals are more likely to be hired than less attractive individuals, particularly for jobs requiring a great deal of interpersonal communication. So widespread is this bias that most institutions now dissuade applicants from attaching a photograph to their applications.

each of the photographs. As expected, Landy and Sigall (1974) found that 'beauty is talented': better grades were given to the attractive female student in both conditions – a finding that has important practical consequences for the way examinations are marked. Furthermore, such biases continue throughout the lifespan: as compared with less attractive individuals, attractive people are more likely to be hired for jobs (see Figure 2.2; Dipboye *et al.* 1977; Swami *et al.* in press, a; Watkins and Johnston 2000) and receive higher starting salaries (Dipboye *et al.* 1975).

Beautiful, therefore innocent

Another area in which attractiveness biases have been found to have a profound effect is in the courtroom, where attractive defendants benefit from more lenient sentencing than less attractive defendants (Cash *et al.* 1977; Mazella and Feingold 1994; Stewart 1984). Of course, it is difficult to gauge the effect of physical attractiveness on perceptions of criminality in real courtrooms, and as a consequence most studies have relied on mock juries. Still, these studies find, almost without exception, that physically attractive individuals are treated more leniently than less attractive individuals, both in terms of perceived guilt and sentencing (Darby and Jeffers 1988; Kulka and Kessler 1978; Solomon and Schopler 1978).

Castellow *et al.* (1990) expressed this effect in quantitative terms: less attractive defendants were 2.5 times more likely to be found guilty by mock jurors than were attractive defendants. Similarly, guilty verdicts were 2.7 times more likely when the plaintiff was attractive than when she was less attractive. More worryingly, Stewart (1980) showed that physical attractiveness, as a factor affecting judgements of criminality, was not restricted to mock jurors: real-life judges were also found to respond the same way mock jurors do when sentencing. That is, in the eyes of judges, the more attractive the defendant, the more he or she is deserving of a lenient sentence.

Other studies have shown that mock jurors consider sexual harassment more likely when the defendant is less attractive, or when the plaintiff is attractive (Castellow *et al.* 1990; Wuensch and Moore 2004). In simulated rape trials, for example, attractive defendants were sentenced more leniently than unattractive defendants, and defendants who were accused of raping an unattractive victim were less likely to be perceived as guilty than those were accused of raping an attractive victim (Jacobson 1981). It may be that (mock) jurors perceive physically attractive litigants as also having other socially desirable characteristics, thus rating them higher than less attractive litigants on attributes such as sociability and intelligence (Castellow *et al.* 1990).

However, some research suggests that the attractiveness bias is moderated by the type of crime for which the defendant is charged. In particular, the attractiveness–leniency effect decreases in strength when the defendant 'uses' his or her attractiveness in committing a crime (Sigall and Ostrove 1975). For

instance, when an attractive (mock) female defendant was accused of burg-
lary, a crime unrelated to her attractiveness, she received a more lenient
sentence than an unattractive defendant. By contrast, when the defendant
'used' her attractiveness in the crime (a swindle), the advantages of attractiveness in sentencing were lost (Sigall and Ostrove 1975; but see Wuensch
et al. 1991).

To date, the literature on the practical consequences of the attractiveness
bias remains relatively underdeveloped, but it is potentially as important as
any other aspect of physical attractiveness that has been studied. Indeed, it is
interesting that employment discrimination based on physical attractiveness
is still permitted, despite legislation prohibiting employment decisions based
on other non-occupation-related factors such as ethnicity, sex and disability
(Watkins and Johnston 2000). Nevertheless, when and how often appearance-
based decisions occur remains in dispute. Experimental studies have certainly
shown that it does occur, but inevitably the specific results are sometimes
equivocal.

As an example, Heilman and Saruwatari (1979) showed that attractiveness
can not only be a benefit but also a handicap to women seeking employment. They found that attractive women were penalised for their appearance
when attempting to gain entry to managerial positions, although physical
beauty worked in their favour when they sought access to non-managerial
jobs. Similarly, Shahani-Denning and Plumitallo (1993) showed that when
an employee had committed a mistake, supervisors were more likely to perceive those who were attractive as failing because of a lack of effort. By
contrast, those who were less attractive were perceived as failing because
of bad luck, suggesting that they may fare better when found guilty of
misbehaviour.

This may mirror an important exception to the attractiveness bias, what
some researchers have termed the 'dark side' of beauty (Bassili 1981; Dermer
and Thiel 1975). Cash and Janda (1984) later termed this the 'what is beautiful is self-centred bias', on the basis that attractive people are sometimes
perceived as vain and egotistical (see Figure 2.3). However, one concern
with this literature, as Shahani-Denning *et al.* (1993) have pointed out, is
that they are typically based on photographs rather than face-to-face interviews. When more sophisticated experimental paradigms are used, the literature reveals greater support for the 'beautiful is good' bias, rather than the
'dark side' of beauty (Musumeci and Shahani-Denning 1996; Podratz and
Dipboye 2002).

Explaining the attractiveness bias

Despite the wealth of evidence documenting the attractiveness bias, an
important question remains: why do we judge others differentially based on
their appearance? Various explanations have been posited to explain this bias,
though most rely on some form of social learning perspective (Dion 1986).

Figure 2.3 What is beautiful is not always good: beauty may also have a 'dark side',
   particularly if attractive individuals are perceived as vain and egotistical.

The most developed of these sees the attractiveness bias as a stereotype that
can be meaningfully understood in terms of the theory of 'implicit personality' (Ashmore 1981; Ashmore *et al.* 1986). In this view, the attractiveness bias
is seen as part of a larger set of knowledge structures that individuals use to
make sense of other people's behaviours.

According to Eagly *et al.* (1991), the attractiveness bias reflects inferential
relations between physical attractiveness and personal attributes. When forming first impressions of an individual, we attempt to identify him or her
with established schemas, and this leads to the formation of stereotypes and
implicit judgements associated with such stereotypes. This approach proposes that the social categories of 'attractive' and 'unattractive' people are
associated in our minds with various dimensions of personality. For example,
if we believe that 'attractive people are outgoing', when we meet someone we
consider attractive, we are likely to believe that he or she is outgoing rather
than introverted.

But rather than proposing that the attractiveness bias is unidimensional
(for example, that beauty is good), implicit personality theorists have demonstrated that the evaluative dimension can be partitioned into content-specific
types of evaluative meaning (Kim and Rosenberg 1989; Rosenberg 1977),
such as social competence, intellectual ability, prosocial behaviour, and psychological or emotional stability. The impact of a person's physical attractiveness on another individual's inferences about personality can be explained by
the specific content of these inferences (see Figure 2.4).

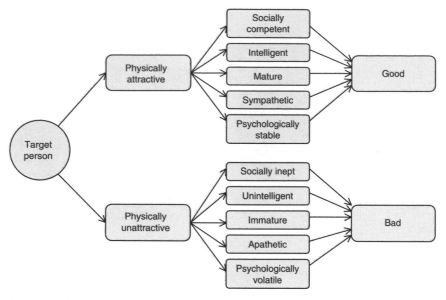

Figure 2.4 A simple example of impression formation.

In practice, however, physical beauty may be more strongly linked to some dimensions of implicit personality theories than others. In their review of the attractiveness bias, Eagly *et al.* (1991) argued that physical attractiveness was most strongly associated with social competence, a category that involved interpersonal skills, sociability, and the outcomes of social competence such as popularity (this is sometimes referred to as the concept of 'emotional intelligence'; Bradberry and Greaves 2005). Other evaluative dimensions, such as intellectual competence, varied in how closely they were psychologically connected to physical attractiveness.

Moreover, the results of Eagly and colleagues' (1991) meta-analysis showed that the strength of the physical attractiveness stereotype was affected by information other than physical attractiveness. That is, the attractiveness bias was weaker when participants received individuating information along with attractiveness cues. Other research supports this idea: in a celebrated study, Argyle and McHenry (1971) showed that when shown photographs as stimuli, participants rated individuals wearing spectacles as more intelligent than those not wearing spectacles. However, this effect disappeared when the same individuals were shown communicating on video-recordings, suggesting that the individuating information provided by such recordings allowed participations to be more discriminating in their perceptions. This would seems to suggest that physical attractiveness may be less important in the perception of friends, family members and co-workers than in the perception of strangers, because we have considerable additional, 'moderating' information about people close to us.

Acquiring the attractiveness bias

A central tenet of the theory of implicit personality is that the attractiveness bias is learned within social and cultural contexts. Eagly *et al.* (1991) have suggested two general ways in which this learning occurs: first, by direct observations of attractive and less attractive people in our social environment; second, by exposure to cultural representations of attractive and less attractive people. It is also possible that physical attractiveness is aesthetically pleasing and may, therefore, elicit positive affect that leads perceivers to infer that attractive people have favourable characteristics.

In terms of direct observation, it seems likely that perceivers observe more attractive people being favourably treated by others in everyday social interactions. For example, numerous reviews of the literature and studies have shown that attractive people are more popular with peers and receive preferential treatment (Adams 1982; Dion 1981, 1986; Feingold 1990). People may then assume that these favourable reactions are educed, not simply by physical attractiveness, but also by positive aspects of behaviour and personality. In other words, we see attractive individuals being fêted in their interactions with others, and consequently come to believe that positive behaviour directed towards them is a result of their physical attractiveness and associated qualities.

In practice, we learn such biases when we are very young by observing the interactions of our parents and peers. Adams and Crane (1980) reported that parents and teachers of preschool children expected their children to favour attractive children and adults when judging the relative attractiveness of a stimulus person. Furthermore, the attractiveness bias among preschool children was related to their mothers' and teachers' expectations, suggesting that social learning may be particularly important in influencing children's acquisition of the stereotype.

Dion (1986) has also discussed the learning of the attractiveness bias in terms of negative reinforcement. She speculated that certain types of encounters with childhood peers may be particularly likely to influence the attractiveness bias, especially the teasing or ridicule of unattractive children (Berscheid *et al.* 1973). These types of encounters reinforce attractiveness stereotyping not only in children who participate in such negative behaviour, but also among children who simply observe the encounter (see Figure 2.5). In addition, insofar as physical attractiveness is positively associated with children's popularity with their peers (Kleck *et al.* 1974), it increases the likelihood that socially desirable characteristics will be attributed to them by other children (Dion 1986).

In terms of cultural messages about appearance, Eco (2004) has documented a long tradition within western European and North American cultural spheres associating beauty with goodness and ugliness with its opposite (see Figure 2.6). In mass media outlets, particularly advertising and popular television, attractive individuals are imbued with all sorts of positive qualities

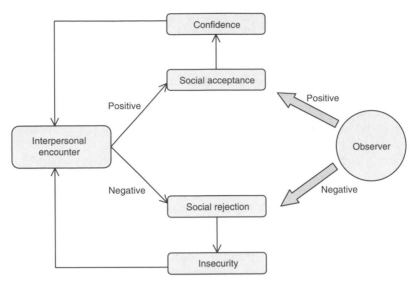

Figure 2.5 Positive and negative reinforcement of the attractiveness bias.

Figure 2.6 In most cultures, particularly in the West, the good are often portrayed as being beautiful or handsome, while the bad are hideous: the story of the beautiful Cinderella and her ugly step-sisters captures this notion precisely. Copyright © Hulton-Deutsch Collection/CORBIS.

(Greenberg *et al.* 2003; Harwood and Anderson 2002). Downs and Harrison (1985), for instance, examined the verbal content of television advertisements, and found statements extolling the virtues of attractiveness to be common. Another study looked at several decades of top box office grossing films, and concluded that, on a variety of measures, attractive characters were portrayed more favourably than unattractive characters (Smith *et al.* 1999).

This phenomenon is particularly striking when we consider sources of media aimed at children, where the message is overwhelming that beauty is good. In their study of children's videos and books, Herbozo and colleagues (2004) discovered that messages emphasising the importance of physical appearance are present in many children's videos, though not as often in the books they read. Another study by Klein and Shiffman (2006) found that the physical appearance of animated cartoon characters was related to many different variables, including intelligence, antisocial behaviour and emotional states. In all such cases, the overriding tendency was for cartoons to provide positive messages about being attractive and negative messages about being unattractive.

The attractiveness bias across cultures

If the attractiveness bias is learned within cultural environments, then it would be useful to ask to what extent the bias is prevalent in non-Western spheres of influence. To date, much of the research examining the physical attractiveness bias has been conducted in North America (Shaffer *et al.* 2000), where there is evidence that the 'beauty is good' stereotype affects the impressions of different ethnic groups (Adams 1978; Stephan and Langlois 1984). Rosenblatt (1974), however, questioned whether physical attractiveness is important in all cultures, especially in those cultures where assigning importance to one's appearance would contravene social norms. There is some evidence to support this suggestion: Rosenblatt and Cozby (1972) found that the function that attractiveness plays varies with the cultural context.

Other cross-cultural research suggests that the attractiveness bias may be more pronounced in cultures that emphasise individualism over group-oriented values (Dion 1986). In their review of various cultural dimensions, Fiske *et al.* (1998) referred to two culturally patterned social systems or 'psyches': the individualistic, Euro-American (sometimes referred to as 'Western') cultural dimension and the collectivist, East Asian (or 'Eastern') dimension. In general, people in individualistic cultures have an independent self: they emphasise their individuality, remain largely unaffected by social contexts and maintain clear boundaries between the self and others. By contrast, people in collectivist cultures tend to have an interdependent self, where self–other boundaries are more diffuse and individuals are highly interconnected with their social group. The distinction between the two kinds of self has important implications for how individuals relate to others in their cultures, and may also affect stereotypes such as the attractiveness bias.

Specifically, Dion (1986) suggested that personal characteristics such as physical attractiveness, particularly facial attractiveness, may be more individuating compared to other personal attributes such as sex and age, which are associated with various roles or social identities. Thus, evaluating others based on physical attractiveness may be frowned upon in cultural contexts that stress more collectivist values. Dion *et al.* (1990) provided some evidence for this hypothesis when they found less stereotyping of personality traits among students in Canada who were relatively high in their degree of involvement in the Chinese community. Dion *et al.* (1990) concluded that participants who identified more strongly with elements of a collectivist society were less inclined to rely on such individuating cues as facial attractiveness when assessing a person's character or personality.

Chen *et al.* (1997), however, have argued that the physical attractiveness stereotype may be just as strong across cultures; rather, it is the *content* of the stereotypes that varies between individualist and collectivist cultures. In support of this theory, Chen *et al.* (1997) found that Taiwanese undergraduates held physical attractiveness stereotypes, but only on highly desirable or socially undesirable traits. However, no physical attractiveness stereotype effect was observed for traits of intermediate desirability, suggesting a difference with the way in which the bias is enacted in more individualistic contexts. Of course, in an increasingly globalised world, many of the individualistic characteristics associated with the West are becoming more prominent in Eastern cultures. It is thus possible that highly modernised individuals in collectivist cultures will display physical attractiveness biases that are similar to those of Western individuals, although further research is necessary to resolve these issues (Shaffer *et al.* 2000).

Conclusion

The effects of physical attractiveness, according to Langlois *et al.* (2000: 404), are 'robust and pandemic'. That is, they extend beyond initial impressions of strangers to our actual interactions with people we know in our everyday lives. Despite what we are told by age-old aphorisms and conventional wisdom, we tend to agree about who is and who is not attractive, and on that basis form judgements about others. In general, being physically attractive appears to be an advantage for children and adults in most contemporary settings, and the magnitude of attractiveness effects is roughly the same as, or larger than, that of other important variables in the social sciences. On this basis, it is not unreasonable to ask just what are the characteristics or attributes we find attractive in others. Of the many attempts to answer this question, perhaps the most elaborate is provided by evolutionary psychologists.

3 Darwin, sexual selection and the peacock's tail

Personal beauty is a greater recommendation than any letter of introduction.
Aristotle, Greek philosopher (384–322 BC)

Remember that the most beautiful things in the world are the most useless: peacocks and lilies, for instance.
John Ruskin, British art critic (*The Stones of Venice*, 1853)

A currently very popular explanation for why we find certain characteristics in others physically attractive is based on evolution and biology. For several decades now, psychologists have endeavoured to incorporate in their writings ideas and theories gleaned from the natural sciences. Indeed, some writers have even described psychology as a 'bio-social science' or as 'biopsychology' (Pinel 1993), which emphasises the role that biology plays (or should play) in understanding human behaviour. The most recent example of biopsychology is what has come to be known as 'evolutionary psychology', that is, the application of Darwinian evolutionary theory for the illumination of contemporary human behaviour (Barrett *et al.* 2002; Bereczkei 2000; Buss 2005; Palmer and Palmer 2002).

It has been said that there were three great thinkers of the nineteenth century that influenced the way human beings view themselves: Charles Darwin, Sigmund Freud and Karl Marx. Each has had a powerful impact on thinking, well beyond their original interests during their lifetime. They shaped how we view ourselves and our place in the universe – how we define, understand and explain human behaviour and nature. It would not be difficult to make the case that, of the three, the most lasting legacy for how we view the natural world was provided by Darwin. Indeed, it sometimes seems as though the 'high points' of Marxism and psychoanalysis have passed, while that of Darwinism is still on the ascendant.

Given the explanatory power of Darwin's thesis, it comes as no surprise that evolutionary theory has captured the imagination of psychologists from a wide range of schools. The appeal of Darwin's theory (indeed, not unlike the theories of Freud or Marx) is its parsimony, distinctiveness and universality.

And unlike competitors to the throne of explaining the natural world, such as creationism and other pseudo-sciences, there is so much evidence in favour of evolutionary theory that it is almost inconceivable that it is not a fact (Swami 2006a). Moreover, the fundamental principles of evolutionary theory are clear, testable and easily understood, which makes it intuitively appealing. Predictably, then, popular books on evolutionary psychology currently occupy the shelves of most respectable bookstores and enjoy widespread appeal (Buss 1994, 1999; Palmer and Palmer 2002).

Within academic circles, too, evolutionary psychology has become a dominant strand of psychological thought (Barkow *et al.* 1992; Dennett 1995; Pinker 1997, 2002), and it is not surprising that evolutionary psychologists have had much to say about physical attractiveness. The first comprehensive exploration of physical attraction as a product of evolution was presented in the late 1970s, when Don Symons published his *Evolution of Human Sexuality* (1979). This work inspired others to approach the science of physical attractiveness from an evolutionary point of view, and over the past several decades, research conducted within an evolutionary framework has intensified dramatically.

Whereas social psychologists have tended to concentrate, as we saw in Chapter 2, on the social consequences of physical attractiveness, evolutionary psychologists have attempted to answer two rather different questions: precisely *what* are the physical markers of attractiveness and *why* are they important? In this chapter, we provide one answer to the question of *why*, and in the next chapter we highlight several answers to the question of *what*. Before doing so, however, and in order to better understand the task at hand, it is necessary to understand what is meant by evolutionary psychology.

Evolution and psychology

With very few exceptions, most scientists today agree on the central propositions of Darwin's theory of evolution by natural selection. In brief, this states that all organisms of a particular species show variation in their behavioural, morphological or physiological traits – their 'phenotype'. A part of this variation between individuals is heritable; that is, some of the variation will be passed on from one generation to the next. For example, as a result of being more effective competitors (at finding food, mating, avoiding predators, and so on), some individuals will leave more offspring than others because the particular traits they possess give them some advantage over others lacking those traits. The offspring of such individuals inherit the successful traits from their parents, and when such tendencies are sustained over many generations, it can lead to the formation of new species (Darwin 1887/1959). This observation underscores the familiar phrase, 'survival of the fittest' (see Figure 3.1)

While scientists have never actually witnessed the emergence of new species, the fact of evolution is as well established as anything else that science has

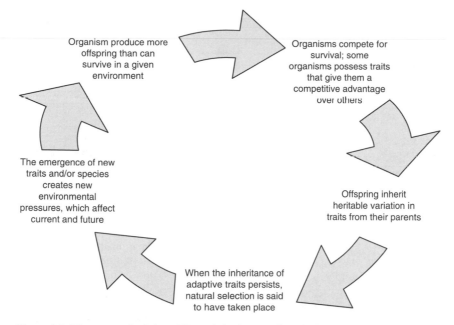

Figure 3.1 The core principles of Darwin's theory of evolution by natural selection.

ascertained, and it is extremely unlikely that its core propositions will be proven wrong (Swami 2006a). For evolutionary psychologists, this fact of evolution is of great importance in explaining contemporary human behaviour. At a fundamental level, they point out that all humans beings are the result of an evolutionary process that has gone on for millions of years. More than this, evolutionary psychologists take the basic tenets of Darwin's theory and apply them specifically to human psychological functioning, in the expectation that evolution has important things to say about human behaviour.

Evolutionary psychology can be described as consisting of four or five core commitments (see Table 3.1). First, evolutionary psychologists propose that human behaviour can be understood by examining the structure of the human brain, which in turn should be understood as a product of the human genome. For some, evolutionary psychology is, therefore, a genocentric programme: many aspects of human behaviour are explained as the product of unfolding genotypes. In other words, instructions for 'building' organisms are prescribed by the genes, which are also the vehicles for transmitting information from one generation to the next (Crawford 1998). In this sense, evolutionary psychology might be said to prescribe an innate origin for many cognitive processes, which are only 'triggered' by experience (Plotkin 1994).

Second, evolutionary psychological arguments reason that recent history (that is, the past 10,000 years or so) is too short to have produced significant changes in the human genome. Rather, the human genome as we know it today evolved in the 'environment of evolutionary adaptedness' (Tooby and

Table 3.1 The core propositions of evolutionary psychology

Hypothesis	Explanation	Outcome
Genocentrism	Human morphology, physiology and psychology should be properly understood as the products of the genes.	Genes prescribe unfolding programmes that are calibrated and fine-tuned by the environment.
Thesis of ancient provenance	Human beings are adapted to the 'environment of evolutionary adaptedness'.	Humans may behave maladaptively in contemporary environments.
Adaptationism	Many human behaviours are psychological adaptations to the 'environment of evolutionary adaptedness'.	It is possible to prescribe an adaptationist argument for most human behaviours.
Monomorphic mind thesis	The human mind is a collection of specialised mental 'tools' brought into play at different times in response to different situations.	Men and women have evolved different mental modules as a result of different evolutionary pressures.
Universality	There is a uniform and universal human nature.	Some cognitive mechanisms operate in a stable and predictable manner across a wide range of environments.

Cosmides 1990a), a period in human evolutionary history that is usually operationalised as sometime in the late Stone Age or Pleistocene (the epoch spanning 1.8 million to 10,000 years ago). Evolutionary psychologists argue that our brains are primarily adapted to conditions prevailing in this environment of evolutionary adaptedness; that is, natural selection produced adaptations that evolved in response to specific pressures in those past physical and geographic environments (Pinker 1997; Symons 1987, 1989). In light of this 'thesis of ancient provenance' (Plotkin 1997), contemporary humans may sometimes behave non-adaptively because our 'Stone Age minds' are not designed to respond adaptively to agricultural or industrial lifestyles (Symons 1989, 1990, 1992).

A third key aspect of evolutionary psychology is the claim that the human brain exhibits 'massive modularity'. Evolutionary psychologists see the human mind as a collection of 'hundreds or thousands' of specialised mental tools that are brought into play at different times in response to different situations (Tooby and Cosmides 1995: 1189). Our Pleistocene ancestors, it is argued, faced a wide range of adaptive problems, and a successful solution in one problem domain (for example, acquiring mates) could not transfer to another domain (for example, avoiding predators). Thus, each adaptive problem would have selected for the evolution of its own dedicated problem-solving mechanism – not unlike a Swiss Army knife, with its many tools adapted for different functions. Thus inspired, evolutionary psychologists have postulated evolved modules for all manner of behaviours, from incest avoidance to sexual attraction, jealousy to alliance formation. In their totality, these modules are said to represent underlying 'human nature', which cannot easily be changed (Buss 1995; Jones 1999).

Finally, since evolved modules are adaptations to the environment of evolutionary adaptedness, evolutionary psychologists propose that 'humans must share a complex, species-typical and species-specific architecture of adaptations' (Tooby and Cosmides 1992: 38). In other words, to the extent that all humans share the same psychological modules, there is a universal and uniform human nature (Tooby and Cosmides 1990b, 1992). To be sure, many evolutionary psychologists do not deny the existence of some cross-cultural differences, but others maintain that at least some cognitive mechanisms are relatively inflexible to environmental conditions and may operate in a stable and predictable manner across a wide range of extant environments (Singh 1993a).

Sexual selection

For some researchers, the adaptationist framework of evolutionary psychology offers a unique and unparalleled way of explaining what characteristics are considered physically attractive and why they are important. In this view, we find others attractive as a result of their possessing specific traits and features that have been shaped by past evolutionary history. But we, the perceivers, also have features, traits or predispositions that lead us to find some features more attractive than others. In other words, what we find beautiful in others, and what features they have acquired, are both the products of evolution (Symons 1995).

Darwin explained this phenomenon of finding certain attributes preferable in others, and others in turn enhancing those attributes, through his process of 'sexual selection'. Writing in *The Descent of Man, and Selection in Relation to Sex* (1871), Darwin argued that his theory of natural selection could not explain extravagant male features, such as the peacock's tail, because such features actually decrease survival ability. When a peacock spreads its tail, for instance, it is 'attractive' to peahens, but also very conspicuous to predators. Darwin reasoned, therefore, that in any sexually reproducing species, any heritable trait that compromises survival may spread through the species because it helps in competing for sexual mates.

In his writings, Darwin distinguished between male competition for female mates and female choice of male mates. Nevertheless, he also recognised that female choice and male competition are often two sides of the same coin: mate choice by one sex implies competition by the other sex. The latter can take place either through direct 'interference competition' (for example, physical fights over the opposite sex) or through indirect 'exploitation competition' (for example, struggles to find and seduce the opposite sex). Darwin had no real explanation of why it is the male of the species that usually competes harder for mates (see Plate 1) – why males court and females choose – though he offered an impressive amount of evidence that this pattern holds for a wide range of species (Darwin 1871).

While Darwin certainly recognised the importance of his theory of sexual selection, most of his contemporaries considered the theory to be Darwin's least successful idea (Huxley 1938). It was not until the 1970s that the theory of sexual selection experienced a revival in fortune. In a centenary volume on sexual selection, Trivers (1972) finally provided an explanation of why males court and females choose, when he argued that the higher levels of necessary 'parental investment' by females of most species make females a limiting resource over which males must compete (see below). In the following decade, there was an explosion of interest in sexual selection, with new behavioural experiments on animals (Møller 1988) and important writings on sexual selection (Bateson 1983; Blum and Blum 1979; de Waal 1982; Dunbar 1988). Today, while natural selection provides the conceptual foundation for evolutionary psychology, actual research more often takes places within the framework of sexual selection.

Runaway selection

Due to their exaggerated nature, mate-attracting signals can prove to be a hindrance to an organism. In many species of birds (including Darwin's favoured peacock), bright colourations and showy ornaments attract potential mates, but also capture the attention of predators. Many species of fish are also brightly coloured, exposing themselves to predators in the hope of finding a mate. Some features – such as deer antlers – also require time and energy to be maximally attractive, and are thus costly investments (see Plate 2). The question, therefore, arises as to why – if survival of the fittest is the rule of thumb – such apparent liabilities are allowed to persist?

One of the first attempts at an answer was provided by Fisher (1915, 1930), one of the few early biologists to take sexual selection seriously. Fisher viewed mate preferences themselves as legitimate biological traits subject to heritable variation, and this insight led him to postulate a process called 'runaway sexual selection'. This refers to an evolutionary positive feedback loop between female preferences for certain male features, and the male features themselves. Given a suitable push in the right direction (for example, an initial bias in female preferences), Fisher's model could account for the exaggerated male traits seen in many species.

For instance, if a male trait (say, coloured spots) and female preference are genetically determined, then females who mate with spotted males will go on to produce spotted male offspring and female offspring who express a preference for spots. These 'sexy sons' will go on to produce large numbers of offspring since females will prefer to mate with them, while female offspring will prefer to mate with other 'sexy' males and go on to have successful sons themselves (see Figure 3.2). So merely by mating with a male who possesses 'attractive' spots, a female can achieve high fitness (Andersson 1982).

A recent conceptualisation that builds on runaway sexual selection is the 'sensory bias model' (Kirkpatrick and Ryan 1991). In this model, one sex has a bias to prefer individuals of particular qualities because that bias has advantages in realms other than mating. In Figure 3.2, for example, green spots may be preferred in males because greenness is a signal of fruit availability. A sensory bias among females to be attracted to green spots, therefore, 'spills over' into domains other than food selection. Thus, if green spots in one sex is preferred in mates due to a sensory bias in the other sex, genes disposing stronger preferences for green spots could spread because they become linked with genes predisposing green spots.

As might be predicted, most species typically favour displays that are louder, larger, more colourful, more varied and more novel than average (Miller 1993), but such perceptual biases also vary substantially across species. For instance, organisms that eat green berries may evolve green-sensitive eyes, which would tend to favour green spots; whereas organisms that eat red berries may evolve red-sensitive eyes that favour red spots (Miller 1998). Nevertheless, this model does not assume an association between a signal and any underlying quality; the feature does not convey any truthful information for the benefit of the perceiver. Rather, it may initially evolve as a result of a bias in some other domain, whereafter runaway selection enhances the trait in one sex while 'building' perceptual mechanisms in the observing sex.

Good genes

In contrast to the theories of runaway selection and sensory bias, most evolutionary psychologists argue that the physical traits that individuals find attractive were selected to act as signals of some underlying quality in its possessors (Rowe and Houle 1996), such as superior 'good health' or 'good condition' (Gangestad and Kaplan 2005; Grammer *et al.* 2003). Individuals in superior health or condition may make better mates for a variety of reasons: they may possess 'fitter' genes to pass on to offspring, they may be better able to provide material benefits such as protection or food, or they may have greater fertility and the ability to reproduce (simply put, they have better reproductive potential). To return to our clichéd example borrowed from Darwin, peacocks with inferior tails may get eaten more often by predators (Petrie 1992), so tail quality may reflect some underlying quality that correlates with predator escape ability. Peahens may have evolved, therefore, to choose males for tail quality, and peacocks consequently to display large, healthy tails (Petrie *et al.* 1991).

Traditionally, good-genes theorists argued that what was being signalled by good genes was really 'good health'. The Hamilton–Zuk parasite model of sexual selection (Hamilton and Zuk 1982), for example, proposed that

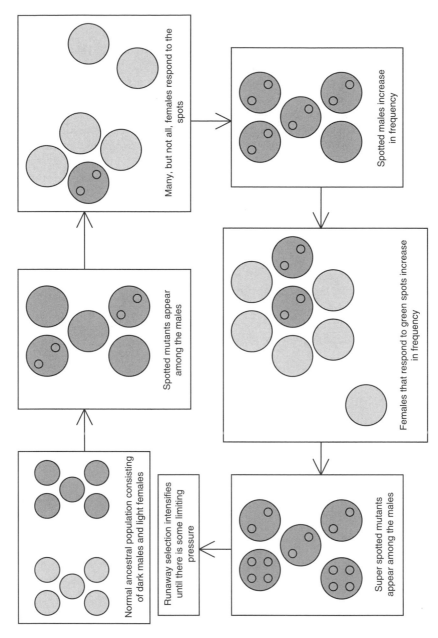

Figure 3.2 An example of runaway sexual selection of spotted mutants.

evolution endows mate seekers with an attraction toward potential mates whose observable traits indicate freedom from parasites and, by extension, resistance to infectious disease (or better 'health'). For example, Møller (1991) showed that, in male barn swallows, greater tail length is indicative of disease resistance and longevity (see Figure 3.3). Thus, female barn swallows that choose a mate with a longer tail would tend to augment the health of its offspring, to the extent that such immune competence is heritable (Soler *et al.* 1998).

Of course, different pathogens are prevalent in different environments at different times. Genotypes that are selected because they are resistant to one particular disease at one point in time may be selected against in the future because they lack resistance to a new pathogen. The genotype favoured in a given environment would, therefore, be constantly changing on account of the continual 'arms race' between pathogens and their hosts. In this

Figure 3.3 In male barn swallows, greater tail length is indicative of disease resistance and longevity. Female barn swallows that choose a mate with a longer tail would, therefore, tend to augment the health of their offspring.

situation, females would be expected to improve the genetic quality of their offspring by selecting for disease-resistant mates, using exaggerated traits as their cue. The possession of an exaggerated trait requires a male to be healthy if the trait is to be displayed to its best advantage, and females can thus assess the health of their partner by the 'loudness' of their signals (Zuk 1991, 1992).

On the other hand, recent conceptualisations have suggested that the equating of good genes with good health is possibly too broad (Gangestad and Kaplan 2005). For instance, in some situations, it may be advantageous for individuals to spend extravagantly on signals in order to attract mates, even if this reduces their overall health. In addition, traits associated with good genes may have other advantages, so it may be useful to develop costly, extravagant signals even if it decreases long-term survivorship or health. This is not to say that the presence of disease markers and health are not important to mate selection; rather, good genes may not necessarily signal good health per se, as much as it signals good 'condition' (Gangestad and Kaplan 2005).

Still, how can organisms be sure that indicators of health or condition are honest signals and not mere deceptions? Zahavi (1975) proposed that it is the very costliness of a feature that ensures its honesty: animals signal that they are of superior quality with a 'handicap'. This is the theoretical constraint that a signal must be costly in order to be reliable, otherwise they could be easily faked (Zahavi 1975). In other words, individuals who can 'afford' a large handicap may be expected to be more viable than individuals who have smaller handicapping traits (Andersson 1986; Iwasa *et al.* 1991). It is this fact that renders the handicapping trait an 'honest' signal of viability.

While we have considered the Fisher-Zahavian and good genes models separately, it should be pointed out that they need not be exclusive (Andersson 1986; Heywood 1989). Recent theoretical contributions by Kokko and her colleagues have attempted to integrate the sensory bias model, good genes hypothesis and runaway selection (Kokko 2001; Kokko *et al.* 2003, 2006). For instance, a sensory bias for green spots may become increasingly strong in successive generations (see Figure 3.2), but only the most high quality males will be able to maintain the costs of displaying those green spots. Thus sensory biases ultimately result in good genes displays. In this sense, the different models of sexual selection should really be seen as non-exclusive and interrelated.

Mate choice preferences

As the example of the peacock and the peahen suggests, in most sexually reproducing species it is the male of the species that courts and the female that chooses. While Darwin (1871) had no real explanation for this difference, Bateman (1948) and Trivers (1972) both pointed out that, in almost all sexually reproducing species, males tend to produce small gametes (sperm) whereas females produce large gametes (ova). And since females invest more matter and energy into producing each egg than males invest in producing each sperm, eggs form more of a limiting resource for males than sperm do for females. In addition, the costs of internal fertilisation, gestation, and long-term lactation are especially high for women, leading to even greater differences between males and females (Symons 1979).

These minimum costs that each sex must 'pay' in order to produce off-spring is called 'parental investment', and refers to any characteristic or behaviour of a parent that enhances the ability of an offspring to survive and reproduce at a cost to the parent's fitness. Evolutionary psychologists derive their hypotheses about mate preferences from these facts about minimum parental investment. In a classic article, Trivers (1985) argued that when there is a sex asymmetry in parental investment (that is, when one sex invests more in offspring than the other), selection will tend to make the higher investing sex 'choosier' in the mating market, because that sex stands to lose more by making a poor choices. This greater choosiness on the part of one sex, in turn, forces members of the opposite sex to compete among one another to be chosen.

Trivers' (1985) theory, however, also predicts that in species where the parental investment of both sexes is high, such as in humans, both males and females will be highly selective in choosing mates. Of course, the physiological investment by women still exceeds that by men, but human offspring are heavily dependent on parental care for many years after birth. Since repro-ductive success requires that offspring themselves survive to reproduce, human offspring need to be nurtured at least until they are able to survive on their own. And this, according to evolutionary psychologists, is why male parental investment is important in humans: in evolutionary history, men could enhance the reproductive potential of their offspring by providing parental care.

Yet, the parental investment provided by women in all cultures still exceeds that provided by men (Einon 2007). This is what we should expect, evolution-ary psychologists argue, given another sex asymmetry in humans. With internal fertilisation, a woman can always be sure that the offspring she births are hers. But because internal fertilisation is coupled with concealed ovulation in females, no man can be completely certain that his partner's offspring really are his (Einon 2007). This is known as the problem of 'paternity uncertainty': given the possibility that a man's supposed offspring are not truly his own, there is always the chance that he is investing in another man's offspring. So, because human male parental investment could potentially be misspent, evo-lution will have 'designed' men to deliver a lower level of parental investment than women as a means of protecting against that possibility.

In sum, because men provided a fairly high level of parental investment throughout evolutionary history, they (like women) have evolved to be very selective in choosing a partner with whom they will jointly invest in offspring. However, because the two sexes provided different *forms* of parental invest-ment throughout human evolutionary history, each sex has evolved to prefer as mates those members of the opposite sex who show signs of being able to provide the forms of parental investment in which that sex is specialised in human evolutionary history (Kenrick *et al.* 1996).

Under the rubric of 'sexual strategies', evolutionary psychologists have postulated integrated sets of adaptations that organise and guide an individual's reproductive effort (Buss 1994). Such adaptations influence things like how individuals select mates, what characteristics they look for in others, how much mating effort they expend and so on (Gangestad and Simpson 2000). In this view, women have evolved to find attractive men who can provide direct benefits (care, resources and so on), whereas men have evolved to find attractive women at peak reproductive potential. And because these differences are assumed to follow from evolutionary adaptations, they are predicted to occur in all societies; that is, they are cross-cultural universals (Buss 1989). Thus, it becomes possible to describe what both men and women find physically attractive in the opposite sex and why.

Quality detection

How can women and men accurately detect whether members of the opposite sex possess the qualities they desire? A man's ability to provide direct benefits cannot easily be directly detected, just as the number of children a woman is likely to bear in her lifetime is not readily detectable. The answer, evolutionary psychologists tell us, is that women have evolved to be attracted to desirable qualities of men that are correlated with the ability to provide indirect resources. Similarly, men have evolved to be attracted to detectable qualities of women that are correlated with peak reproductive potential (Buss 1994; Buss and Schmitt 1993).

In the evolutionary psychological scheme, women solved their 'detection problem' by evolving a preference for high status (particularly in long-term relationships) over other considerations like attractiveness. This is because, the higher a man is in status, the greater his ability to control resources. High status in most societies is associated with wealth and power; it may also be associated with intelligence, emotional stability, and conscientiousness, which are themselves desirable traits (Furnham 2001). Consequently, rivalry among men to attract women focuses on acquiring and displaying cues of resources. In men, then, beauty may only be 'wallet deep', as some have sardonically suggested (Drury 2000: 90).

Men, on the other hand, solved the problem of detecting peak reproductive potential in women by favouring features that signal high reproductive potential, youth or fertility (Buss 1989; Pawłowski and Dunbar 1999; Symons 1979), rather than attributes that signal, say, status. According to Buss (1994: 53), these features include 'full lips, clear skin, smooth skin, clear eyes, lustrous hair, good muscle tone and body fat distribution . . . a bouncy youthful gait, an animated facial expression and a high energy level'. These features are said to signal that a woman is at her peak reproductive potential. In short, then, while both men and women may value the same characteristics in a partner (such as attractiveness, status, emotional stability and so on), they weight these characteristics differently as a result of their evolutionary endowments.

In support of these predictions, evolutionary psychologists have relied on all manner of qualitative and quantitative experiences. For example, some have studied personal advertisements, which provide a good encapsulation of people's mate choice preferences (Kenrick and Keefe 1992; Waynforth and Dunbar 1995). Studies have shown that newspaper advertisements for hetero-sexual partners placed by women in different parts of the world put a strong emphasis on indices of wealth or status, or indices that indicate some will-ingness to invest in the relationship itself (Greenlees and McGrew 1994; Wiederman 1993). The explanation is that women who are able to gain access to more resources, especially in traditional economies, are able to invest more in their offspring and thereby increase the survival and reproductive chances of their offspring (Borgerhoff Mulder 1989; Voland 1988).

By contrast, newspaper advertisements placed by men show a different pat-tern of preferences: they put a strong emphasis on cues of physical attractive-ness in prospective partners (Buss 1987; Buss and Barnes 1986), while other traits – such as wealth or status – receive much less emphasis. As might be predicted from an evolutionary psychological analysis, cues of physical attractiveness are interpreted as indices of reproductive potential in women. Since physical attractiveness changes predictably with age, and age is a good correlate of fertility in women, such cues provide an indirect measure of a woman's fertility.

These preferences have also been found using more conventional psycho-logical experiments. Buss (1989; see also Buss *et al.* 1990) used a questionnaire format to explore mate choice preferences in more than 30 different cultures, and found that women place a strong emphasis on cues related to wealth and status, while men tend to place an overwhelming emphasis on physical attrac-tiveness. Similarly, in a review of the literature on mate choice preferences, Grammer (1989) found that women use more cues than men when evaluating prospective mates. Men typically prioritise physical attractiveness, while women consider many different traits including both social and economic status. Similar findings have been found by ethnographers and anthropolo-gists: men in many tribal societies prize youth above all else in their prospective brides (Borgerhoff Mulder 1988).

This, then, is the basis for evolutionary psychology's theorising about phys-ical attractiveness. Women will tend to find attractive cues in men that signal the possession, or likelihood of possession, of resources and the likelihood of providing parental care. Men, on the other hand, will tend to find attractive cues in women that signal peak reproductive potential, youthfulness or some combination of the two. Combined with the theory of sexual selection, these hypotheses have generated a vast number of psychological studies concerning the attributes that men and women find attractive in opposite-sex partners, some of which are discussed in the following chapter.

Conclusion

Evolutionary psychology has earned a degree of cachet for its remarks about the evolutionary origins of mate choice. Certainly, not everyone is in agreement with the view put forward by evolutionary psychologists that the male preference for youth and the female preference for high status are adaptations designed by evolution (Eagly and Wood 1999; Foley 1996; Luszyk 2001). Alexander Pope, an English poet of the eighteenth century, mirrored just this sentiment when he wrote: 'There should be, methinks, as little merit in loving a woman for her beauty as in loving a man for his prosperity; both being equally subject to change.'

Nevertheless, others have been happy to conduct research within the evolutionary psychological framework, and this has spurred the rapid dissemination of studies concerning the evolutionary origins of physical attractiveness preferences. Certainly, evolutionary psychology has allowed researchers to derive and test a number of very specific hypotheses about physical attractiveness. These studies do not necessarily prove the validity of the overarching theory, but the sheer number of studies deriving from evolutionary psychology has acted as a real impetus for research in this area.

4   The naked woman and man

A handsome woman is a jewel; a good woman is a treasure.
Muslih-un-Din Saadi, Persian poet (1184–1291)

The average man is more interested in a woman who is interested in him than
he is in a woman with beautiful legs.
Marlene Dietrich, actress (1901–1992)

What's female beauty, but an air divine,
Through which the mind's all-gentle graces shine!
They, like the Sun, irradiate all between;
The body charms, because the soul is seen.
Edward Young, English poet ('Satire VI: On Women', 1728)

Evolutionary psychology is not merely concerned with general principles that
govern what men and women look for in a potential partner, but also takes an
interest in the specific physical attributes that they use to make their judgements. In exploring mate choice, we have seen how there are general principles that underpin and guide the partner preferences of women and men. In
brief, men are concerned with mating with women at peak reproductive
potential, whereas women seek men that possess resources and can provide
parental care to offspring. However, the detection problem means that men
and women will pay attention to sexually selected cues that signal each of
these qualities in opposite-sex partners.

Sexually selected signals typically emerge at sexual maturity under the influence of the sex hormones, primarily testosterone and oestrogen in humans,
and are appropriately timed to influence the process of mate selection (Gould
and Gould 1989). Traditionally, the theory of sexual selection has been concerned with explaining exaggerated and maladaptive phenotypes, such as the
plumage of peacocks. However, sexually selected traits do not necessarily
impose costs in terms of decreased survival rates (Buss 1987). For example,
Barber (1995) notes that the silver back of the adult male gorilla is a signal of
social status that attracts females, but does not confer any known cost in
terms of decreased survival probability.

A great deal of evolutionary psychological research has examined the sexually selected physical characteristics that men and women find attractive in opposite-sex potential partners. In practice, this has involved many different component parts of the human body, as well as adornments and non-physical traits (see Table 4.1). Perhaps not surprisingly, given its impact on social interaction, most scholarly research and artistic imagination has focused on the human face (Ferrario *et al.* 1995; Furnham and Reeves 2006), but more recent work has focused on the body. In this chapter, we review

Table 4.1 In theory, the science of physical attractiveness has the potential to investigate almost any aspect of the human body and face. Below is a list of some of these (adapted from Patzer 2006: 1051)

Body component	Examples
Static measures	Height, torso, extremities
Hair	Length, colour, style, presence/absence of body hair
Skin	Colour, absence of blemishes, quality
Eyes	Colour, shape
Nose	Shape, size
Lips	Fullness, colour
Mouth	Oral hygiene
Face	Presence/absence of facial hair, neoteny, masculinity, symmetry
Shoulders	Breadth, shape
Figure	Symmetry, proportion, waist-to-hip ratio, waist-to-chest ratio
Posterior/buttocks	Shape, size, firmness
Weight	Overall weight, weight distribution, weight scaled for height (body mass index)
Muscularity	Muscle location and size, muscle tone
Stomach	Size, shape, muscularity
Arms	Symmetry, length, size, proportionality to body
Hands	Symmetry, size, skin
Fingers	Symmetry, length, skin, nails, cuticles
Legs	Symmetry, length, size, proportionality to body
Feet	Symmetry, size, skin
Procedures	Routine hygiene, hairstyle
Adornments	Clothing, jewellery, cosmetics
Dynamic	Body language, personal space, ageing, walking gait, dance personality and other non-physical attributes

some of the most widely researched characteristics that have fallen under the purview of evolutionary psychology.

These are not ranked in any order of importance, and the review is certainly not exhaustive (see Morris 1987 for more extensive coverage). Our aim in this chapter, rather, is to provide a number of prominent examples of research inspired by evolutionary psychology. As a final caution, it is worth bearing in mind that an individual's decisions in terms of mate choice, as in every other aspect of real life, are contingent. In other words, no matter how attractive we are, or how attractive we find other individuals, there is no guarantee that the attraction will be mutual. Mate choice criteria are almost always contingent on circumstances, a fact we return to in subsequent chapters.

Youthfulness

The Passionate Pilgrim is a collection of poems attributed to William Shakespeare, although in actual fact only five of the 20 poems can be identified as Shakespeare's. In one of these, Shakespeare (1598/2003) sings of youth:

> Crabbed age and youth cannot live together;
> Youth is full of pleasance, age is full of care;
> Youth like summer morn, age like winter weather;
> Youth like summer brave, age like winter bare.
> Youth is full of sport, age's breadth is short;
> Youth is nimble, age is lame;
> Youth is hot and bold, age is weak and cold;
> Youth is wild, and age is tame.
> Age, I do abhor thee; youth, I do adore thee.

Shakespeare is not alone in extolling the virtues of youth. Given the theoretical model proposed by evolutionary psychologists (see Chapter 3), it is hardly surprising that many of the features they are interested in are also markers of youth. This is because the mate value of potential partners will depend not just on their expected parental care or the genetic contribution to offspring, but also on their 'fecundity', the likelihood that mating will result in conception and the birth of offspring (Symons 1979). Mating with someone who looks youthful increases the probability of him or her having high reproductive potential.

Studies have shown that ratings of physical attractiveness for men and women decline with age (McLellan and McKelvie 1993), although these effects are more pronounced for the latter. While women are rated as less feminine with increasing age (Arking 1998), ratings of male masculinity do not appear to be affected to the same degree (Deutsch *et al.* 1986). This finding is sometimes attributed to a 'double standard' of ageing in Western societies, but for evolutionary psychologists, they support the idea that standards of attractiveness for men are less stringent and less connected with youth than they are for women.

The best markers of youthfulness can be found on the face, as attested to by the growing industry devoted to anti-ageing treatments and products (Junqueira *et al.* 1995). In one study, Cunningham (1986) reported that men from five populations judged faces that looked younger than the actual age to be more attractive than faces that appeared age appropriate or older than the actual age. Consequently, he suggested, *looking* young may be more import- ant than actually *being* young. In addition, altering facial features in the direction of youth results in higher ratings of attractiveness, which mirrors the pattern in the real world where female models have younger looking faces than the general population (Jones 1996).

Some early theorising suggested that the preference for younger looking faces reflects a preference for neoteny or 'babyness' (Cunningham 1986; Johnston and Franklin 1993), defined as those features that tend to elicit a nurturant response. Neotenous features are particularly important for female facial attractiveness: women with baby-like features (such as large, widely spaced eyes and a small nose and chin) are typically judged to be the most attractive. Cross-cultural support for this was provided by studies with African-American, Asian, Hispanic and Taiwanese participants, whose judgements of women from their own cultural background gave the same result (Cunningham *et al.* 1995; Zebrowitz *et al.* 1993).

Jones (1995, 1996) proposed that facial attractiveness, especially in women, may be underlined by the sensory bias theory of sexual selection; that is, the preference for facial attractiveness may have arisen 'accidentally' from a pre- ference unrelated to mating. Given men's preference for youthfulness in women, he argues, women with exaggerated youthful facial features will have had an advantage in competition for men. The male preference for facial indicators of age-related fertility is thus seen as a sensory bias that selected for facial neoteny in women (Jones 1996). In other words, facial neoteny is a 'supernormal' cue of youth, not a cue of actual phenotypic or genetic quality (Thornhill and Grammer 1999).

In recent years, however, this theory has come up against a number of critics, who point out that some attractive feminine features are not baby-like. For example, the high cheekbone in attractive female faces is in marked con- trast to the protruding, puffy cheeks of babies (Grammer and Atzwanger 1994). More recent evolutionary psychological theories of facial attractive- ness have stressed the role of sexually dimorphic facial features, which, it is argued, are markers of underlying quality.

Facial sexual dimorphism

Differences in the secondary sexual characteristics between males and females of a species are referred to as 'sexual dimorphisms', and can range from subtle differences in size to extreme horns or colour patterns. Examples include male deer antlers, the elaborate tails of peacocks, the horns of the rhinoceros beetle, and certain facial features in humans (see Figure 4.1). As even the briefest of glances informs us, the facial features of men and women differ quite considerably. Although there are some features that are attractive in both male and female faces, such as prominent cheekbones and a wide smile (Forgas 1987), there are other features that work in opposite directions. Indeed, some evolutionary psychologists have proposed that having facial features that are 'sex-typical' enhances physical attractiveness for men and women.

For women, it has been said, facial 'femininity' (for example, a small nose and chin, and large eyes) signals underlying reproductive condition and the ability to dedicate energy to offspring. Although facial femininity does not change dramatically with changing circumstances, Gangestad and Scheyd (2005) proposed that it could index a woman's history of energy balance appropriate for reproduction. The advantages of being attracted to women with such a history (at least in ancestral populations) include the association between facial femininity and direct benefits (such as lower rates of disease) and indirect factors (genetic benefits to offspring). As predicted by this view, studies have found a strong positive correlation between participants' ratings of women's facial femininity and attractiveness (Koehler *et al.* 2004; Rhodes

Figure 4.1 In human beings, the facial features of men and women differ quite considerably. A typically masculine face is characterised by a broad jaw and large forehead, whereas a typically feminine face is characterised by large eyes and a small nose.

et al. 2003). Using computer averaging and morphing techniques, for instance, two studies showed that exaggerated femininity is considered attractive in female faces (Johnston *et al.* 2001; Perret *et al.* 1998).

For men, on the other hand, facial 'masculinity' (for example, a broad jaw) is thought to be a costly ornament, insofar as increasingly masculine features reduce men's resistance to disease and parasites (Folstad and Karter 1992). According to Gangestad and Scheyd (2005), this trade-off arises as a consequence of the dual effect of androgens on ornamentation (higher androgens result in larger ornamentation) and immune function (androgens impair immune function). Nevertheless, the net result is that masculine features are associated with certain desired features: across cultures men with masculine faces are perceived as being more socially dominant (Mazur *et al.* 1984).

One explanation for this association is that testosterone promotes male mating effort, and that men's underlying condition affects the extent to which they can effectively dedicate effort to mating. Variation in condition, therefore, gives rise to variation in testosterone metabolism, which can cause variation in facial masculinity during adolescence. Consistent with this interpretation, some studies have found positive associations between male facial masculinity and reported health (Rhodes *et al.* 2003) and attractiveness (Grammer and Thornhill 1994; Penton-Voak *et al.* 2001). In terms of the latter, for example, Johnston *et al.* (2001) had women identify an average, an attractive and a masculine face along a continuum of masculine and feminine faces, and reported that the selected attractive face was on the masculine side of average.

Nevertheless, some studies have also found that feminine features are sometimes attractive on male faces (Little *et al.* 2001), while others show no consistency in sexually dimorphic features that are considered attractive (Scheib *et al.* 1999). If, as has been suggested, male facial masculinity varies with condition, why do women not consistently prefer masculine faces? Perrett *et al.* (1998) have proposed that women actually seek a 'trade-off' between good mates and good fathers, and that more feminine faces suggest better fathering abilities. As this view hypothesises, men with feminine faces are perceived to be warmer, more agreeable and more honest than men with masculine faces (Fink and Penton-Voak 2002).

Other evidence relating to this is the finding that women's preferences vary with their menstrual cycle. Women prefer more masculine faces at around the time of ovulation, but more feminine faces at other times (Penton-Voak *et al.* 1999b). In addition, when women are close to ovulation, they are also attracted to the scent of symmetrical men (Gangestad and Thornhill 1998), deep, masculine male voices (Puts 2005) and more confident, intersexually competitive male behavioural displays (Gangestad *et al.* 2004). These changes in preferences across the menstrual cycle may reflect female decisions to weigh signals of heritable condition more heavily when they are fertile.

As the preceding section on youthfulness indicates, however, not everyone is in agreement that facial femininity or masculinity signal underlying condition (Jones 1996). Importantly, in their review of the literature, Weeden and Sabini (2005) found little evidence that facial attractiveness was correlated with actual health, while Feingold (1992) proposed that perceived associations between masculine features and sociability actually have very little basis in fact. Still, research on preferences for facial masculinity and femininity remains a vibrant avenue of scientific study.

Beards

In his writings on sexual selection, Darwin (1871) conjectured that the relative hairlessness of humans compared to nearly all other mammals is the result of sexual selection. He reasoned that since, compared to men, the bodies of women are nearly hairless, hairlessness is an atypical case of selection by men at some time in prehistory. Barber (1995) has extended this argument to beards: facial hair, he proposed, is a good candidate of a sexually selected character in human beings. Beards emerge at puberty and do not have any apparent survival value, given that they seem not to be necessary for women or children (see Figure 4.2). Thus, if beards were a sexually selected trait in human evolutionary history, we should expect that women find men with fuller beards more attractive than clean-shaven men (Freedman 1969a).

A number of studies seem to indicate that men with fuller beards are rated more favourably along a number of dimensions, including being older looking as well as more masculine, dominant, courageous and confident (Addison 1989; Kenny and Fletcher 1973; Pancer and Meindl 1978; Reed and Blunk 1990; Roll and Verinis 1971). In one study in which the level of beardedness of male faces was experimentally manipulated, ratings of physical attractiveness increased with greater quantity of facial hair (Hatfield and Sprecher 1986). Another study asked several students to shave off their beards in a stepwise fashion until they were completely clean-shaven (Pellegrini 1973). Participants then rated photographs of the students, and it was found that students with full beards were considered more attractive, mature and confident. Similarly, Wood (1986) found that putting on a false beard and taking a look in the mirror increased self-perceived masculinity.

Historically, beards have also been treated with great care and veneration (Peterkin 2001). Among the Catti, an ancient German tribe, young men were not allowed to shave or cut their hair until they had slain their first enemy, and it was customary among many such tribes to grow large, full beards. For the ancient Romans too, a bearded man was a proverbial expression for a man of virtue, and was associated with knowledge and wisdom. 'Beards in olden times,' wrote Thomas Macaulay, 'were the emblems of wisdom and piety.'

Barber (1995) proposed that, in evolutionary history, beards may have been intimidating to rivals as they constituted an advertisement of social

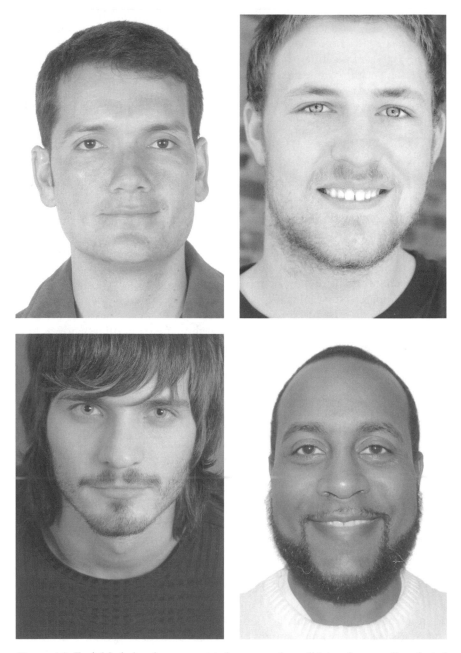

Figure 4.2 Facial hair has been suggested as a good candidate of a sexually selected trait in human beings: beards emerge at puberty and do not have any apparent survival value. But do all women find men with fuller beards more attractive than clean-shaven men?

dominance. Because a man's beard increases in size (and presumably social impact) with age, and because men's social status tends to increase with age, Barber (1995) suggested that women who favoured beardedness as a cue to maturity and hence social dominance would have been reproductively more successful than those who did not. Similarly, Freedman (1969a) earlier argued that beards increase the perceived status of men and may increase the social distance between rival men.

However, the available evidence suggests that there may also be substantial individual differences in perceptions of beardedness. For example, Feinman and Gill (1977) simply asked women if they found the beard attractive, and most stated that they did not. Other evidence suggests that bearded men are not always judged positively: in some studies, bearded men are perceived as dirtier (Kenny and Fletcher 1973), less attractive (Wogalter and Hosie 1991) and only sometimes more intelligent (Addison 1989), older, and more mature than clean-shaven men (Cunningham *et al.* 1990; Wogalter and Hosie 1991).

Other anecdotal evidence suggests that the beard is, or was, not found attractive in all cultures. For the ancient Egyptians, facial hair was associated with mourning and, with the exception of a pencil-thin moustache, they generally found beards unattractive. Some sociologists have also pointed out that the beard (like hairstyles and hair colour in general) is intrinsically open to changes in fashion and cultural dictates (Bunkin and Williams 2000; Peterkin 2001). This suggests that attitudes toward beardedness have little basis in evolutionary history, but follow changes in fashion (at least in modern times) or result from random 'attitude drift' (Mazur 1986).

Certainly, there is some evidence that the beard, at least in terms of length, may be a site for changing fashions. While full beards remained in fashion until the turn of the twentieth century, this began to change particularly following World War I, when disease and chemical weapons necessitated that soldiers shave their beards. Mass marketing that popularised being clean-shaven then ensured that beardlessness became the only acceptable style for decades (Bunkin and Williams 2000). From the 1920s to the 1960s, beards were virtually non-existent in mainstream North American and Western European societies, and the few who wore beards often faced a degree of prejudice.

Beards, together with long hair (see below), were reintroduced to mainstream society in Western Europe and North America by the radical sociopolitical movements of the mid-1960s. As depicted in *Winter Soldier*, for example, many Vietnam War veterans who turned against the war grew long hair and beards as a reaction against being clean-shaven while serving as soldiers. Nevertheless, the trend of the full-flowing beard in mainstream culture subsided again in the mid-1980s and today, with the exception of some religions, few men sport fully grown beards. Indeed, at different points in recent history, the male beard has been imbued with religious attributes not generally associated with attractiveness, including celibacy and holiness.

Cranial hair

There are many interesting features of cranial or head hair from an evolutionary psychological perspective (see Plate 3). These include the quality and quantity of cranial hair; hair length, colour and lustre may also be important signals (Graham and Jouhar 1981). Indeed, hair is so powerful an individual marker that people are often described in terms of hair colour, at least in the West (Bull and Hawkes 1982). Hair is also fetishistically treated in some cultures: it is a crowning glory and for many a sense of great worry, pride or pure entertainment. Nor has hair escaped the attention of poets and lyricists: in *The Merchant of Venice*, for example, Shakespeare (1596/2003) has Bassanio say of Portia:

> Her name is Portia, nothing undervalued
> To Cato's daughter, Brutus' Portia;
> Nor is the wide world ignorant of her worth,
> For the four winds blow in from every coast
> Renowned suitors, and her sunny locks
> Hang on her temples like a golden fleece,
> Which makes her seat of Belmont Colcho's strond,
> And many Jasons come in quest of her.

A recent example of an evolutionary psychological approach to cranial hair is provided by Frost (2006), who proposed that blonde hair evolved at the end of the last Ice Age (10,000 to 11,000 years ago) by means of sexual selection. During that period, the European region likely experienced severe food shortages. The only sustenance would have come from herds of wild animals, but finding them required arduous hunting trips in which numerous men died, leading to a high ratio of surviving women to men. As a consequence, argues Frost (2006), blonde hair and blue eyes evolved among northern European women to make them 'stand out' from their rivals at a time of fierce competition for scarce males.

Applied to contemporary settings, Frost's (2006) suggestion is not that humans have a universal preference for blonde individuals – which brings to mind Anita Loos' comic novel, *Gentleman Prefer Blondes* (or the film adaptation starring Marilyn Monroe and Jane Russell). Rather, Frost (2006) makes an argument for the concept of a 'rare-colour advantage'. When an individual is faced with potential mates of equal value, she or he will tend to select the one that 'stands out' the most, the one with the rarest colour morph. Certainly, evidence of a rare-colour advantage exists in some non-human species, such as red flour beetles and leafroller moths (Hughes *et al.* 1999; Simchuk 2001).

But is a rare-colour advantage also evident among humans? In one early study, Thelen (1983) presented three series of slides showing blonde and brunette women and asked men to select the one from each series that they would most prefer to marry. The first series showed six brunettes, the second one brunette and five blondes and the third one brunette and eleven blondes. Thelen (1983) showed that for the same brunette, preference increased significantly from the first to the third series. In other words, preference for the brunette increased in proportion to the rarity of her hair colour. More recently, Schweder (1994) reported that women tend to change their hair colour and style to a type that is less common in the general population.

On the other hand, there is also evidence that perceptions of hair colour vary with changing fashions and media icons. Rich and Cash (1993) examined the frequency with which different hair colours were represented in women's magazines over four decades. They concluded that the percentage of blondes was overrepresented in the magazines, with the exception of the 1960s, when Jackie Kennedy – a brunette – became *the* style icon in much of North America, if not internationally. More generally in the West, blondes tend to be perceived as more attractive, seductive and outgoing, although they may also be perceived as untrustworthy, manipulative and promiscuous (Lawson 1971).

Much less is known about the effects of greying hair on attractiveness. One might argue that, insofar as grey hair is associated with age, it should be perceived as unattractive. After all, 'Grey hairs are death's blossoms', as Friedrich von Schiller, the German poet and philosopher, put it. Yet, others have found beauty in greying hair, including the artist Maria Dewing:

> Grey hair is beautiful in itself, and so softening to the complexion and so picturesque in its effect that many a woman who has been plain in her youth is, by its beneficent influence, transformed into a handsome woman.

Fewer studies have dealt with hair length, although a handful of studies have taken an interest in male-pattern baldness (Hankins *et al.* 1979; Henss 2001; Roll and Verinis 1971; Wells *et al.* 1995). In one study, Cash (1990) found that baldness caused lower ratings of physical and social attractiveness, personal likeability and life success. In the same study, however, baldness was also associated with high ratings of intelligence and over-estimates of age. Cash (1990) suggests that, because baldness comes with age in men predisposed to it, it may be a useful cue for age. Of course, some men attempt to conceal their baldness by wearing false hair, and their doing so appears dependent on personality traits (Franzoi *et al.* 1990; Gosselin 1984).

By contrast, men with long hair have been judged to be more feminine, non-conforming and youthful, and less potent, educated and intelligent than men with short hair (Pancer and Meindl 1978; Peterson and Curran 1976). However, these studies were conducted at a time in Western political history when the length of a man's hair was equated with sociopolitical activism. Fewer studies have examined women's hair length, though Terry and Krantz (1993) did find that long hair in women was associated with decreased social forcefulness. This was attributed to long female hair softening the contour of the face and increasing the youthful look of the face.

Body hair

Attitudes toward hair on the human body have also been explained as an evolutionary adaptation. Barber (1995) proposed that hairlessness of the skin, especially in women, is a sexually attractive feminine trait because hairlessness is a sign of youth. As women age, increasing testosterone levels cause growth of body hair, and to the extent that this occurs, absence of body hair would be correlated with fecundity and youthfulness. However, the association between hairlessness and youthfulness as an evolutionary outcome is not entirely clear.

For one thing, a completely hairless female body is more accurately a sign of prepubescence, when women have very low reproductive potential. In addition, attitudes towards body hair (including armpit and pubic hair) more often reflect cultural and personal norms, and can range from pleasure to revulsion for both the presence and absence of such hair. In most Western societies, it became a public trend during the late twentieth century, particularly for women, to reduce or remove their body hair, and sexual images of the hairless woman in advertising and other media have been raised as the major reason for this development.

Similarly for men, excessive chest hair is a symbol of virility and masculinity in some cultures, while other societies display a hairless male body as a sign of youthfulness. In contemporary Western societies, there appears to be a preoccupation among men with body hair depilation, that is the removal of body hair below the neck. One study found that more than 60 per cent of men interviewed engaged in body hair depilation (Boroughs *et al.* 2005), the best explanation for this practice being a socially constructed ideal of masculine attractiveness.

Skin tone

In almost all cultures, men and women differ in their complexions: in general, women are fairer, while men tend to be darker (see Plate 4; Frost 2005; Jablonski and Chaplin 2000). This difference in the level of skin pigmentation appears to be a product of natural selection: because the production of vitamin D (and hence, decreased pigmentation) is important during pregnancy and lactation, natural selection has favoured lighter skin tone in women (Jablonski and Chaplin 2000). Further, Frost (2006) suggests that sexual selection targeted this difference, resulting in lightened European skin tone (Frost 1994a, 1994b; Manning *et al.* 2004), which may explain cross-cultural differences in skin tone.

But do men and women hold strong preferences for skin tone in an opposite-sex partner? A robust finding within the anthropological literature is a preference, within ethnic groups, for women with skin tones somewhat lighter than the local average (van den Berghe and Frost 1986). In Western societies, for example, blonde hair and fair skin are associated with sexual attractiveness, particularly for women (Guthrie 1976). But this phenomenon is not limited to the West: van den Berghe and Frost (1986) found that, of the 51 societies for which relevant data were available, 47 preferred lighter toned skin in women. Conversely, there is some evidence that, within ethnic groups, women prefer darker complexioned men (Aoki 2002; Frost 1988, 2005; van den Berghe and Frost 1986).

Across ethnic groups, however, the picture is complicated by the different ways in which evolutionary and sociocultural patterns interact. On the one hand, when given the choice, individuals tend to idealise skin tones that mirror the norm within their own ethnic group. For instance, Swami *et al.* (2007e) presented participants from eight distinct national settings with images of women that ranged in skin tone from pale to dark. They found that what was attractive was local: Barbadians, for instance, rated as more attractive darker skin tones than Britons or Austrians.

Skin tone preferences are further complicated by the legacy of colonialism and racism in some societies, which has meant a denigration of darker skin tones (Ducille 1996; Hall 1995; Russell *et al.* 1992; Swami 2007). In almost all societies that suffered colonial occupation (and in many others that did not), the imperial agenda clearly associated fairness of skin with goodness and power. Nor was this merely enforced through racist laws: Hall (1995) has described how concepts of blackness were derided and denigrated in art and culture. For example, many paintings of the eighteenth and nineteenth centuries show an upper class, white woman with one or more black servants who are often depicted holding out pearls, coral, or other valuables to their mistresses (see Plate 5). Both the servants and their offerings come from Africa and they are all signs in the social construction that marked the women as fair and beautiful (Hall 1995; Swami 2007). Even today, individuals with dark-toned skin face more discrimination than individuals with light-toned skin (Frisby 2006; Keenan 1996; Leslie 1995), and European (Caucasoid) features are accorded higher status, even within some minority ethnic groups (Maddox 2004; Thompson and Keith 2001).

There is also a strong association between skin tone and social status (Keith and Herring 1991). In many pre-industrial societies, having tanned skin signifies that a person has to work outdoors for much of the day, and consequently is likely to be poor and uneducated. At different points in history – in ancient Egypt and China, for instance – having pale skin was considered more attractive, as lighter skin tones signified that a person was wealthy enough to avoid manual labour. Indeed, women and goddesses depicted in ancient Chinese drawings are often fair skinned, a trait typically associated with girls from royalty or nobility who could afford to stay indoors most of the time.

By contrast, in some industrial societies, having pale skin is considered unattractive, as it is perceived as an unhealthy sign that a person works in polluted urban areas with weakened sunlight. It is not surprising, therefore, that skin tanning is currently experiencing a growth in popularity in the West and some Eastern subcultures, such as the *ganguro* of Japan. Despite ultra-violet radiation being a central risk factor in the development of skin cancers (Armstrong and Kricker 2001; Diepgen and Mahler 2002), a tan has a posi-tive effect on the appearance of both women and men (Bond and Cash 1992; Broadstock *et al.* 1992; Hill 2002; Jackson and Aiken 2000; Miller *et al.* 1990; Sahay and Piran 1997; Smith *et al.* 2007).

Sociocultural influences, specifically the media, peers and family, play an important role in the formation of tanning attitudes (Cafri *et al.* 2006). Some theorists have proposed that higher incomes, in combination with ease of travel to warmer climates during the winter, have allowed skin tone to become an ubiquitous symbol of a person's occupation. In developed societies in the West, being able to get a tan serves as a symbol of status, a message relayed to individuals through the mass media and social interactions (Jackson and Aiken 2000; Wichstrom 1994). In a recent study, participants who viewed magazine advertisements with tan models had higher ratings than controls (who viewed neutral stimuli) on the importance of tanning to overall attrac-tiveness, suggesting that this form of media causes greater positive evaluation of a tan appearance (Lee *et al.* 2004).

Thus, while some studies have supported a preference for skin tones lighter than the local average, skin tone preferences may also vary systematically in relation to perceived socioeconomic status. When a skin tone, whether light or dark, is associated with low socioeconomic status, it tends not to be valued and is, therefore, considered less attractive. This pattern seems in accord with the suggestion that in most, if not all, human societies, people compete for prestige (Henrich and Gil-White 2001). Indeed, Frederick *et al.* (2005) have suggested that the body may be an important arena for prestige competition. While they limited their discussion to the salience of male muscularity and female body shape or thinness, skin tone ideals may be a site for prestige competition that affects both sexes.

Fluctuating asymmetry

One of the great controversies in the history of art stems from the unexpected finding of asymmetries in the facial features of the *Venus de Milo*, one of the famous sculptures currently in the Louvre in Paris (Swami 2007). In actual fact, most people are aware that they are not perfectly symmetrical, whether in the shape of their eyes and ears, their hands or breasts, or even their smile. Many people also have asymmetric eyebrow control and facial lines or wrin-kles. These asymmetries often increase or at the very least become more notice-able over time. In the scientific literature, these asymmetries are referred to as 'fluctuating asymmetries', or small deviations from perfect bilateral symmetry in traits that on average show no directional asymmetry (Simmons *et al.* 2004).

For many evolutionary psychologists, departures from perfect symmetry are assumed to be the result of environmental stressors such as reduced nutrition, disease and parasitic infections. In other words, external factors such as pollutants, pathogens and physical trauma adversely affect symmetrical development. Greater symmetry is thus assumed to reflect the presence of 'good genes' in the sense that individuals are able to resist environmental stressors. In short, evolutionary psychologists argue that only the healthiest of the population possess the ability to develop symmetry in spite of harsh environment conditions (Thornhill and Gangestad 1993).

Fluctuating asymmetry has been found to be important for plants and animals when faced with the struggle for survival, mates and reproduction (Møller 1996; Møller and Swaddle 1997; Møller and Thornhill 1998; Swaddle and Cuthill 1994; Thornhill 1992). Barn swallow females, for example, prefer males with symmetric tails over males with asymmetric tails (Møller 1992), and female peahens prefer males with long tails containing large numbers of bilaterally symmetrical eye spots (Petrie *et al.* 1991). The assumption in such studies is that, if mate choice results in paired structures or ornaments, then both the size and symmetry of ornaments might function as reliable indicators of mate quality.

What is the evidence that symmetry matters for humans? For one thing, a common feature in early forms of human art, and especially face and body painting, is the use of symmetrical designs (see Figure 4.3; Boas 1955; Brain 1979; Ebin 1979). Traditionally, the preference for symmetry in face and body painting was attributed to cultural processes, but it is now believed that this cannot be the whole story. One reason is that many cultures showing the preference are temporally and geographically isolated (Lévi-Strauss 1963) and another is that it does not appear to be affected by learning (Rentschler *et al.* 1998; Washburn and Humphrey 2001). It seems plausible, as some

 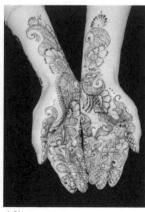 

4.3a   4.3b   4.3c

Figure 4.3 A common feature in many forms of body art, especially tribal face and body painting is the use of symmetrical designs. Figure 4.3c Copyright © Jim Zuckerman/CORBIS.

evolutionary psychologists have proposed, that the preference of symmetry is an evolutionary bias that has affected cultural practices (Cárdenas and Harris 2006).

Indeed, studies have shown that more symmetric men attract more sexual partners and have sex more often (Thornhill and Gangestad 1999), and that the frequency of women's orgasms is correlated with low fluctuating asymmetry in male partners (Thornhill *et al.* 1995). However, these studies have not directly measured the effect of fluctuating asymmetry on the attractiveness of an individual, and it would be useful to ask to what extent fluctuating asymmetry decreases ratings of attractiveness. In practice, evolutionary psychological studies of fluctuating asymmetry have considered the body and face as separate entities.

In terms of facial symmetry, one line of research has studied the symmetry of faces that have been manipulated either to enhance or reduce symmetry. Several such studies have shown a preference for face symmetry in attractiveness judgements for both male and female faces (Koehler *et al.* 2002; Perrett *et al.* 1999; Rhodes *et al.* 2001a,2001b). Similarly, Rhodes *et al.* (1999) found that blending faces with mirror images to create symmetry resulted in more attractive symmetric images. However, other studies have found such symmetric images less attractive (Swaddle and Cuthill 1995) or have shown no preference (Noor and Evans 2003).

One limitation of these studies is that, while they provide some evidence that a preference of symmetry exists, they do not answer the question of how much it matters. It is possible that symmetry matters, but that it matters very little in comparison with other facial characteristics such as sexually dimorphic traits (Gangestad and Scheyd 2005). Scheib and colleagues (1999), for example, found that both facial and body symmetry predict men's facial attractiveness, but facial symmetry predicted just as well the attractiveness of half-faces which possess minimal cues of symmetry. Jaw size, prominent cheekbones and healthier looking skin have all been shown to covary with symmetry, and may account for its association with attractiveness (Gangestad and Thornhill 2003; Jones *et al.* 2004).

Fewer studies have attempted to examine the effect of fluctuating asymmetry on bodily attractiveness, and those that have done so do not provide compelling evidence either way. Singh (1995a) used line drawings of the female figure that varied in body shape and breast asymmetry, and reported evidence that both variables mattered for attractiveness judgements. However, the effects for breast asymmetry were small and probably covaried with perceived age of the figures. In his study, Singh (1995a) created breast asymmetry by having one breast sag noticeably, and this may have resulted in raters judging the drawn figure to be significantly older, a suggestion corroborated by other studies (Furnham *et al.* 2006).

More recent research has used better technological designs to get at the same question. Tovée *et al.* (2000) conducted a computer-enhanced symmetry study comparing the photographs of 25 women's bodies with manipulated images of those photographs to produce perfect symmetry. When observers were asked to rate these images for attractiveness, there did not seem to be any difference in their rating of normal images (varying in symmetry) and morphed (completely symmetric) versions. However, when observers were presented with the unaltered image and its symmetric version simultaneously, and were forced to choose the more attractive of the two, they tended to choose the symmetric version. The effect, however, was slight and suggests that although symmetry may matter for judgements of women's attractiveness, it probably matters very little.

One explanation for the weak association between symmetry and attractiveness is that fluctuating asymmetry is in fact a poor indicator of underlying quality or 'good genes'. One widely cited study by Shackelford and Larsen (1997) had undergraduates keep daily journals of various health symptoms for a month, and reported that low face fluctuating asymmetry was associated with better physiological health. However, Weeden and Sabini (2005) recalculated the correlations in this study and suggest that the relationship between face fluctuating asymmetry and physiological health is weak. Moreover, their examination of two other studies that reached similar conclusions (Rhodes *et al.* 2001b; Tomkinson and Olds 2000) also casts doubt on the association between health and fluctuating facial asymmetry. The same is also true of studies correlating bodily symmetry with health, where the relationship is modest at best (Weeden and Sabini 2005).

Height and stature

Preferences for women's and men's height is a topic that is relatively under-researched, which is quite surprising given the importance of height in popular culture and the relative ease and reliability of its measurement (Freedman 1969b). Indeed, there are studies reporting that height has a profound impact on a person's disposition and personality, so much so that the psychologist Alfred Adler once coined the phrase 'Napoleon complex' to describe cases where a person's short stature makes her or him feel inadequate. Among such individuals, short stature may lead to an inferiority complex and the adoption of over-aggressive behaviour to compensate for lack of height and power.

In humans beings, height is a sexually dimorphic characteristic: on average, and across most ethnic groups, men are several inches taller than women (Gillis and Avis 1980). Evolutionary psychologists have proposed that tallness in men is associated with 'good genes', as is reflected by their greater reproductive success than men of average height. Pawłowski *et al.* (2000) showed that taller than average men had more children than matched men of average height: on average, each metre in residual stature (adjusted for age and natal location) was worth one whole offspring over a lifetime. Similarly, Nettle (2002a) showed that, in a cohort of British men, taller than average men had a higher lifetime number of cohabiting partners and decreased probabilities of childlessness or having no major relationship.

In accordance with this line of thinking, evolutionary psychologists cite numerous examples of taller men being considered more attractive than men of average height. For instance, women express direct preferences for men who are taller than they are (Pawłowski 2003), and taller men also receive more responses in personal advertisements (Pawłowski and Koziel 2002). In addition, women have been found to go out with their taller dates more often than their shorter dates (Sheppard and Strathman 1989), and the majority of women who place newspaper advertisements specify height as an important attribute in a partner (Jackson and Ervin 1992). In short (forgive the pun), tallness is attractive in men because of its association with observed reproductive success differentials. Indeed, men with the highest reproductive success in Nettle's (2002a) study were the same height (1.80 metres) as those stated most attractive by women in a study by Hensley (1994).

By contrast, the available evidence suggests that there is no advantage for women in terms of reproductive success in being taller than average (Nettle 2002b). That is, being taller than average does not seem to affect the reproductive success of women in the same way that it does for men. This seems in line with the suggestion that there is a tendency for men to choose women shorter than themselves in mate choice judgements (Gillis and Avis 1980). Height is less important to the physical attractiveness of women, and men find women of average height most attractive and date them most often (Jackson and Ervin 1992; Sheppard and Strathman 1989).

However, it remains unclear to what extent height plays an independent role in physical attractiveness. As Weeden and Sabini (2005) point out, height may be important in mating decisions (as are other characteristics, such as education, political orientation, and so on) and yet not be 'attractive' in the sense that it affects judgements of how attractive men are. A great deal of anecdotal and some empirical evidence would also seem to suggest that individuals actually prefer a complementary height partner, but often settle for one whose height meets basic social stereotypes (for women, taller than her; for men, shorter than him; Cameron *et al.* 1977; Hensley 1994; Martel and Billier 1987). Indeed, assortative mating for height is common in Western societies (Susanne and Lepage 1988), as well as some non-Western groups (Ahmad *et al.* 1985).

In addition, some studies have found that men of average height are actually considered more attractive as dates than either very tall or very short men (Graziano *et al.* 1978). Short men are also sometimes considered more likeable, suggesting that tall height may be perceived as intimidating (Graziano *et al.* 1978). Finally, some research suggests that greater height is actually associated with poor health and mortality (Gunnell *et al.* 2003b; Samaras *et al.* 1999; Shors *et al.* 2001). Although this does not necessarily rule out a good genes explanation – especially as height may provide evolutionarily relevant advantages beyond just being a costly signal (the ability to intimidate rivals, for example) – it does suggest that the explanation should be applied with caution.

Complicating this picture further is the association between height and socioeconomic status. In their review of studies on height and workplace success, Judge and Cable (2004) found that height was significantly correlated with success and earnings. Their results suggested 'that an individual who is 72 in. tall would be predicted to earn almost [US] $166,000 more across a 30-year career than an individual who is 65 in. tall' (Judge and Cable 2004: 437). To explain the association between height and workplace success, Judge and Cable (2004) proposed a model in which height affects success through several mediating processes (see Figure 4.4).

First, height affects how individuals regard themselves (self-esteem) and how individuals are regarded by others (social esteem). Social and self-esteem affect an individual's job performance as well as their supervisor's evaluation of their work. This, in turn, affects success in their careers. Consistent with their model, Judge and Cable (2004) found that height was related to job performance, although not as strongly as it is related to social or self-esteem. Specifically, their evidence suggested that height was more predictive of subjective ratings than objective outcomes. In other words, height predicts how observers perceive and evaluate others more than it predicts actual performance.

These findings suggest that, in addition to possible innate predispositions, women may learn to prefer cues that are reliable indices of resources, in this case cues of greater height (Barrett *et al.* 2002). Such learning may occur either through direct experience or through cultural transmission of certain rules regarding behaviour. Indeed, the available evidence suggests that taller men do indeed have greater social and economic success (Higham and Carment 1992; Jackson and Ervin 1992; Kurtz 1969; Lester and Sheehan 1980; Stogdill 1948; Young and French 1998), which supports the idea of learning by observation.

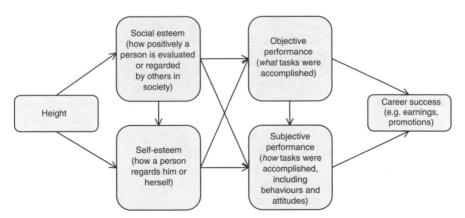

Figure 4.4 The relationship between height and job performance (adapted from Judge and Cable 2004: 429).

Leg length

A related concept when it comes to studies of human height is the wealth of anecdotal evidence suggesting that some men have a preference for longer legs in women (Morris 1987). Fashion and runway models are on average 11 cm taller than normal women (Tovée *et al.* 1997), and much of this difference can be related to differences in leg length. Surprisingly few studies, however, have examined the effect of leg length on physical attractiveness. In a recent exception, Swami *et al.* (2006) argued that one attribute that may explain the preference for leg length is the leg-to-body ratio (LBR). Because the LBR is relatively easy to measure, it is often used as criteria for the study of nutrition and development, especially among children (Albanes *et al.* 1988).

From an evolutionary perspective, there are a number of different reasons why the LBR may be important in aesthetic judgements of men and women. One possibility is that the LBR is a signal or cue of both stable childhood development as well as current well-being. In terms of the former, the interruption of growth at any stage of the life cycle results in a relatively long torso and short legs (Leitch 1951). If the rate of growth is sufficiently slowed down (for example, due to nutritional deficiencies or psychological stress), the adult will have shorter legs relative to the trunk. Indeed, some studies suggest that leg length measured in childhood may be the component of stature most sensitive to environmental influences. In addition, longer leg length relative to the torso is associated with various life outcomes including reduced risk of coronary heart disease, diabetes resistance, low blood pressure, better cardiovascular profiles, lower adult mortality and reduced risk of cancer (Davey Smith *et al.* 2001; Gunnell *et al.* 2003a, 2003b).

From this perspective, it might be predicted that a higher LBR will be preferred in both men and women because it is both an indicator of the ability to resist developmental insults and current health. However, when Swami *et al.* (2006a) tested this hypothesis using line drawings that varied in five levels of LBR (see Figure 4.5), they found a preference for a higher LBR in women, but not in men, suggesting that the LBR plays a differential role in judgements of men and women. Because the LBR is a sexually dimorphic feature, with women tending to have higher LBRs than men, it is possible that a higher LBR is associated with femininity, while a shorter LBR is associated with masculinity. Moreover, because peak growth occurs during adolescence, a higher LBR may also be a cue of youthfulness, which is more greatly valued in women. Thus, sexual dimorphism in LBR may have evolved due to men's preference for women with higher, youthful LBRs.

However, these studies are far from conclusive, and more work is required to elucidate the ways in which leg length may be associated with attractiveness in men and women. Swami *et al.* (2006c) have also raised the possibility that their findings could be explained by sociocultural attitudes and preferences toward leg length relative to the torso. As documented by

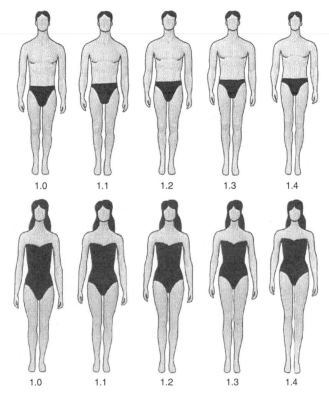

Figure 4.5 Figures used to test leg-to-body ratio preferences (ratios are noted below each image) (from Swami *et al.* 2006).

Morris (1987), exposure of women's legs has long been considered to be sexually appealing, at least in Western contexts. At different periods, the amount of female leg flesh considered appropriate for exposure has varied considerably. By contrast, men's legs have attracted far less attention, which may be explicable in terms of fashion dictates (Morris 1987). Alternatively, it is possible that other components of the male leg may be considered attractive, such as muscularity. The latter is consistent with the idea that muscularity is an important component of men's physical attractiveness, at least in terms of upper body shape (Maisey *et al.* 1999; Swami and Tovée 2005a).

Nevertheless, the LBR seems to underpin the popular notion that leg length is an important feature of women's physical attractiveness. At present, it remains unclear to what extent preferences for LBR can be associated with preference for overall height, and it is possible that the LBR may only be utilised once other attributes (such as body weight and perhaps overall height) have been 'filtered out' (Fan 2007). And aside from leg length, leg shape may also be expected to play a role in overall attractiveness. As an example, high heels tend to accentuate the calf, which is itself considered attractive by some.

Foot size

Another sexually dimorphic feature in humans is foot size: in general, women tend to have smaller feet than men (Fessler *et al.* 2005a). It has been suggested by Fessler *et al.* (2005b) that this sexual dimorphism in foot size is the product of sexual selection for smaller female feet. They point out that children's feet are smaller than those of adults, and so a small adult foot may be a cue of youthfulness (Barber 1995). In addition, in adult women, foot size increases with both age and parity, a pattern which supports the idea that foot size is associated with youth.

Using line drawings of men and women that varied only in regard to relative foot size, Fessler and colleagues (2005b) found that small foot size was generally preferred for women while average foot size was preferred for men in several distinct cultures. They proposed that this supports the idea that foot size in women is a sexually selected trait, especially considering that dimorphism in foot size is not explicable in terms of natural selection alone. Given the costs to fitness of falls during pregnancy associated with small foot size, it might be expected that natural selection would have favoured larger foot size relative to stature in women compared to men. That the opposite pattern occurs suggests that sexual selection has shaped women's foot size, and men's continuing preference for small feet in women.

Nevertheless, caution should be exercised in applying the findings of Fessler, *et al.* (2005b) to such cultural practices as foot binding, a custom common in China until the early twentieth century (see Figure 4.6). This practice involved wrapping the feet of young women in bandages to prevent normal growth, thus ensuring that the feet remained small and highly deformed. Fessler *et al.*'s (2005) results might suggest that such practices began because men find small feet attractive, but it is a common misconception that men found the deformed foot, in the flesh, erotic. Most often, men would never see the bound woman's feet, as most traditional cultures conceal the feet in clothing. In addition, sociologists have argued that binding the foot was meant to keep women dependent on men, because with the foot bound they could not walk, stand up straight or even support their weight without leaning on a man.

Voice

Evolutionary psychologists are not merely concerned with the physical characteristics of the human body, but also with non-physical characteristics like the voice (Puts 2005; Puts *et al.* 2006). It has been speculated that during human evolutionary history voice may have been an important feature of mate choice, particularly at night when vision was compromised (Hughes *et al.* 2002). This is because, quite aside from content, the sound of an

Figure 4.6 Foot binding was a common practice in China until the early twentieth century, and involved wrapping the feet of young women in bandages to prevent normal growth. Copyright © Michael S. Yamashita/CORBIS.

individual's voice provides important information about a variety of biologically relevant features such as sociodemographics, fluctuating asymmetry and sexual behaviour (Collins 2000; Dabbs and Mallinger 1999).

For example, listeners who hear voice samples can infer the speaker's socioeconomic status (Ellis 1967; Harms 1963), personality traits (Zuckerman and Driver 1989), and emotional and mental state attributes related to deception (Ekman *et al.* 1976; Streeter *et al.* 1977). Listeners are also capable of estimating the age, height and weight of speakers with the same degree of accuracy achieved by estimating photographs (Krauss *et al.* 2002). Hughes *et al.* (2002) further found that individuals with symmetrical morphological traits were rated as having more attractive voices, and as deviations from bilateral symmetry increased, ratings of voice attractiveness decreased.

Hughes *et al.* (2002) point out that vocal development is influenced and modified by activational sex hormones during adolescence. Oestrogen and progesterone shape the mature female voice, while testosterone modifies the male voice (Abitbol *et al.* 1999). The same hormones that affect voice have also been implicated in the development of sex-specific body configuration features, such as the shoulder-to-hip and waist-to-hip ratios in men and women respectively (see Chapter 5). Thus, Hughes *et al.* (2004) report that the voices of women with low waist-to-hip ratios and men with larger shoulder-to-hip ratios are judged to be more attractive than the voices of women with high waist-to-hip ratios and men with low shoulder-to-hip ratios. Hughes *et al.* (2004) also found associations between voice attractiveness ratings and different features of self-reported sexual behaviour, including age of first sexual experience and number of sexual partners.

Individuals with attractive voices are perceived more favourably and as having more desirable personality characteristics (Zuckerman and Driver 1989). Furthermore, the higher the ratings of voice attractiveness, the more the speaker is judged to be similar to the rater and the more the rater would like to affiliate with the speaker (Miyake and Zuckerman 1993). Some authors have termed this the 'vocal attractiveness stereotype' (Zuckerman and Driver 1989; Zuckerman *et al.* 1990), and Hughes *et al.* (2004) suggest this stereotype may promote sexual opportunities.

Putting Humpty Dumpty back together

In *An Essay on Criticism* (1711), Alexander Pope wrote: 'Tis not a lip, or eye, we beauty call/But the joint force and full result of all.' He was highlighting the popular belief that beauty is not found in the individual characteristics of an individual, but in their totality. Given the wide range of physical characteristics considered in this chapter, it might be asked to what extent these attributes interact with each other to determine overall physical attractiveness. After all, when we see an individual we see much more than just the sum of her or his body parts (Swami 2007). This is consistent with the idea that it makes little sense that there should be a psychologically adapted module eliciting preferences for each such trait, particularly if a more general mechanism (for example, 'choose a good mate') is more plausible (Sterelny and Griffiths 1999).

Surprisingly, however, very little research has examined this possibility, and existing work has tended to focus on the relative contributions of the face and body to physical attractiveness. Of the two, the face has been shown to have the stronger influence on attractiveness judgements than body characteristics like the waist-to-hip ratio or body weight (Furnham *et al.* 2001). For example, Mueser *et al.* (1984) found that attractiveness ratings of women's faces explained a larger proportion of the variance in ratings of whole figure than ratings of the body alone. This implies that people tend to utilise facial cues more than the body when forming judgements of overall attractiveness. This is perhaps not surprising: the face is the most information-dense part of the body (Symons 1979) and is thus likely to provide clues to underlying condition.

On the other hand, Thornhill and Grammer (1999) have suggested that the face and body should be considered as 'one ornament that signals quality'. In their study, they found that attractiveness ratings of women's faces, backs and front were positively correlated, which they took to suggest a single ornament, or elaborate trait that functions in competition for mates, that signals hormonal health. Specifically, they argued that the effects of oestrogen in the development of sexually dimorphic features of women's faces and bodies would give rise to consistent external signals throughout the face and body. And to the extent that the development of other sexually dimorphic traits (such as the LBR, height and voice) falls under the influence of sex hormones, then these too might be considered part of that single ornament.

Of course, this does not rule out the possibility of 'trade-offs' among various parts of the signal under certain circumstances. For example, in some situations, signalling with fat deposits on the buttocks may allow women to more successfully attract mates, and in such a scenario the importance of these fat deposits may override that of facial attractiveness (see Chapter 6). Or again, an obese (and therefore unhealthy) individual may have the 'optimal' waist-to-hip ratio in terms of evolved psychologies (Tovée *et al.* 2002), and in such a situation judgements of body weight may 'trump' that of body shape (see Chapter 5).

Of course, there is utility for researchers in isolating certain traits one at a time, as long as the research does not stop there. The examples highlighted in this chapter suggest that, ultimately, Humpty Dumpty needs to be put back together again. Deconstructing the body in terms of its individual components may be useful for research purposes, but the absence of an holistic approach will undoubtedly hinder our understanding of what it means to be physically attractive (Armstrong 2004; Swami 2007).

Conclusion

In this chapter, we looked at a number of morphological traits of the human body that men and women find attractive. With most of these traits, the underlying logic derived from evolutionary psychology is that men have evolved to find attractive cues that signal reproductive value or health. Women, on the other hand, have evolved to find attractive those cues that signal resources-acquiring potential in men. To the extent that these characteristics are honest signals of underlying quality or condition, men and women who mate with partners with such characteristics will obtain a reproductive advantage.

Clearly, ascertaining which feature (if any) is the most important, and how these characteristics influence attractiveness in combination, is a difficult task. Nevertheless, evolutionary psychology has provided a starting point for such an endeavour and the utility of these and other attributes continues to be debated. In the next chapter, we consider in more detail the attributes of women's and men's bodies that have generated the most debate between evolutionary psychologists and sociocultural theorists: preferences for women's and men's body shape and weight.

5 Of hourglasses and triangles

Human body weight and shape

Beauty, *n.* The power by which a woman charms a lover and terrifies a husband.

Ambrose Bierce, American satirist (*The Devil's Dictionary*, 1911)

In life, as in art, the beautiful moves in curves.

Edward George Bulwer-Lytton, English novelist
(*What Will He Do with It?*, 1858)

In the previous chapter, we examined some of the physical characteristics that men and women find attractive in a potential partner. While studies have shown many of these attributes to be important in judgements of physical attractiveness, the vast majority of studies have tended to focus on two aspects of the human body that are the most ubiquitous and politicised: body shape and weight. In this chapter, we consider evolutionary psychological arguments for why we find certain body shapes attractive in men and women. This serves to illustrate the research methodology that many evolutionary psychologists have relied upon, as well as the difficulty in ascribing a singular explanation for results obtained through such techniques.

Men's body shape

Traditionally, a great deal of psychological research has concentrated on the attributes that define women's physical attractiveness, and fewer studies have considered what makes men's bodies attractive. Swami (2007) proposed a number of reasons for this, including the greater preponderance of male researchers studying physical attractiveness and the evolutionary psychological idea that women are less interested in the attractiveness of male partners than they are in cues that signal resource possession. However, recent research has attempted to rectify this oversight, and it is now widely acknowledged that women, at least in some cultures, hold strong beliefs about what constitutes the ideal male body.

Barber (1995) suggested that some aspects of the male body could be sexually selected. Early studies highlighted the fact that ratings of men's attractiveness were enhanced with increasing masculinity, and bodily features that signal dominance or masculinity were considered to be especially important. For example, the shoulders of men, their upper-body musculature and biceps have all been suggested as characteristics that determine male attractiveness. Importantly, these features are all more developed in men than in women (Ross and Ward 1982), and are influenced by testosterone levels (Björntorp 1987).

On the other hand, using silhouettes as stimuli, a number of studies have shown that women tend to prefer moderately developed male torsos rather than extremely muscular physiques (Barber 1995). However, most of these studies have not looked explicitly at male bodily physique, but have used line drawings that focus on the waist-to-hip ratio (WHR, the ratio of the width of the waist to the width of the hips). These studies report a preferred WHR of 0.90 to 0.95 in men (Furnham *et al.* 1997, 2001; Henss 1995; Lynch and Zellner 1999; Singh 1995b), and it has been suggested that this is because such ratios are 'optimally healthy' for men (Singh 1995b). There is little evidence to suggest, however, that male WHRs between 0.90 and 0.95 are strongly associated with health outcomes (Weeden and Sabini 2005). Moreover, a great deal of research indicates that lower-body shape, which is what the WHR measures, may be relatively unimportant when both women and men judge men's bodies for physical attractiveness. Rather, they are more concerned with upper-body build, and many men indicate a desire to increase torso and arm muscularity.

Of triangles

Fortunately, a number of studies have used better sets of stimuli to examine the preferences of women and men for male bodily attractiveness. Some studies have relied on line drawings based on 'somatypes' that Sheldon and his colleagues defined and measured (1940, 1954). These authors argued that a person's body could be rated as having a degree of three independent dimensions or somatypes: endomorphy (fatness or softness), mesomorphy (muscularity) and ectomorphy (leanness). Dixson *et al.* (2003) had women rate line drawings of paradigmatic examples of Sheldon *et al.*'s (1940, 1954) three somatypes along with an average stimulus. They found that women showed a strong preference for the mesomorph type, followed by the average, then ectomorph, and finally endomorph.

Other studies have examined the relative contribution of overall body weight (as measured by the body mass index, BMI), upper-body shape (measured by the waist-to-chest ratio, or WCR – the ratio of the width of the waist to the width of the chest) and lower-body shape (WHR) to attractiveness ratings of men's bodies. These studies, using photographic and three-dimensional images (see Figure 5.1), have shown that while the WHR, BMI and WCR are all significant contributors to men's bodily attractiveness, WCR is the

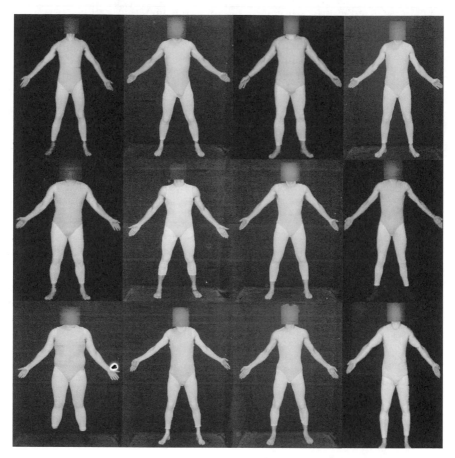

Figure 5.1 Examples of the photographic stimuli used in the study by Maisey *et al.*
(1999). Images are not arranged in any particular order and are reproduced
here with kind permission of Martin Tovée.

primary determinant and accounts for the greatest amount of variance in
attractiveness ratings (Fan 2007; Fan *et al.* 2005; Maisey *et al.* 1999; Swami
and Tovée 2005a; Swami and Tovée, in press b; Swami *et al.* 2007i). In the study
by Maisey and colleagues (1999), for example, WCR accounted for 56 per
cent of the variance of attractiveness ratings, with lower WCRs (indicating
larger chests relative to waists) increasing ratings of attractiveness. In the
study by Dixson *et al.* (2003) too there was a general preference for low WCRs.

Women are thought to prefer men whose torsos have an 'inverted triangle'
shape, that is, a narrow waist and broad chest and shoulders (see Figure 5.2),
which is consistent with physical strength and muscle development in the
upper body. These findings are comparable with other studies using line drawings, which show that women prefer men with a 'V-shape' (wider shoulders
than chest, which is, in turn, wider than the hips; Frederick and Haselton

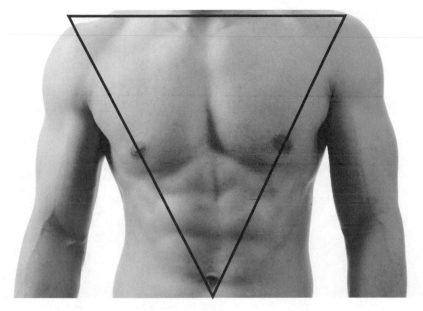

Figure 5.2 In socioeconomically developed societies, women find attractive men whose torsos have an 'inverted triangle' shape, that is, a narrow waist and a broad chest and shoulders.

2003; Furnham and Radley 1989; Lavrakas 1975; Salusso-Deonier *et al.* 1993). For example, Hovath (1979) found that shoulder width was a good predictor of the attractiveness of male line drawings, and that the WCR accounted for almost all of the variance in bodily attractiveness for the stimuli used. Similarly, self-reports by women of what they consider important about a man's body suggest that the WCR is an important consideration (Franzoi and Herzog 1987).

Moreover, a wealth of evidence suggests that being muscular is an important component of historical messages about men's attractiveness (see Figure 5.3), as well as contemporary men's ideal body image (Fisher *et al.* 2002; Jacobi and Cash 1994; Jones 2001; McCreary and Sasse 2000, 2002; O'Dea and Rawsthorne 2001; Phillips and Diaz 1997; Pope *et al.* 2000). Among adolescent boys, for example, resistance training activities are a popular means of gaining muscle mass (Ricciardelli and McCabe 2003), and when boys are asked where they would like to be more muscular, they typically want larger pectorals, biceps and shoulders (Drewnowski and Yee 1987; Huenemann *et al.* 1966).

Interestingly, however, to be considered attractive, it is not sufficient for a man to simply have a V-shaped body. Rather, body weight is an important additional consideration (Fan *et al.* 2005; Maisey *et al.* 1999; Swami and Tovée 2005a, in press b; Swami *et al.* 2007i). In the study by Maisey *et al.* (1999), while BMI was a smaller predictor of attractiveness ratings, it nevertheless

Figure 5.3 Being muscular is an important component of historical messages about men's attractiveness, as is often depicted by ancient statues of heroic men.

accounted for 13 per cent of the variance in a curvilinear relationship. That is, BMIs towards the lower end of the normal weight range were judged as most attractive, with drop-offs on both sides of this peak (see Figure 5.4). Other studies have shown that, for self-ratings of attractiveness, men in overweight and underweight BMI ranges rate themselves less attractive than men in normal weight samples (Cash and Hicks 1990; McCreary and Sadava 2001). Additionally, studies using line drawings have shown that overweight male figures are consistently judged the least attractive (Fallon and Rozin 1985; Furnham *et al.* 1997; Henss 1995).

Another study varied several parameters of male silhouettes including the presence or absence of a protruding abdomen, slouched versus straight shoulders, neck girth and a V-shaped versus pillar-shaped body (Gitter *et al.* 1982). When undergraduates in the United States and Israel rated the line drawings for attractiveness, the body characteristic that accounted for the

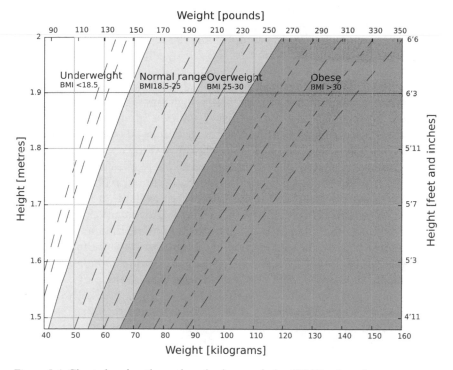

Figure 5.4 Chart showing the various body mass index (BMI) categories.

greatest variance was the presence versus absence of a protruding abdomen, which accounted for 53 per cent of the variance across cultures. This result contrasts somewhat with the studies finding chest size in relation to waist size to be the primary determinant, but is corroborated by a contemporary preoccupation with abdominal stomach muscles (Baker 1997). In short, then, the evidence suggests that to be considered attractive men would do well to show a simultaneous presence of high muscularity and low fatness (and possibly leanness of the abdomen).

Men's body shape and health

A 'traditional' good genes hypothesis of men's physical attractiveness might suggest that men with low WCRs and body weights within the normal BMI range are considered attractive because they are also optimally healthy (and possibly have greater resource accrual). However, the evidence does not appear to support this argument. In particular, studies that have included measures of mesomorphy in examining health outcomes suggest that both increased mesomorphy and increased endomorphy are actually risk factors for, among other conditions, cardiovascular disease (Malina *et al.* 1997; Williams *et al.* 2000). Men's increased body size from muscularity may be associated with higher attractiveness, but it is also associated with poorer health outcomes (Weeden and Sabini 2005), recalling something Plautus wrote in *Miles Gloriosus* (*c.*2 BC/1997): 'It is a great plague to be too handsome a man.'

However, there may be advantages accrued by building a bigger signal of mesomorphy, which offset more long-term complications associated with health and well-being (Kaplan and Gangestad 2005). For example, increased muscularity may intimidate rival men (deterring them from making cuckoldry attempts) or provide enhanced defensive abilities. In such a scenario, the health costs of developing increased muscularity may be outweighed by their benefits, which may also be passed on to offspring (Wong and Candolin 2005).

In a similar vein, Barber (1995) has suggested that women may have evolved to find men with a certain physique attractive because this body shape was beneficial to men in past evolutionary history. For example, it is possible that a low WCR, which is associated with physical strength and upper-body muscle development, was an adaptation for intrasexual competition among men in our evolutionary past, either via direct fighting or through intimidation. An alternative explanation is that upper-body strength is an adaptation for hunting large animals, which Barber (1995) argued was a predominantly male activity in the environment of evolutionary adaptedness. Thus, if women are adapted to select men who would make 'good hunters', then they should be attracted to men with a mesomorphic body shape as this physique would most likely have been successful at hunting.

While Barber's (1995) suggestions are certainly plausible, for the moment they remain conjectures given our lack of relevant knowledge about past evolutionary environments to which evolutionary psychologists argue we are adapted. In a sense, they are 'Just-So Stories', a metaphor that Gould (1980) used to describe some aspects of the evolutionary psychological paradigm. The 'Just-So Stories' of evolutionary psychology, named after Rudyard Kipling's book of fables describing, for example, 'How the Leopard Got his Spots', cannot stand as an example of genuine scientific explanation. Moreover, it should be remembered that social constructionist explanations for why we find the muscular ideal attractive in men are just as plausible as evolutionary psychological explanations, and we encounter some of these in subsequent chapters (see Chapters 7 and 8).

Women's body shape

Among human beings, it is women who have tended to be considered more attractive when rated by both men and women (Jackson 1992), and female appearance receives more attention than male appearance, even across cultures (Ford and Beach 1952). Indeed, it is much easier to find examples of the adoration of feminine rather than masculine beauty within literary record. As Jean-Antoine Petit-Senn put it: 'There is no beauty on earth which exceeds the natural loveliness of woman.' So too within the arts: depictions of idealised feminine beauty far outweigh those depicting the ideal man.

What for the art historian John Berger (1977) was an unfair emphasis on women's attractiveness as a result of men's dominance in most societies – what he termed the 'male gaze' – is for evolutionary psychologists a natural result of evolutionary history. Competition among women for high-quality men resulted in the evolution of various physical cues signalling women's reproductive potential. Among the attributes that some evolutionary psychologists argue signal the reproductive capacity of a woman is her breasts.

At first glance, female breasts would seem to be a primary candidate of a sexually selected signal in humans. Permanently large breasts are an evolutionary novelty in primates (Montagna 1983), and in humans breasts are perceived as an important component of sexual attractiveness, at least in some cultures (Ford and Beach 1952). This is underscored by the willingness of women to undergo breast augmentation surgery in order to enhance their physical attractiveness: in the United States alone, there are some 300,000 breast augmentations each year (American Association of Plastic Surgeons 2005). Of course, women may choose breast augmentation surgery for different reasons (aesthetic purposes, relieve physical discomfort, and so on; Fallon 1990), but the comparable frequencies of both augmentations and reductions suggest that, as far as breasts are concerned, both smallness and largeness may be experienced as undesirable or unattractive.

There appears, however, to be little evidence to suggest that breast size is associated with fertility, lactational output or health (Barber 1995), which would seem to rule out a 'good genes' explanation for why men find female breasts attractive. An alternative explanation is that female breasts evolved under runaway selection as a sign of nulliparousity in women. Because breasts develop most intensely at the beginning of the reproductive age, some researchers have suggested that breasts evolved as a sexual signal of reproductive value rather than fecundity as such (Barber 1995; Cant 1981). In short, because breasts are a signal of reproductive age, men should have evolved mechanisms eliciting preferences accordingly (Marlowe 1998). In particular, men should find large breasts more attractive than small breasts because this is a larger signal of reproductive value.

However, when psychologists have included breast size as a variable in their studies of physical attractiveness, they have generally not found consistent preferences. For instance, it was reported by Kleinke and Staneski (1980) that medium breasts evoked the most favourable ratings from participants of both sexes, when written stimuli were used. In another study, using colour photographs, the same experimenters found that women with smaller breasts were rated as competent, ambitious, intelligent, moral and modest. Women with large breasts were judged to have the opposite characteristics by both female and male participants. On the other hand, using silhouettes of the female figure that varied in breast size, Furnham and Swami (2007) found that participants rated small breast size as the most physically attractive.

Gitter *et al.* (1983) also conducted a study with male and female participants, but in contrast to the above findings their results suggested that men preferred large breasts whereas smaller breasts were rated more favourably by women. Yet, large breasts on overweight women are not considered especially attractive: Low (1979) suggested that only slim women with large breasts would be thought of as attractive. This was also the conclusion of Furnham *et al.* (1998), who found that the attractiveness of breast size varied according to the shape and size of the body, with large breasts consistently enhancing attractiveness ratings so long as the figures were slender.

Clearly, existing studies do not present a conclusive picture of what is considered an attractive breast size in women. Related evidence that breast size preferences are highly variable was documented by Mazur (1986), who showed that 'ideal' breast size grew continually from its flat period in the 1920s to the large-breasted ideal of the early 1960s. Since then, in tandem with a societal idealisation of extreme thinness, preferred breast size has become smaller, although there has been a recent trend towards large-breasted figures in media appealing to men (Koff and Benevage 1998). Certainly, size is only one of several characteristics that can affect preferences for upper body shape, but it is the most public variable and a principal way in which women's breasts have come to be embodied in popular culture (Mazur 1986).

Recent studies have suggested that breast size may be the least important characteristic in men's ratings of women's physical attractiveness, after body weight and shape (Furnham *et al.* 2006; see Figure 5.5). On the other hand, it is unclear whether such variability in preferences remains true when cross-cultural samples are included, although there is every reason to believe that this is the case (Swami *et al.* 2007b, 2007d). In short, then, breast size does not appear to be a reliable predictor of physical attractiveness, despite being a good candidate for having evolved by sexual selection (Barber 1995).

Of hourglasses

Glance through any contemporary fashion or glamour magazine and it becomes clear that what is beautiful is also slim, perhaps even dangerously so. For example, Tovée and his colleagues (1997) compiled the biometric measurements of 300 fashion models and 300 glamour models, and found that they were consistently underweight in terms of BMI. Research on Miss America contestants and *Playboy* centrefolds has also shown that the 'ideal' became increasingly thinner over a 20-year period, between 1959 and 1978, while American women actually became 4 per cent heavier (Garner *et al.* 1980; see also Freese and Meland 2002; Voracek and Fisher 2002). Follow-up studies showed that this trend continued between 1979 and 1988 (Wiseman *et al.* 1992), and possibly even into the millennium (Seifert 2005; Sypeck *et al.* 2004, 2006). These studies would seem to suggest that body weight should be of primary importance in Western men's judgements about women's bodily attractiveness (Swami 2006b).

Not so, say some evolutionary psychologists. In a series of ground-breaking studies, Singh (1993a, 1993b, 1994a, 1994b, 1994c, 1995a, 1995b; Singh and

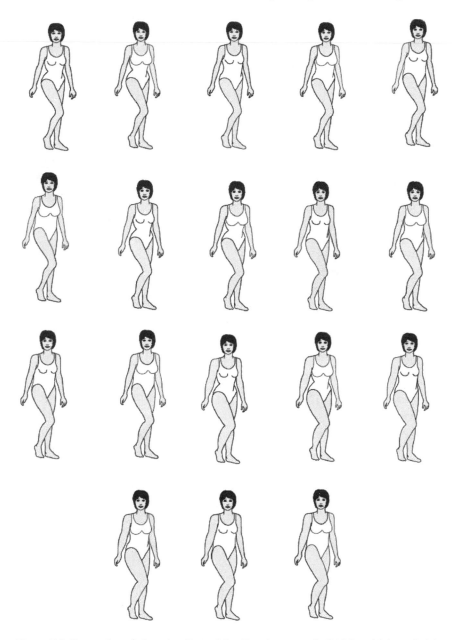

Figure 5.5 Examples of the stimuli used by Furnham *et al.* (2006), which varied in several levels of breast size, waist-to-hip ratio and body weight. In this study, breast size was found to have the smallest effect on ratings of physical attractiveness.

Luis 1995; Singh and Young 1995) highlighted that, while overall body weight is the most noticeable change caused by pubertal onset, this change does not take into account the sex-dependent anatomical distribution of fat deposits. While the body shape of boys and girls is more or less similar before puberty, the sex hormones – primarily oestrogen and testosterone – regulate the deposit and utilisation of fat from various anatomical areas during pubertal onset (LaVelle 1995; Leong 2006).

For most women, fat (or adipose tissue) deposit is inhibited in the abdominal region and stimulated in the gluteofemoral region (buttocks and thighs) more than in any other region of the body. This engenders what is known as a 'gynoid' fat distribution. For most men, on the other hand, fat deposit is stimulated in the abdominal region and inhibited in the gluteofemoral region, giving rise to an 'android' fat distribution (Björntorp 1991, 1997; Rebuffé-Scrive 1988, 1991). It is this sexually dimorphic body fat distribution that underscores body shape differences between the women and men (Molarius *et al.* 1999), and is typically quantified by measuring the ratio of the circumference of the waist to the circumference of the hips. This measurement is known as the waist-to-hip ratio (WHR), and closely related to the classic 'hourglass' figure in women (see Figure 5.6; Singh 2006).

For healthy, pre-menopausal Caucasian women, the range of WHRs has been shown to be between 0.67 and 0.80 (Lanska *et al.* 1985); for healthy Caucasian men, it ranges from 0.85 to 0.95 (Jones *et al.* 1986; Marti *et al.* 1991). Women typically maintain a lower WHR than men through adulthood, although the WHR approaches the masculine range after menopause (Arechiga *et al.* 2001; Kirschner and Samojlik 1991). This increase in WHR in menopausal women is most likely caused by the reduction in oestrogen levels, which increases fat deposit in the abdominal region. This interpretation is corroborated by studies showing that, when women and men are administered oestrogen compounds, their WHRs tend to become lower over time (Kirschner and Samojlik 1991; Pasquali *et al.* 1999).

In short, then, there are sex-typical differences in the pattern of fat distribution as a function of the sex hormones. Combining this with an evolutionary psychological approach, Singh proposed that the risk for various diseases depends not only on the degree of obesity as measured by BMI, but also on the anatomical location of fat deposits (Guo *et al.* 1994; Kissebah and Krakower 1994). In other words, the WHR is systematically related to a variety of life outcomes, with a low WHR being associated with better outcomes in women. In particular, the WHR is a risk factor for cardiovascular disorders, adult-onset diabetes, hypertension, endometrial, ovarian and breast cancer, and gall bladder disease (Folsom *et al.* 1993; Huang *et al.* 1999; Misra and Vikram 2003).

In addition, Singh argued that the WHR signals all the conditions that affect women's reproductive status (see Kirchengast and Huber 1999; Waass *et al.* 1997). Women with higher WHRs have more irregular menstrual cycles (van Hooff *et al.* 2000), and the WHR becomes significantly lower during

Figure 5.6 The waist-to-hip ratio is quantified by measuring the ratio of the circumference of the waist to the circumference of the hips, and a low waist-to-hip ratio is closely related to the classic 'hourglass' figure in women. Copyright © Bettmann/CORBIS.

ovulation compared to non-ovulatory phases of the menstrual cycle (Singh *et al.* 2000). The probability of successful pregnancy induction is also affected by WHR: women participating in donor insemination programmes have a lower probability of conception if their WHR is greater than 0.80, after controlling for age, BMI and parity (Zaadstra *et al.* 1993). Married women with a higher WHR also have more difficulty becoming pregnant and have their first live birth at a later age than married women with lower WHRs (Kaye *et al.* 1990). On the basis of such evidence, Singh concluded that women's susceptibility to various major physical diseases and fertility is reliably conveyed by the size of the WHR.

The ideal waist-to-hip ratio

One of the main problems facing our hunter-gatherer ancestors during the Pleistocene epoch, say evolutionary psychologists, was the identification of mate value. Singh (1993a) proposed that, to overcome this problem, 'perceptual mechanisms' or mental modules evolved in men to detect and use information conveyed by the WHR in determining a woman's attractiveness as a potential mate. Because of its association with health and fertility outcomes, men will have evolved to use the WHR as a direct assessment of women's underlying quality. And so, Singh (1993a) argued, it should be possible to systematically change men's evaluations of women's attractiveness by manipulating the size of the WHR.

To test this idea, Singh (1993a, 1993b) developed a set of 12 line drawings of the female figure, which were systematically varied with respect to overall body weight (underweight, normal weight, and overweight) and the WHR (see Figure 5.7). Within each weight category, line drawings represented four levels of the WHR by changing the waist size. In a series of experiments using these drawings, Singh (1993a, 1993b, 1994c; Singh and Luis 1995) described a negative correlation between WHR and female attractiveness. That is, line drawings with gynoid WHRs (0.70 and 0.80) were judged as the most attractive, and ratings decreased with increasing WHR. Although the body weight categories also had an effect, within each weight category, figures with the lower WHR were judged to be more attractive than other figures in those groups.

Using Singh's original set of line drawings, the preference for low WHRs has been replicated with participants in the United States (Singh 1994c), Britain (Furnham *et al.* 1997) and Germany (Henss 1995). But lest it be said that line drawings do not reflect actual mate preferences as they occur in real life, studies have also examined the effect of WHR in field studies with real people. Mikash and Bailey (1999) reported that women with low WHRs have more sexual partners than women with high WHRs, whereas Hughes and Gallup (2003) found that young women with low WHRs also report earlier ages of first intercourse. In addition, aesthetic plastic surgery that redistributes body fat to make the body more proportionate without altering BMI appears to increase ratings of attractiveness (Roberts and Weinfield 2005; Singh and Randall 2007).

In combination, these studies indicate that, to be considered attractive, a woman should have a low WHR and fall within the normal body weight range. For Singh (1993a: 304), the WHR 'acts as a wide first-pass filter, which would automatically exclude women who are unhealthy or who have low reproductive capacity'. It is only after this 'culturally invariant' filter is passed that other features such as the face, skin or weight (which may vary between cultures) become utilised in final mate selection. Some researchers have even gone so far as to suggest that dieting is a 'natural' strategy employed by women attempting to achieve the ideal WHR. While Singh's research was framed in terms of the

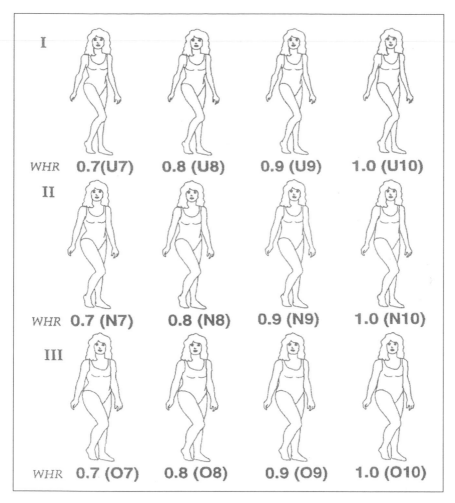

WHR 0.7(U7)   0.8 (U8)   0.9 (U9)   1.0 (U10)

WHR 0.7 (N7)   0.8 (N8)   0.9 (N9)   1.0 (N10)

WHR 0.7 (O7)   0.8 (O8)   0.9 (O9)   1.0 (O10)

Figure 5.7 Singh's original set of female line drawings varying in four levels of waist-to-hip ratio and three levels of body weight. Used with kind permission of Devendra Singh.

comparison of low WHR to high WHRs, some evolutionary psychologists have suggested a specific preference for a WHR of 0.70 (which happened to be the lower end of WHRs used in Singh's studies). In one of the more enthusiastic endorsements of this hypothesis, Burnham and Phelan (2000: 144) wrote that 'there's something about that 0.7 that only a gene could love'.

Critical tests

For various reasons, the WHR hypothesis of women's physical attractiveness – and in particular, the notion that the WHR acts as a 'first-pass filter' – has attracted an enormous amount of controversy, debate and sometimes even heated polemic. A great many pages in scientific journals, academic books and the popular press have been devoted to women's WHRs, and it seems this book is no exception. Still, determining the relative importance of the WHR in judgements of attractiveness is not an end in itself; rather, it may have important consequences in other areas. At a scholarly level, for example, the WHR hypothesis of attractiveness is often held up as a paragon of the evolutionary psychological approach, which would make it an important hypothesis to be tested critically.

One of the first studies to criticise Singh's research was a paper by Tassinary and Hansen (1998), which took issue with the fact that research on the WHR and women's attractiveness had been restricted to the set of line drawings developed by Singh. Tassinary and Hansen (1998) suggested that the use of Singh's line drawings to depict variations in WHR lacked 'ecological validity'. As Singh himself had indicated, line drawing stimuli are often impoverished and unrealistic, and rely on a single original image from which modifications are made. Indeed, Furnham and Reeves (2006) have pointed out that the WHR manipulations used in Singh's line drawings are, in reality, crude approximations made on the basis of two-dimensional stimuli. Careful measurements showed that figures which Singh claimed had the 0.70 WHR, for example, had actual ratios of 0.69, 0.70 and 0.75 (Furnham and Reeves 2006).

Tassinary and Hansen (1998) therefore proposed that it was ecologically unrealistic to show modified versions of the same stimulus and expect each to be rated on its own merits. To examine this issue, they developed a set of their own line drawings comprising 27 female figures that varied in weight (light, moderate, heavy), waist size (small, medium, large) and hip size (small, medium, large). With this new set of images, they found the weight of the figures to be more important in judgements of physical attractiveness than the WHR. Light and moderate weight figures were judged to be much more attractive than the heavy figures, whereas moderate weight and heavy figures were judged to be much more fecund than the light figures.

For Tassinary and Hansen (1998), these results suggested to them that the association between WHR and attractiveness was an artefact of a limited stimulus set. They went on to write that their finding 'constitutes a clear and unambiguous disconfirmation of the WHR hypothesis' (Tassinary and Hansen 1998: 154–155). Like other numerical formulas of attractiveness, they believed the WHR hypothesis would 'eventually be understood to be a dimensionless number with great intuitive appeal but with highly circumscribed explanatory or predictive efficacy with respect to aesthetic judgements' (Tassinary and Hansen 1998: 155).

More recently, Streeter and McBurney (2003) failed to replicate the positive relationship between WHR and attractiveness reported by Tassinary and Hansen (1998). Using a set of photographic stimuli, they found that when perceived body weight was statistically controlled, an inverse relationship between WHR and attractiveness was found to be significant. That is, a low

WHR was considered maximally attractive when the effect of body weight was removed. However, they were quick to point out that the arguments in favour of WHR as an important predictor of attractiveness independent of weight were purely empirical: they did not dispute the fact that WHR only predicts preference when the effect of weight is removed (but see McBurney and Streeter 2007).

A number of other studies have also attempted to overcome the ecological problems associated with line drawings, again finding a significant effect of WHR (Singh 2002). Henss (2000), for instance, designed a study using full frontal photographs that included the face and breasts of different women with computer-altered WHRs. Using this new set of stimuli, Henss (2000) found support for Singh's argument that the WHR is an essential attribute of the attractiveness of the female figure. Like Streeter and McBurney (2003), however, Henss (2000) also pointed out that whenever both WHR and overall body weight have been manipulated, it is evident that weight accounts for more variance than WHR. All the evidence, he concluded, underlines the fact that the WHR plays a less potent role than the weight category or the face.

This was also the conclusion of Forestell *et al.* (2004), who used Tassinary and Hansen's line drawings to test the degree to which various body shape characteristics influence women's ratings of attractiveness of female figures. Their results showed that participants' preferred figures had WHRs around 0.70, but as body size increased, larger WHRs tended to be preferred. Figures with small and medium waists and hips were generally preferred regardless of body weight, but figures with large hips were preferred less, regardless of other shape characteristics. It seems likely, therefore, that body weight, waist size and hip size all interact to influence the attractiveness of female figures (Furnham *et al.* 2005, 2006; Swami and Furnham 2006), although this has in no way stifled the controversy.

The relative importance of body shape and weight

Just as some studies have taken issue with the line drawings used in the extant WHR research, so others have asked whether the WHR really acts as a 'first-pass filter' of women's attractiveness. Whereas the use of line drawings meant that body weight could only be generalised as vague categories, utilising technologically advanced sets of stimuli has allowed researchers to be more precise in their definitions of body weight. In such studies, body weight is typically measured using BMI, where BMIs below 18.5 are considered underweight, BMIs between 18.5 and 25 normal weight, BMIs between 25 and 30 overweight, and BMIs over 30 obese (Bray 1998; Figure 5.3).

These studies attest to the important role played by body weight in determining women's attractiveness ratings, often much more strongly than WHR. This is a point made by Tovée and colleagues (Smith *et al.* 2007a; Tovée *et al.* 1997, 1998, 1999), who took issue with the extant WHR research. They argued that it is erroneous to believe that the weight of figures is held constant when body shape is altered (Tovée and Cornelissen 2001). That is, modifying line drawings by altering the width of waist not only alters the WHR but also apparent BMI, and so it is impossible to say whether attractiveness ratings are being made on the basis of WHR, BMI, or both (Tovée and Cornelissen 1999; Tovée *et al.* 1999). Almost all previous studies, they argue, have made this error, and so it is likely that the importance attributed to WHR in previous studies was an artefact of covarying WHR with BMI.

To investigate the relative importance of BMI and WHR in the perception of women's attractiveness, Tovée and colleagues struck upon a seemingly intuitive solution: they used images of real women, for whom BMI and WHR were known precisely (see Figure 5.8). They could, therefore, estimate the effects of both these variables separately. Indeed, their analyses showed that, although both shape and body mass are significant predictors of women's attractiveness, BMI was a far more important factor than WHR (Tovée and Cornelissen 2001; Tovée *et al.* 1998, 1999). In their studies, BMI accounted for more than 70 per cent of the variance in attractiveness ratings, whereas WHR accounts for little more than 2 per cent. In other words, the importance of BMI to ratings of attractiveness was about 35 times greater than that of WHR. Nor is this finding limited to participants in Britain: using the same methodological paradigm, Swami and colleagues have reported similar findings in Europe, Polynesia, East and Southeast Asia and Africa (see Table 5.1).

In their research, Tovée and his colleagues used the widest range of BMI and WHR values available, and so it might be argued that the relative ranges of BMI and WHR are unequal. The apparent importance of BMI in such studies, therefore, could be due to the greater relative variation in body weight than in WHR (Singh 2002). To address this issue, Tovée *et al.* (2002) used images of women's bodies where the range of BMI values was strictly controlled (giving WHR an 'advantage'), but WHR still failed to emerge as a strong determinant of attractiveness ratings.

In a second experiment, Tovée and colleagues (2002) 'disturbed' the natural relationship between the WHR and BMI. Normally, BMI and WHR tend to be positively correlated in the female population, that is, women with a higher BMI tend to have a less curvaceous shape. Instead, Tovée *et al.* (2002) chose a set of photographs that demonstrated an inverse correlation between BMI and WHR, that is, a group in which as the women become heavier they also become more curvaceous. Even though the relative ranges of WHR and BMI should favour WHR in this sample of images, BMI again emerged as the dominant predictor. In other words, women with a low BMI and a high WHR were judged as more attractive, rather than women with a high BMI and a low WHR.

Importantly, these results hold when women were presented in profile, as opposed to a frontal view (Tovée and Cornelissen 2001) and when different methodological designs and stimuli are used (Puhl and Boland 2001; Thornhill

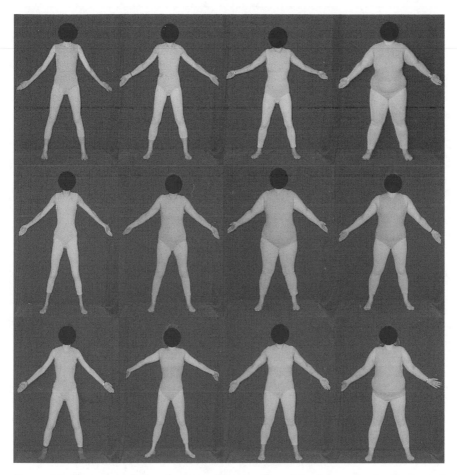

Figure 5.8 Examples of the photographic stimuli used in the studies by Tovée and
colleagues (1997, 1998). Images are not arranged in any particular order
and are reproduced here with kind permission of Martin Tovée.

and Grammer 1999; Wilson *et al.* 2005). Studies using three-dimensional
images, for example, have found evidence consistent with the hypothesis that
BMI is the dominant determinant of women's attractiveness (Smith *et al.*
2007a). For example, Fan and colleagues (2004) argued that observers estimate
the body weight of women's bodies from their volumes, what in their study was
described as the ratio of volume over the square of chin height. They therefore defined a new parameter called the volume-height index (VHI), which
has a strong linear relationship with BMI. In their study, Fan *et al.* (2004)
found that the VHI gave a better prediction of women's attractiveness than
BMI, leading them to suggest that VHI is used as an estimation of BMI in
the visual assessment of physical attractiveness. In sum, then, the available
evidence suggests that it is unlikely that the WHR acts as a 'first-pass filter'

Table 5.1 Studies reporting that body weight is the better predictor of women's attractiveness than WHR

Continent	Nation	References
Africa	South Africa	Tovée *et al.* (2006)
	Tanzania (Hadza tribe)	Marlowe and Wetsman (2001); Wetsman and Marlowe (1998)
Americas	Canada	Wilson *et al.* (2005)
	Peru (Matsigenka tribe)	Yu and Shepard (1998)
	United States of America	Puhl and Boland (2001)
Asia	Japan	Swami *et al.* (2006b)
	Malaysia	Swami and Tovée (2005b); Swami *et al.* (2007g)
	Thailand	Swami and Tovée (2007a)
Australasia	Independent Samoa	Swami *et al.* (2007g)
Europe	Britain	Smith *et al.* (2007); Swami and Tovée (2005b); Tovée *et al.* (1997, 1998, 2002)
	Finland	Swami and Tovée (2007)
	Greece	Swami *et al.* (2006a)
	Portugal	Swami *et al.* (in press, b)
	Spain	Swami *et al.* (in press, b)

of women's attractiveness, and that women's body weight is a much better predictor of attractiveness ratings.

Body weight, WHR and health

Could there be an evolutionary psychological reason why men find certain body weights attractive in women? Tovée and his colleagues have suggested that there are advantages to using BMI as a basis for mate selection, as BMI provides a reliable cue to women's health (Manson *et al.* 1995; Willet *et al.* 1995) and reproductive potential (Frisch 1987, 1988; Lake *et al.* 1997; Reid and van Vugt 1987; Wang *et al.* 2000), just as Singh argued in the case of WHR. For example, obesity is usually associated with complications of pregnancy, menstrual irregularities and infertility, among other things (National Heart, Lung and Blood Institute 1998). Severely underweight women also experience menstrual irregularities and non-ovulation (De Souza and Metzger 1991), and anorexia nervosa is associated with higher miscarriage rates, higher premature birth rates and lower birth weights (Bulik *et al.* 1999).

Put together, the balance between the optimal BMI for health and fertility in women centres on a BMI value of about 19–20. In most studies, a BMI in this range (which is at the low end of the normal weight category) is also the preferred BMI for physical attractiveness. For example, Tovée and colleagues (2003) had women use a computer programme that manipulated a picture of a body to add or remove fat from particular areas. On average, women using the programme set the ideal female BMI at just over 20. Other studies support this conclusion: for self-ratings of attractiveness, women in the overweight BMI range rate themselves as least attractive (Cash and Hicks 1990), and women in the underweight BMI range, or low end of the normal weight range, consider themselves the most attractive (McCreary and Sadava 2001).

Tovée *et al.* (2002) have further argued that the WHR is limited in its utility, which may explain why it is such a poor predictor of attractiveness ratings of women. They cite the example of anorexic women, who are amenorrhoiec (and, therefore, have low reproductive potential), but who nevertheless could have WHRs akin to those of healthy women. In other words, a woman with an effective fertility of zero could have the same WHR as a woman with normal fertility. In addition, there is evidence to suggest that the sexual dimorphism in the WHR may be highly variable, depending on multiple aetiological factors such as culture, environment and genetic inheritance (Abitbol 1996). If these suggestions are substantiated, it would suggest that the WHR is an unreliable cue on which to base judgements of attractiveness.

Furthermore, there is evidence to suggest that the WHR is an equivocal predictor of health and reproductive potential, contrary to the evidence Singh presented. For instance, some studies have shown that waist circumference alone is a better measure than WHR in determining overall health risks (National Heart, Lung and Blood Institute 1998) and risk for cardiovascular disease (Lean *et al.* 1995). Two other studies observed that waist and hip circumference are independently related in opposite directions to risk factors such as high insulin levels (Bigaard *et al.* 2004; Seidell *et al.* 2001). Not surprisingly, then, recent studies have highlighted the possibility that the waist and hips may have a differential effect on attractiveness ratings (Rozmus-Wrzesinska and Pawłowski 2005). When photographs of women with WHR manipulated either by hip or waist changes are used, attractiveness seems to be more influenced by changes in waist than hip size.

Conclusion

It can sometimes seem that, in debating whether BMI or WHR is the stronger predictor of women's attractiveness, researchers are quibbling over minor points of contention. Nevertheless, it is important for scientists to engage in lively debate and discussion, which serves only to drive forward our understanding of human behaviours. And here, despite evidence suggesting that the WHR and BMI are highly correlated (Jasienka *et al.* 2004), the available data highlights the fact that BMI and WHR have independent contributions to attractiveness judgements of women (Pawłowski and Dunbar 2005; Smith *et al.* 2007a), with BMI having the stronger effect of the two. What should we make of these findings?

In general, the salience of the WHR as a primary attractiveness criterion appears to decrease as the ecological validity of the stimuli increases (Voracek and Fisher 2006). That is, as researchers have used better sets of stimuli to test the WHR hypothesis, mounting evidence seems to support the conclusion that the WHR is not the first-pass filter of women's attractiveness that Singh argued it to be. Moreover, it is very difficult to judge a person's WHR if he or she is viewed at an angle, or if a person is in motion, which makes the WHR a poor visual proxy. As Tovée and Cornelissen (2001: 400) put it:

> If a physical feature has only a comparatively weak visual proxy, then it does not matter how good a predictor it is of health and fertility, it will play only a secondary role in sexual selection. This may be true of WHR and could explain why it plays a subsidiary role to BMI, which has a more reliable visual proxy.

In this sense, it seems more likely that the real first-pass filter of women's (and possibly men's) attractiveness is body weight. Indeed, body size is perhaps the most ubiquitous characteristics of an individual seen at a distance (Voracek and Fisher 2006). The WHR, on the other hand, may only be indirectly involved in judgements of attractiveness. Converging lines of research suggest that the WHR may be primarily used as a means of discriminating broad categories, such as distinguishing women from men (Johnson and Tassinary 2005, 2007), or non-pregnant from pregnant women (Furnham and Reeves 2006; Tovée *et al.* 2002). Using three-dimensional stimuli that incorporated motion, for example, Johnson and Tassinary (2005) reported that the WHR (particularly the motion of the hips and waist) was primarily involved in raters' judgements of sex, and not attractiveness.

In short, then, the evidence we have reviewed in this chapter would seem to suggest that the WHR hypothesis of women's attractiveness has been over-stated. A woman's body weight may be the more important criterion of her physical attractiveness, which is in line with both popular belief and time-series analyses (Freese and Meland 2002; Garner *et al.* 1980; Sypeck *et al.* 2004, 2006; Voracek and Fisher 2002; Wiseman *et al.* 1992). Still, the one thing shared by both the WHR and BMI hypotheses of women's attractiveness considered in this chapter is that they both accept that physical attractiveness acts as a cue for some underlying quality (health or reproductive potential). This is evident both in Singh's idea that the WHR acts as a cue for repro-ductive potential, and Tovée's counter-argument that BMI is a more useful signal of overall health and fertility. In the next chapter, we consider studies of physical attractiveness that take a more critical stance towards evolutionary psychological explanations of attractiveness.

6   The Venus of Willendorf, Rubens and milking huts

Ask a toad what is beauty . . . he will answer that it is a female with two great round eyes coming out of her little head, a large flat head, a yellow belly and a brown back. Question a Negro from Guinea, beauty for him is an oily black skin, sunken eyes and squat nose.
                    Voltaire, French writer (*Beauty: The Philosophical Dictionary*, 1764)

Beauty comes in all sizes – not just size 5.
                    Roseanne Barr, actress (1952–)

In a world of hunchbacks, a fine figure becomes a monstrosity.
                    Honoré de Balzac, French novelist (1799–1850)

An important tenet of the evolutionary psychological programme, as we saw in Chapter 3, is that all human beings are the products of the same process of evolution, and therefore share a similar 'architecture of adaptations'. That is, all human beings share the same genetic make-up and, hence, the same psychological modules that govern human behaviour. Where differences in behaviour between individuals, cultures or societies do exist, these are explained as being due to environmental factors that 'trigger' different responses from the same, underlying mental structure.

In practice, however, some evolutionary psychologists have sought to show that a number of behaviours are universal to all human beings across time and culture (but see Gangestad *et al.* 2006). In contrast to this approach, anthropologists, sociologists and cross-cultural psychologists have explored, emphasised and rejoiced in the fact that many social behaviours and practices are different between cultures. This is particularly true of anthropology, with its emphasis on cultural relativity and in-depth examinations of the context in which behaviours take place (Boas 1911). Any comprehensive account of human behaviour, in this account, should *expect* cross-cultural or temporal differences in human behaviour. In this chapter, we examine the issue of cultural relativity as it applies to our earlier investigation of preferences for body weight and shape.

Playboy centrefolds and Miss America

Let us return, first, to Singh's waist-to-hip ratio (WHR) hypothesis of women's attractiveness. A central tenet of his evolutionary psychological approach was that a low WHR has always been considered attractive, regardless of the historical period or culture (Singh 1995b; Singh *et al.* 2007). From an evolutionary psychological perspective, this seems obvious enough. All men faced the same problems of mate selection in evolutionary history, and because all contemporary men are the descendants of ancestral populations, so they should share the notion of a low female WHR as being attractive. When it comes to depicting the 'ideal' woman in art, literature or fashion, therefore, she will most likely have a low WHR (Singh 2006).

So, for example, Singh (1995b) reported there has been remarkable consistency in the WHRs of both *Playboy* centrefolds and Miss America pageant winners across time. Assuming that these women are representative icons of venerated beauty and sexually desirable standards, the consistency in their WHRs is taken as *prima facie* evidence of an evolved basis for a preference for a low WHR (Buss 1999; Etcoff 1999). In other words, *Playboy* centrefolds and Miss America winners tend to have WHRs in the 'attractive range' because it is exactly this that men have evolved to find attractive.

In actual fact, the evidence in favour of this hypothesis does not seem to stand up to scrutiny (Voracek and Fisher 2002). For instance, Freese and Meland (2002) showed that Singh's assertion that all *Playboy* centrefolds and Miss America contestants fall into a narrow range of WHR values was erroneous. In reality, the actual range of WHR values of Miss America pageant winners and *Playboy* centrefolds is much wider than what was claimed, and at the very least the narrow ranges reported by Singh (1995b) do not encompass most of the members of either sample. Freese and Meland (2002) showed, for example, that winners of the Miss America pageant had WHRs ranging from 0.61 to 0.78, whereas the overall range for *Playboy* centrefolds was even wider (0.53 to 0.79). Furthermore, correlations between WHR and a linear measure of the time of pageant victory or magazine appearance showed that the WHRs of Miss America contestants and *Playboy* centrefolds have changed over time (Freese and Meland 2002).

Nor are such temporal differences limited to *Playboy* centrefolds and Miss America pageant winners; rather, a great deal of evidence exists to suggest that idealised figures of women's bodily beauty, at least in the West, have not remained static (Sarwer *et al.* 2002). In the first half of the nineteenth century in Victorian England, for example, the most popular ideal was a strong, statuesque woman (see Figure 6.1). The more slender, 'fainting' beauty – which is closer to Singh's exalted image of idealised beauty – only became prominent later in the nineteenth century, particularly as a means of associating feminine beauty with powerlessness at a time when the women's liberation struggle was growing in strength (Swami 2007).

Following World War I, a very different image of feminine beauty emerged,

6.1a   6.1b   6.1c

6.1d   6.1e

Figure 6.1 Despite the proclamations of some evolutionary psychologists, it is clear
that the 'ideal' female body has not remained static throughout the ages,
fluctuating as it has from the 'statuesque' Victorian ideal to the curvaceousness of the 1950s, the 'slender curves' of the 1960s to the curveless
ideal of the 1970s. Figure 6.1a copyright © Underwood and Underwood/
CORBIS, Figures 6.1b-d copyright © Bettmann/CORBIS, Figure 6.1e
copyright © Photo B. D. V./CORBIS.

one that was androgynous, curveless and almost boyish in shape. Indeed, the
mean bust-to-hip measurements of Miss America winners in the 1920s was
about 32-25-35 (Mazur 1986). Even when this ideal was replaced by more
curvaceous models in the 1930s (when the average bust line of Miss America
winners grew by two inches), they conspicuously lacked extraneous fat, had a
slim lower body and a flat abdomen (Mazur 1986). This ideal, in turn, was
replaced in the early 1950s by more curvaceous physical ideals, typified by the
voluptuous, hourglass figure of Marilyn Monroe (Fallon 1990).

By the mid-1960s, the weights of Miss America winners and *Playboy* centre-folds gradually declined, while height increased (Garner *et al.* 1980). During this period, the bust and hips of Miss America winners remained symmetrical, but the height of contestants rose by an average of one inch, while weight fell by an average of five pounds per decade (Mazur 1986). In combination with this, the ideal torso required an unnatural curvature, with fat distributed away from the waist to the hips and breasts. Similar to the beauty icons of the late nineteenth century, Western culture during the 1960s admired the slender curves of icons such as Audrey Hepburn and Grace Kelly (Sarwer *et al.* 2002).

By the late 1960s, dramatically thinner icons such as Twiggy became the new ideal, and this super-thin notion of beauty has remained the defining characteristic of physical beauty in the West (Fallon 1990). In conjunction with being thin, the ideal had also become increasingly tubular with time: one study of English fashion models from the years 1967 to 1987 found that, while the models' height and waist sizes increased significantly over the time period, there was no corresponding change in their hip measurements, resulting in higher WHRs (Morris *et al.* 1989). But being thin was now the key to being physically attractive (Spitzer *et al.* 1999): by the 1980s, the majority of Miss America winners had a body mass index of less than 18.5 (Rubinstein and Caballero 2000), which is considered clinically underweight, and sometimes also displayed signs of anorexia nervosa (Wiseman *et al.* 1992). Comparable historical trends have shown that models depicted in women's magazines have also become increasingly thin with time (Guillen and Barr 1994; Silverstein *et al.* 1986), as have cover models on fashion magazines (Sypeck *et al.* 2004).

Such studies suggest that the preferred body shape for women has changed markedly from the very curvaceous hourglass to a less curvaceous shape (Fallon 1990; Garner *et al.* 1980). In short, the WHRs of 'icons' of beauty have been much more variable than Singh suggested, and the average WHR of these 'icons' has changed considerably over time. If further evidence were needed of these changing ideals, one might also look to the proportions of the Barbie doll, which has undergone a radical transformation of its own since the late 1950s – though her proportions remain extreme relative to the general population (Norton *et al.* 1996).

The waist-to-hip ratio in art

A similar permutation of the idea of an evolved male preference for low female WHRs is the suggestion that, despite local aesthetic canons, artists cross-culturally and cross-generationally have almost always represented female WHRs in the healthy and fertile range (Singh 2006; Singh *et al.* 2000). That is, despite differences in local taste, cultural conditions and economic factors, almost all cultures and generations share a particular notion of a low WHR as healthy and, therefore, attractive (see Figure 6.2). Thus, Singh *et al.* (2000) measured the WHRs of some 300 ancient sculptures from India,

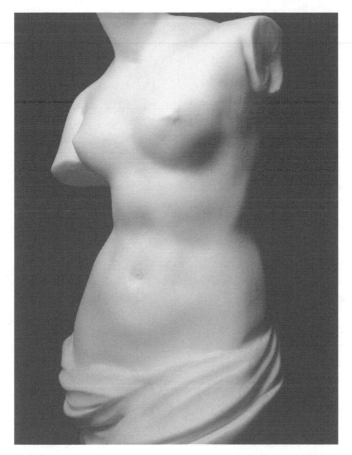

Figure 6.2 According to some evolutionary psychologists, a low waist-to-hip ratio can be found in sculptures of beautiful women across disparate cultures, regardless of differences in local taste, cultural conditions or economic factors.

Egypt, Greece and some African tribes, and reported remarkable similarity in depictions of a low WHR as attractive in all four cultural groups.

One concern with this idea, as Swami (2007) has pointed out, is that different cultural groups and historical epochs have used figurines and sculptures for very different reasons, some of which may have little to do with aesthetic tastes and canons. Swami (2007) uses the example of the *Venus de Milo*, perhaps one of the most famous statues in art history and one with an 'attractive' WHR in the evolutionary psychological sense, to show that there were a range of historical, religious and sociocultural meanings associated with the statue, which make it impossible to say whether it truly was held up as an example of ideal beauty in ancient times. In short, ancient statues and sculptures may have served very different functions than those attributed to them by modern-day evolutionary psychologists.

Moreover, it is clearly not the case that all artists have depicted women with low WHRs as being maximally attractive. Swami *et al.* (2007d), for example, made measurements of nearly 30 female nudes depicted in paintings by the Flemish painter Pieter Pauwel Rubens, considered one of the most important artists of the seventeenth century and whose stylised plump figures became the definition of exuberant sensuality in baroque painting (giving rise to the term 'Rubenesque'). By taking such measurements, they showed that the range of WHRs of Rubens' women were highly variable, but in general were much higher than what is considered attractive in the evolutionary psychological scheme (see Plate 6). Nor was Rubens' taste idiosyncratic: the available evidence suggests that the 'ideal' woman in seventeenth- and eighteenth-century Europe was plump, even overweight, by today's standards (Swami 2007).

The Venus figurines

It is also quite surprising that psychologists who favour the WHR hypothesis of attractiveness have not considered the measurements of the Venus figurines and reliefs (Swami 2007). These are small figurines and representations depicting obese women with extreme WHRs (Passemard 1938): because they generally date from the Late Stone Age, they would appear to be the perfect specimen for the evolutionary psychological thesis, as they may offer an insight into the mind of ancestral human populations. Characteristically, these figures have robust hips and buttocks, while the arms and legs are often reduced (Jelínek 1975). Some figurines are portrayed with large, hanging breasts, while engravings are much closer to the stylised outlines of animal bodies such as horses, bison and mammoths.

In general, the figurines – like the Venus of Lausssel or the Venus of Willendorf (see Figure 6.3) – are extremely fat-bodied and resemble a spherical ellipsoid. It would be wrong, however, to assume that because these figures depicted obese women that this was the usual case during that period (Graziosi 1960). The living conditions of the Late Stone Age were extremely difficult and women of this period were unlikely to have had so much food as to be able to achieve the obese figures depicted by carvings and engravings (Wood 2006). These obese figures, therefore, were more likely images with sexual and economic implications (Jelínek 1975; Leroi-Gourhan 1968; Ucko 1962).

Some research suggests that the Venus figurines may not be fertility goddesses, but depictions of actual women idolised for their obesity (Sandars 1968). This is further indicated by the fact that any likeness is noticed only in the torso; otherwise the Venus figurines have no faces, unnaturally thin arms and no feet (Rice 1982). Moreover, the fact that numerous examples of this type of female figure, all generally exhibiting the same essential characteristics – large stomachs and breasts, featureless faces, miniscule or missing feet – have been found over a broad geographical area ranging from France to Siberia, suggests that some system of shared perception of a particular type of woman existed during this period in evolutionary history.

Figure 6.3 Figurines like the Venus of Willendorf typically have robust hips and buttocks, while the arms and legs are often reduced. In general, the figurines
are extremely fat bodied and resemble a spherical ellipsoid.

A somewhat different explanation derives from the fact that images of
women, mostly figurines of the same type as the Venus figurines and dating to
the Paleolithic period, far outnumber images of men. This has led to specula-
tion about the place of women in Stone Age society (Ehrenberg 1989; Nelson
1997). Some have argued that these female figures denote the existence, during this period, of a prominent female deity, typically identified as the Earth
Mother or the Mother Goddess. On the basis of this assumption, it has been
suggested that, unlike today, women played a considerably more important, if
not dominant, role in Paleolithic society; that possibly a matriarchy existed
and women ruled. Thus, the Venus figurines may be a representation at once
of the Mother Goddess and a special living woman; one represented in the
form or guise of the other (Russell 1998).

These figurines are important because they corroborate the suggestion that not all generations of human beings have shared the same notions of an 'attractive' body size. Of course, like other statuettes and artistic representations, we should be careful about reading too much into the Venus figurines (Swami 2007), especially since archaeologists cannot be completely certain what purpose they served in ancestral human populations. But given that they are unlikely to have been aberrations, and originate from the period during which evolutionary psychologists claim the architecture of the human mind was 'built', their existence certainly raises very interesting questions for the WHR hypothesis of attractiveness.

The waist-to-hip ratio across cultures

One of the most fruitful avenues of research ever since Singh proposed his theory of the WHR being a first-pass filter of women's physical attractiveness has been cross-cultural work. Indeed, the preference for a low WHR has been replicated in a wide range of countries (see Table 6.1), and this is usually taken as evidence for the universal and culturally invariant nature of the WHR as a signal for mate selection. In addition, some researchers have reported that the winners of non-Western beauty pageants also exhibit low WHRs within the 'optimal' range (Leung *et al.* 2001). These studies seem in line with Singh's (1993a) argument that the 'psychological mechanism' governing preferences for a low WHR in men is universal because it was an adaptive assessment of female mate value in human evolutionary history.

However, a common factor shared by all these studies, which makes the claim unwarranted, is that they were carried out in relatively developed, industrial societies. A different way of substantiating Singh's claims would be to examine the WHR preferences of hunter-gatherer or forager groups that are still in existence today. Evolutionary psychologists have been eager to study such groups because they typically assume that foragers represent a lifestyle that existed during the environment of evolutionary adaptedness. Of course, this claim is doubtful and takes an unnecessarily static view of human development and history (Caro and Borgerhoff Mulder 1987; Shennan 2000). Rather, existing forager groups are likely to have been highly influenced by their association with more powerful agricultural societies in recent history (Foley 1988). Nevertheless, because hunter-gatherer and forager groups provide the only direct observations of human behaviour in the absence of agriculture, and because they generally have limited contact with Western media and values, they are a useful way of testing evolutionary psychological predictions (Marlowe 2005).

In an important test of the WHR hypothesis, Wetsman and Marlowe (1999) examined the preferences of a hunter-gatherer tribe called the Hadza, in Tanzania, who subsist almost exclusively from foraging wild foods. Using line drawings of the female figure, they found that the size of the WHR does not affect Hadza men's judgements of attractiveness. Instead, the Hadza preferred heavy over medium, and medium over lightweight line drawings when selecting for attractiveness, health and desirability as a wife, regardless of WHR. When Marlowe and Wetsman (2001) returned to Tanzania with a new set of line drawings, in which only the WHR was varied, they found that Hadza men still preferred high over low WHRs. Indeed, the authors proposed that this could have been an artefact of the Hadza's preference for heavier women. Wetsman and Marlowe (1999: 226) therefore concluded that the WHR was more likely to act as a 'second-pass filter':

> The first-pass filter could consist of partner preferences based on body weight . . . The influence of WHR may only become relevant when food resources are plentiful enough that the risk of starvation during pregnancy and lactation for women is minimal . . .

Their results were strikingly similar to that of a previous study conducted among another relatively isolated population, the Matsigenka of southern Peru, who practise slash-and-burn agriculture (Yu and Shepard 1998, 1999). Using Singh's original line drawings, the researchers tested three groups of Matsigenka differing in their degree of contact with the outside world (and in the authors' estimation, differing in their degree of 'Westernisation'). The least Westernised group, like the Hadza, ranked figures first by weight (high preferred over low) and only then high WHR over low WHR, once again diametrically opposing findings using participants in industrial societies. The second, moderately Westernised group differed in that they rated low WHR females as being more attractive and more desirable as spouses, but not more healthy. The third and most Westernised group (first contacted 20 to 30 years previously) did not differ in their attractiveness preferences from men in the United States.

As might be expected in an ever-shrinking world, access to relatively isolated hunter-gatherer groups is becoming increasingly difficult. Many cross-cultural researchers have, therefore, relied on the disparity in wealth between developing and developed nations. Furnham *et al.* (2002), for instance, investigated the effect of body weight and WHR on attractiveness ratings of men from Uganda, Greece and Britain. They too found a cultural influence on body weight and shape preferences: although the European data showed an overall preference for the 0.70 WHR, the Ugandan subjects gave the ratio of 0.50 the highest rating.

At first glance, this might seem to support the WHR hypothesis, and indeed a monotonic negative relationship between WHR and perceived attractiveness has been proposed (Singh 1993a). An extrapolation of this relationship would yield the 0.50 ratio as the most attractive WHR, but, remember, the evolutionary psychological hypothesis would also require this ratio to be the most fertile and healthy ratio, which is not what has been reported (Gray *et al.* 2003). Rather, Furnham *et al.* (2002) have argued that Ugandan participants may have shown a preference for the 0.50 ratio because, in real-life populations, a 0.50 ratio could only be achieved by having a small waist and

Table 6.1 Summary of selected studies examining preferences for WHR in different cultures

Reference	Site	Stimuli	Result
Forrestell et al. (2004)	USA	Line drawings	Preference for WHR of about 0.70, but as body weight increased, larger WHRs were preferred
Freedman et al. (2004)	US Caucasian and African-American	Line drawings	African-Americans chose a very low WHR as ideal, but preferred heavier figures
Furnham et al. (1997, 1998, 2001, 2005)	Britain	Line drawings	Low WHR (0.70) rated as most attractive
Furnham et al. (2003)	Kenya and Britain	Line drawings	Low WHR rated as most attractive
Furnham et al. (2002)	Greece, Britain and Uganda	Line drawings	Overall preference for low WHR (0.70) in Britain and Greece, but extremely low WHR preference (0.50) in Uganda
Furnham et al. (2006)	Britain	Modified line drawings	Male participants rated figures with a WHR of 0.60 most highly, while female participants preferred figures with a WHR of 0.80.
Gray et al. (2005)	New Zealand	Line drawings	Extremely low WHRs (0.50, 0.60) preferred over average WHRs (0.70, 0.80)
Henss (1995)	Germany	Line drawings	Low WHR rated as most attractive
Henss (2000)	Germany	Photographs	Low WHR rated as most attractive
Markey et al. (2002)	US Caucasians and Mexican Americans	Line drawings	Low WHR most preferred among parents and pre-adolescents
Marlowe and Wetsman (2001)	Hadza tribe (Tanzania)	Modified line drawings	With no weight variation, high WHR most preferred
Puhl and Boland (2001)	USA	Photographs	High WHR preferred over all weight conditions, but body weight more important than WHR
Rozmus-Wrzesinska and Pawłowski (2005)	Poland	Photographs	Attractiveness more influenced by changes in waist than hip size

Study	Location	Stimulus type	Findings
Singh (1993a, 1993b, 1994a); Singh and Young (1995)	USA	Line drawings	Low WHR most attractive when weight controlled
Singh (2000, 2002)	India	Photographs	Preference for WHRs lower than the local average
Singh (2004)	Azore Islands and Guinea Bissau	Line drawings	Low WHR rated as most attractive
Singh and Luis (1995)	Indonesia	Line drawings	Low WHR rated as most attractive
Streeter and McBurney (2003)	USA	Photographs	Low WHR most attractive when body weight is statistically controlled
Swami and Tovée (2005a)	Malaysia and Britain	Photographs	Low socio-economic status participants preferred higher WHR than high socio-economic status participants, but BMI is a better predictor of ratings than WHR
Tassinary and Hansen (1998)	USA	Modified line drawings	Weight more important factor than WHR
Thornhill and Grammer (1999)	Austria and USA	Photographs	Facial attractiveness overrides preference for low WHR
Sugiyama (2004)	Shiwiar tribe (Ecuador)	Line drawings	Preference for WHRs lower than the local average
Swami et al. (2007a)	Malaysia and Britain	Photographs	Higher WHR judged more attractive by rural Malaysians, compared with urban Malaysians in Malaysia and the UK
Tovée et al. (1997, 1998, 1999)	UK	Photographs	Preference for low over high WHRs, but body weight significantly more important factor than WHR
Wetsman and Marlowe (1999)	Hadza tribe (Tanzania)	Line drawings	WHR does not affect attractiveness judgements; heavier figures preferred over medium-weight and lighter figures
Yu and Shepard (1998)	Matsigenka tribe (Peru)	Line drawings	Least westernised group ranked figures first by weight (high preferred to low) and then high WHR over low WHR; moderately westernised group rated low WHR females as more attractive and more desirable as spouses, but not more healthy; most westernised group did not differ from male participants in the USA

large hips. Because large hips yield the impression of a heavier figure, the Ugandan preference for a 0.50 ratio could be explained as a preference for large figures. Moreover, Furnham *et al.* (2002) found a preference for heavy figures among the Ugandans, while the British and Greek participants preferred light-weight figures, suggesting that body weight matters over and above WHR.

This set of results is similar to that reported by Freedman *et al.* (2004), who examined ethnic differences in men's preferences for ideal body weight and shape in women. This group of researchers found that African American men were more likely to choose heavier figures as ideal than did Caucasian men. Specifically, African American men disliked a low body weight for women more frequently than did their Caucasian counterparts. In addition, both ethnic groups chose figures with a low WHR, but African American men were more likely to choose a very low WHR as ideal. For Freedman *et al.* (2004), the findings emphasised the importance of assessing male preferences for female shape (or WHR), but also showed weight to be a more important cue than WHR in the male selection process. It appears that African American men are more willing to idealise a woman of a heavier body size, with more curves, than do their Caucasian counterparts.

Explaining cross-cultural differences

In short, then, when researchers have examined the WHR preferences of groups not limited to developed, industrial nations, there does not appear to be a universal preference for the same WHRs. Rather, in some groups – typically, hunter-gatherer or forager groups – there is a preference for high over low WHRs, while in others, there appears to be a preference for extremely low WHRs. The common conclusion shared by both these sets of findings is that they are incompatible with the idea that the WHR is a reliable cue of fertility and health. So how might these cross-cultural differences be explained?

One early but now seemingly obsolete explanation rested on the WHR acting as a predictor of child sex. A high preconceptual WHR is a good predictor of having a male child, and so in cultures that 'value' male children, an androgynous body shape should be judged as more attractive. This predictive value of WHR is based on studies measuring women who already have children and correlating their WHRs with the proportion of existing male children. Thus, two studies suggested that women with high WHRs tended to have more sons, and that the preference for women with a high WHR may, therefore, result in selection for increased testosterone levels in children (Manning *et al.* 1996; Singh and Zambarano 1997). Similarly, Manning *et al.* (1999) presented data from a rural Jamaican population which showed that there is a positive association between a woman's waist circumference and her number of sons.

However, an important limitation of these studies is that carrying a male child may alter the WHR in a different way to carrying a female child. If this is correct, then a high WHR may be an effect, rather than a cause, of a child's sex. To test the predictive power of preconceptual WHR and offspring sex, Tovée *et al.* (2001) took WHR measures from 458 women who intended to become pregnant and correlated this with the sex of the subsequent child. They found no significant correlation, suggesting that WHR does not act as a predictor of child sex. In recent years, support for the child-sex-predictor hypothesis of the WHR has consequently waned.

Steatopygia

A different explanation of cross-cultural differences in preferences for WHR has been proposed by Marlowe *et al.* (2005). They argue that the frontal images of women used in most cross-cultural studies do not capture the contribution of the hips, and in particular the buttocks, to actual WHR. When they used line drawings of women in profile, they found that Hadza hunter-gatherers preferred a lower profile WHR (more protruding buttocks) than American men, which is in contrast to their preference for a higher frontal WHR (Marlowe and Wetsman 2001). They therefore concluded that there is, in reality, less disparity in Hadza men's theoretical preferences for actual WHR. In general, they argue, taking into account profile WHR, there is a general preference for low over high WHRs in all societies.

There are, however, a number of limitations to this explanation. First, the line drawings used by Marlowe *et al.* (2005) likely covaried WHR and body weight (Swami *et al.* 2007d, 2007f), a limitation of line drawings in general (see Chapter 5). The images of women with bigger hips and buttocks also appear to have a heavier body weight, and so it is possible that Hadza men, in choosing a profile figure with protruding buttocks, were actually choosing women with a heavier body weight. Second, other studies have suggested that profile WHR or buttock size is a relatively unimportant predictor of attractiveness ratings of women (Swami *et al.* 2007d, 2007f; Tovée and Cornelissen 2001), which is consistent with studies using images of women in frontal view (see Chapter 5). For example, Furnham and Swami (2007) used silhouettes of the female figure and found that buttock size was not an important consideration for British participants when making judgements of women's attractiveness.

Of course, it seems plausible that cultures differ widely in their preferences for such features as buttocks and hip size. Anecdotal evidence would suggest that some cultures or subcultures emphasise larger buttocks or hip size in their attractiveness ideals (Swami *et al.* in press, b). Furthermore, it has been suggested that fat deposits on the buttocks of women, a condition known as 'steatopygia', may be considered attractive by some hunter-gatherer or forager tribes (Morris 1978), which may explain the findings of Marlowe *et al.* (2005). These fat deposits may occur in both sexes, but are usually much larger in women than in men. They develop fully at puberty and are said to be sexually attractive to men in the populations in which they occur (Tobias 1957), such as the Khoikhor of South Africa and the Onges of the Andaman Islands.

It has been argued that steatopygia is an attribute of women's attractiveness independent of the WHR, at least in some tribal or rural groups. It seems unlikely that there is a good genes explanation for this: the fat stored in the buttocks interferes greatly with balance and mobility, and fat stored around the waist would be mechanically more efficient (Pond 1981). Moreover, fat stored in the buttocks generally suffers from poor utilisation (Pond and Mattachs 1987), which rules out the suggestion that it may serve as a reserve for metabolic demands or protection against famine (Symons 1979). It is therefore possible that fat is stored in a more conspicuous location – the buttocks – to provide a clearer advertisement of reproductive prowess (Barber 1995).

Alternatively, it is possible that steatopygia evolved for reasons unconnected to the ability to attract opposite sex partners, and only later became a sign of femininity. For example, some researchers have proposed that aspects of the human body may have evolved so as to increase surface area for thermoregulatory reasons (Einon 2007), as in the case of desert animals such as camels. This seems to be supported by the fact that steatopygia occurs only in very hot climates and that people exhibiting steatopygia are short in stature (short stature promotes heat conservation, so steatopygia would have evolved to aid heat loss).

Regardless, the explanation of cross-cultural differences in preferences for WHR based on the disparity between frontal and profile images seems inadequate. It may very well turn out to be the case that some populations have a preference for larger, protruding buttocks, which explains their preference for higher frontal WHRs (Marlowe *et al.* 2005). However, it is unlikely that this will turn out to be the case universally (Furnham and Swami 2007), which makes it an insufficient explanation for cross-cultural differences in preferences for the WHR.

Facultative adjustments

A more recent evolutionary psychological explanation for cross-cultural WHR preference differences is based on the idea that humans have psychological adaptations to facultatively adjust certain determinants of sexual attraction to local conditions (Symons 1995). In other words, the mental modules that make up the human mind will likely adjust preferences in response to local conditions, and this may explain why some groups have a preference for WHRs that are higher than other groups. This is in fact the argument of Sugiyama (2004, 2005), who made the point that cross-cultural tests of the low WHR hypothesis have used stimuli that were not scaled to local conditions.

Forager women have high fecundity, parasite loads and caloric dependence on fibrous foods, all of which increase their WHRs. Since mate selection should calibrate for local conditions, Sugiyama (2004) proposed that WHR preference mechanisms will assess the local distribution of female WHR, and will recalibrate as conditions change. Instead of expecting uniform cross-cultural preference for a specific WHR value, researchers should anticipate only that WHR values lower than the local average will be attractive, and that the influence of this factor relative to others will vary cross-culturally. In other words, psychological adaptations could instantiate a rule to prefer WHRs somewhat lower than the local female average rather than some absolute size of WHR, as some evolutionary psychologists have suggested.

Thus, taking into account the local distribution of Ecuadorian Shiwiar WHRs, Sugiyama (2004) found that Shiwiar men use female WHRs in a way that is consistent with the hypothesis that WHR assessment is sensitively calibrated to local parameters. The average female WHR of the Shiwiar is not as low as typically found in Western societies, although the average female WHR was still lower than the average male WHR. When Shiwiar men were asked to judge a set of photographic images of women, Sugiyama (2004) found that they judged overweight figures with a low WHR as physically attractive. When differences in body weight were minimised, Shiwiar men preferred lower than locally average female WHRs.

The concept of facultative adjustments is currently a very popular means of explaining cross-cultural differences in WHR preferences (Sugiyama 2005), but is by no means accepted by all. One issue of contention has to do with the conclusions that are drawn from seemingly limited data: after all, studies that have shown a preference for WHRs lower than the local female average have not provided any evidence that such preferences are adaptations, or for the existence of mental modules governing such behaviour. Yet, within the evolutionary psychological scheme, such modules are assumed to exist *a priori*, and evidence in favour of the hypothesis is taken to show the existence of such adapted modules.

When is an adaptation not an adaptation?

In such a scenario, it is worth considering – as an important aside in our current discussions – the adaptationist programme of evolutionary psychology in some detail. As we have seen, evolutionary psychologists have proposed that WHR preferences are an example of an adaptation: men solved the problem of detecting a woman's reproductive potential in the environment of evolutionary adaptedness by evolving 'modules' or psychological mechanisms that elicited preferences for healthy and fertile WHRs. Such an explanatory strategy might be useful, write Gray and colleagues (2003), if three criteria could be satisfied: (a) all traits are adaptations; (b) it is relatively easy and straightforward to characterise adaptations: (c) there are few or no plausible alternative adaptive explanations.

First, are all traits adaptations? Here, it is worrying that the evolutionary psychological paradigm is able to assimilate almost any (and often contra-dictory) contentions, typically explaining these as adaptations to the environment of evolutionary adaptedness (Stainton Rogers and Stainton Rogers 2001). Indeed, Ramachandran (1997) once wrote a satirical essay, 'Why Do Gentlemen Prefer Blondes?', in which he argued that men preferred blondes in order to enable them to detect the early signs of parasitic infest-ation and ageing, both of which indirectly reduce fertility and offspring viability. Certainly, not all evolutionary psychologists were taken in by Ramachandran's (1997) spoof, but some certainly were. It seems, therefore, that the evolutionary psychological paradigm is able to explain almost any data as adaptations; but a theory that is able to explain everything in reality explains very little.

In a seminal paper published in 1979, Gould and Lewontin attacked what they referred to as 'adaptationism', the idea that any arbitrarily selected fea-ture of an organism must have some function that explains its selection over evolutionary time. Using the example of the spandrels on the arches of the Cathedral of San Marco in Venice – there solely as a side effect of the con-struction of the arch – Gould and Lewontin (1979) pointed out that in an object as functionally integrated as an organism, particular features would be constrained by the overall structure and functioning of the organism. And these constraints may well be more important than the optimising tendencies of natural selection in explaining the final structure of the organism (Kitcher 1985, 2004). Of course, evolutionary theory has changed considerably since Gould and Lewontin (1979) took issue with the adaptationist programmes, but their point still stands: there is no reason to expect that any arbitrary trait of humans (or any organism) are adaptations.

Second, we might ask what exactly is the trait or characteristic said to have been shaped an adaptation? The correct characterisation of traits to be given adaptive explanations is by no means obvious, as Lewontin (1978) pointed out in the case of the human chin. The chin is present in humans but absent in our ape relatives, which would make it appear to be an obvious trait. But the chin is actually not a discrete trait at all; rather, it is the consequence of dif-ferent degrees of neoteny in the dentary and alveolar growth fields of the lower jaw. The same issues apply when characterising other purported traits as adaptations: providing evidence of a preference for WHRs lower than the local female average, for example, is not sufficient for ascribing to it an adaptive explanation.

Finally, we might ask if there are any alternative, adaptive explanations available for a particular hypothesis. Certainly, there is no reason to believe that the evolutionary psychological explanation is the only plausible theory accounting for physical attractiveness, and within evolutionary theory more generally it is not uncommon to have different adaptive explanations for a single trait. Returning to the example of WHR preferences, for instance, Gray *et al.* (2003) have proposed that the preference for low WHRs may be better explained ethologically as a by-product of a sensory bias in another domain (see Chapter 3). This argument suggests that the WHR is not a cue of any underlying quality, as some evolutionary psychologists have argued, but rather is a result of a generic psychological mechanism for enhanced responding to exaggerated features, or what are known as 'superstimuli' (Eibl-Eibesfeldt 1970).

A superstimulus is an exaggerated version of a stimulus to which there is an existing response tendency, or any stimulus that elicits a response more strongly than the stimulus that normally releases it. For example, following his extensive analysis of the stimulus features that elicited food begging in the chick of the herring gull, Tinbergen (1957) constructed an artificial super-stimulus consisting of a red knitting needle with three white bands painted round it. This elicited a stronger response than an accurate three-dimensional model of the parent's head (white) and bill (yellow with a red spot). Gray *et al.* (2003) have proposed that the preference for low WHRs found in some studies may be akin to a response to superstimuli.

Among ancestral populations, sex-typical differences in body shape may have evolved for reasons unconnected with the ability to attract sexual partners, such as the need to regulate heat loss (Einon 2007) or different biomechanical constraints on each sex (Burr *et al.* 1977; Pawłowski 2001; Pawłowski and Grabarczyk 2003; Walrath and Glantz 1996). In terms of the former, the sexual dimorphism in human body shape may have been bene-ficial in increasing heat loss in women, especially since the inability to lose excess body heat would have been damaging for pregnant women (Chang *et al.* 1963; Kosambi and Raghavachari 1962; Zelnik 1969). In terms of the latter, Pawłowski and Grabarczyk (2003) have suggested that, because of preg-nancy, bipedal females in the course of evolution would have faced different constraints in the biomechanics of locomotion than did males. Since locomo-tion is presumed to have been an important selection pressure on early humans, it is possible that a different skeletal morphology and body fat distribution evolved in women to permit better body stability. Indeed, this explanation of the origins of body shape differences in humans has the bene-fit of explaining the uniqueness of such human differences among all primate species (Schultz 1969).

Over time, sex differences in body shape may have become associated with sexual attractiveness, and sexual selection will have amplified these differences (Leong 2006). In other words, the preference for a low WHR in women may be a sensory bias, and exaggerating the difference will likely elicit stronger pre-ferences; indeed, this is exactly what Heaney (2000) found in her study. She conducted a study with line drawings based on Singh's original stimuli, but manipulated the waist to include figures with WHRs as low as 0.50 (Singh's original stimuli had only included WHRs within the range of 0.7 to 1.0). The overwhelming preference of her male participants was for figures in the 'normal' weight range with a WHR of 0.50, followed by figures with a WHR of 0.60. In the view of Gray *et al.* (2003), no specific evolved psychological mechanism for adaptive mate selection needs to be invoked to explain these findings. Rather, the preference for low WHRs is better understood as a sensory bias rather than a cue of good genes. Certainly, more work needs to be done to understand how such mechanisms might be generalised in humans, but at the very least the work by Gray *et al.* (2003) highlights the fact that evolutionary psychologists have not presented an unchallenged account of preferences for low WHRs.

It is worth being clear at this stage that we are not necessarily advocating an anti-adaptationist or even an anti-evolutionary psychological explanation of WHR preferences. Our point, rather, is to raise the possibility that a plausible adaptive explanation does not necessarily mean that it must be correct. We believe that once evolutionary psychologists drop some of their more dogmatic theories of universal attractiveness judgements, this will open up the possibility of active mate choice decisions which are not ancestrally constrained (see Chapter 7), and which show much cross-cultural, temporal and inter-individual variability.

Cross-cultural preferences for body weight

On a rather different note, the study by Sugiyama (2004) also raises the issue of body weight once again: when WHR and body weight were not independently assessed, Shiwiar men showed a preference for high WHR figures. This may have to do with the fact that high WHR figures appear to weigh the most among the high-weight images. That is, WHR and body weight are not completely unconfounded in the study by Sugiyama (2004), and given the evidence suggesting that body weight is the more salient predictor of women's attractiveness (see Chapter 5), it is worth asking if there are cross-cultural differences in body weight preferences.

The answer is a resounding yes: over the years, a great deal of anthropological and psychological research has made it very clear that cultures differ widely in their attitudes towards such things as obesity and body fat (Brown and Konner 1987; Cassidy 1991; Sobal and Stunkard 1989). In their groundbreaking ethnography, Ford and Beach (1952) showed that while there may have been a great deal of similarity across cultures when it came to such things as kissing and sexual orientation, preferences for body size were much more variable. While a few – typically socioeconomically developed – cultures express a preference for slim figures (Swami and Tovée 2005b; Swami *et al.* 2006a, 2006b; Smith *et al.* 2007; Tovée *et al.* 1998, 1999, 2002, 2006), a great many 'traditional' cultures prefer plump, and sometimes overweight, women and men.

In such traditional cultures, plumpness is (or was) often symbolically linked with psychological dimensions of self-worth, sexuality and fertility (Brown 1991; Rguibi and Belahsen 2006; Treloar *et al.* 1999), and for women in particular body fat is also a symbol of maternity and nurturance. In such societies, where women often attain status only through motherhood, this symbolic association increases the acceptability of obesity (Holmberg 1946;

Powdermaker 1960). An overweight woman, symbolically, was well taken care of, and she in turn took good care of her children. Fellahin Arabs in Egypt, for example, described the proper woman as 'fat' because she had more room to bear the child, lactated abundantly and gave warmth to her children (Amnar 1954).

Similarly, Teti (1995) describes how, for southern Italians, plumpness was a symbolic marker of prosperity and power, whereas thinness was a symbol of poverty, misery and evil. Other studies suggest that weight gain across the life cycle can be culturally acceptable (Bohannon and Bohannon 1969), even in extreme cases. The most obvious example of this is the seclusion of adolescent girls of elite families in 'milking huts' in parts of Africa and the South Pacific (Brink 1995; Malcom 1925; Popenoe 2003; Randall 1995) in preparation for their 'coming out' and marriage. De Garine (1995) also describes fattening sessions for adolescent men among Maasa pastoralists of Cameroon, for whom gorging on milk and sorghum porridge can increase their perceived strength, beauty, goodness, health and wealth. Moreover, the advantages of plumpness or obesity can be significant in many traditional societies (Pollock 1995a; Scrimshaw and Dietz 1995), and individuals of extreme size such as Sumo wrestlers in Japan can become cultural icons (see Figure 6.4; Hattori 1995).

One particular cultural milieu that has been extensively studied in the ethnographic and anthropological literature is the South Pacific. Traditionally, large bodies have had prestige in Polynesian societies, and were seen as representing high status, power, authority and wealth (Pollock 1995b). Ethnographic observations of Polynesian societies have noted that obesity was particularly common among chiefs and those of high social ranking (Buck 1932), and reports of the Polynesian perception of beauty often referred to fatness or very large body sizes as a primary requisite (van Dijk 1991). On the island of Tahiti in French Polynesia, for example, the ritual process of *ha'apori* (literally, to make fat) involved a purposeful fattening process for men and women, usually from high-ranking families (Oliver 1974; Pollock 1995b).

Ethnographers have since confirmed the positive association between body fat and prestige in the South Pacific, where it is argued that body fat reflects access to food resources (Craig *et al.* 1996; Knight *et al.* 2004; McGarvey 1991; Swami *et al.* 2007g; Wilkinson *et al.* 1994). In her comprehensive ethnography of Fiji, for instance, Becker (1995) reported that Fijian men and women were more tolerant of overweight and obese line drawings than a British comparison. More recently, Brewis and McGarvey (2000) compared Samoans living in three environments with different degrees of modernisation (Samoa, American Samoa and New Zealand) on actual and perceptual measures of body size. Women in the more ecologically modern settings were found to select significantly slimmer ideal body sizes, and they also had the largest bodies on average. It has also been reported that Samoans are unlikely to regard themselves as overweight or obese even when they are very large (Brewis *et al.* 1998).

Figure 6.4 In some cultures, the advantages of plumpness or obesity can be significant, and individuals of extreme size such as Sumo wrestlers in Japan can
become cultural icons. Copyright © Barry Lewis/CORBIS.

Nor are Polynesian samples unique in this regard: in one early cross-
cultural study, Furnham and Alibhai (1983) compared Black Kenyan to
British Caucasian and British Kenyan participants' ratings of line figures
from anorexic to obese. The authors reported that Black Kenyan participants
viewed obese female shapes more positively than either British or British
Kenyan participants, both of which were indistinguishably negative in their
evaluation. A replication in Uganda some ten years later also found the
indigenous African sample to be much more approving of obese female figures than a British comparison group (Furnham and Baguma 1994). Another
study revealed that despite a high prevalence of overweight and obesity,
Sahraoui women of Morocco described their size as appropriate and socially
acceptable (Rguibi and Belahsen 2006).

This line of evidence is further corroborated by a raft of studies (Akan and

Greilo 1995; Perez and Joiner 2003; Poran 2002; Rucker and Cash 1992) and reviews of the literature (Crago *et al.* 1996; Fitzgibbon *et al.* 1998) demonstrating that African Americans have (or had) different attitudes about weight, body shape, and physical attractiveness than Caucasians, with overall less drive for thinness and greater acceptance of larger body proportions. Similar findings have been reported among other ethnic minorities in the United States, such as Mexican Americans and Puerto Rican Americans, who show greater positive evaluation of fatness than Caucasians (Massara 1980, 1989; Rittenbaugh 1982, 1991; Ross and Mirowsky 1983). Nevertheless, it should be said that such ethnic groups are heterogeneous, and upwardly mobile individuals may more closely resemble mainstream American culture in attitudes about obesity and ideal body shape (Stunkard 2000).

Explaining cross-cultural differences

Clearly, then, there are cross-cultural differences in what is perceived as an attractive female body weight. Within the early literature, there was a tendency to associate the preference for plump figures with 'traditional' or 'developing' societies (Ghannam 1997), which is necessarily difficult to define. Indeed, some early theorists viewed the preference for plump figures as a deviant behaviour among 'backward' populations or groups that had yet to be 'enlightened' by Western intervention. While such notions were clearly influenced by the prevailing colonial climate at the time (Swami 2007), they were quite unsatisfactory in explaining why such differences should exist, once cultural prejudices were set aside.

Over the decades, various different theories have been put forward to explain the difference in body weight preference across cultures (Anderson *et al.* 1992; Ember *et al.* 2005). Some have argued that such preferences are related to the relative social dominance of women; others that it depends on the extent to which adolescent sexuality has adverse consequences for girls if they become pregnant. Yet others have proposed that men's preferences for female body weight are entirely arbitrary and determined by local fashions (see Table 6.2). While each of these explanations have been examined and debated in detail, most contemporary research has focused on two related explanations, the first being that body weight preferences are related to ethnicity, and the second that it is related to differences in socioeconomic status (SES).

In the first instance, some psychologists have attempted to explain cross-cultural patterns of body weight preferences through an adaptationist framework. Where Singh argued that evolutionary history endowed men with adaptations for particular WHRs, some researchers have argued that differences in preferred body weight can be explained as an evolutionary adaptation. Tovée and Cornelissen (2001), for instance, made the point that the same ideal BMI as found among Caucasians in the West should not be expected for all racial groups and environments. Rather, different ethnic populations may have differing levels of risk for negative health consequences with changing

Table 6.2 Hypotheses to explain cross-cultural differences in men's preferred female body size (adapted from Anderson et al. 1992; Barrett et al. 2002)

Hypothesis	Rationale	Prediction	Source
Food security	The biological function of fat is to store calories, and attitudes towards fatness therefore a response to food supply	Heavier body weights will be preferred where or when food supplies are unpredictable	Brown and Konner (1987); Sobal and Stunkard (1989)
Small but healthy	A slender body is valued in cultures that experience chronic food shortages because a large body requires more food	Thinness and short stature will be valued where and when food supplies are unreliable	Seckler (1980, 1982)
Climate	Fat has two biological functions: storage of calories and insulation	Heavier body weight will be preferred in colder climates	Anderson et al. (1992)
Male preference	Fat functions to influence the probability of ovulation or success in pregnancy and lactation	Plump women will be seen as more attractive than slender women	Symons (1987)
Adaptive reproductive suppression	A function of female fat is the regulation of the initiation and maintenance of ovulation	Women opt for thinner body shapes in order to reduce fertility so as to minimise risk of unwanted pregnancy	Voland and Voland (1989)
Battle of the sexes	At least one of the above biological functions of female fat had differing implications for the fitness of ancestral men and women	Body fullness as a cue of fertility and women opting for thinner body shapes are in conflict, and which achieves prominence depends on which sex is socially dominant	Messer (1989)
Fraternal interest groups	Menstrual taboos are a tactic by which men consolidate their political position with weak fraternal interest groups	When men's political status is dependent on fraternal interest groups, they will de-emphasise women's fertility, and hence will prefer thinner women	Paige and Paige (1981)
Kirche, Küche, Kinder	The biological function of female fat is the regulation or the probability of ovulation	When pregnancy interferes with women's labour, thinner women will be preferred because they are less fecund	Anderson et al. (1992)
Whims of fashion	There is no biological function of female fat	Men's preferences are purely arbitrary and dictated by fashion	Mazur (1986)

BMI (Kopelman 2000; McKeigue *et al.* 1991; Shetty and James 1994), and, consequently, there may be a different optimal BMI for health and longevity in different ethnic groups. So, where ethnic groups have different optimal BMIs for health and fertility, researchers should expect differences in body weight ideals.

This conclusion, however, has been thrown into doubt by cross-cultural studies that have tested this idea among, for example, Malaysians (Swami and Tovée 2005b) and South African Zulus (Tovée *et al.* 2006). For instance, in their study of preferred women's body weight in Malaysia and Britain, Swami and Tovée (2005b) elicited the preferences of participants of different ethnic origin (Malay, Chinese and Indian) from the same environment. Epidemiological studies have indicated that ethnic Malays, Chinese and Indians in Southeast Asia have different optimal BMIs for risk factors for morbidity and mortality (Deurenberg *et al.* 2002), which would suggest that these ethnic groups should have different preferences for body weight. However, this was not the case: Malays, Chinese and Indians in Kuala Lumpur all had a similar preference for slender figures with a BMI of about 19–20.

Nevertheless, it should be pointed out that what matters may not be the actual association between optimal health and body weight, but rather what is perceived as healthy. If this is the case, then we should expect a strong relationship between ratings of health and attractiveness, which are relatively flexible to changing circumstance. Some evidence for this has been presented by Tovée *et al.* (2007), who showed that ratings of women's health and attractiveness were both highly correlated but also flexible to changing socioeconomic circumstance. With current data sets, however, it is difficult to determine the direction of the relationship between health and attractiveness. The evolutionary psychological model suggests that what is (perceived as) healthy is beautiful, but given the 'halo effects' of physical attractiveness (see Chapter 2), it may be that what is attractive is also healthy.

A different explanation for cross-cultural differences in body weight preferences is based on the idea that these differences are underscored by changes in socioeconomic status. In this view, what matters when considering body weight ideals is not ethnicity or race, but the SES of the group in question (Swami and Tovée 2005b, 2007b; Tovée *et al.* 2006, 2007). In general, low SES observers tend to prefer heavier body weights in both men and women than high SES observers. In their study of Malaysians and Britons, for example, Swami and Tovée (2005b) found a consistent pattern of greater liking for heavier figures with decreasing SES: high SES observers in both Britain and Malaysia were found to consider attractive women with a BMI of about 19–21, while low SES participants perceived an attractive woman as having a BMI of about 23–24 (see Table 6.3).

Similar findings were reported when the Sámi of Finland, the last indigenous population in Europe, were compared with urban Finns in Helsinki (Swami and Tovée 2007b), when South African Zulus were compared with South Africans in Britain (Tovée *et al.* 2006, 2007), when rural Samoans were

Table 6.3 Swami and Tovée (2005b) found a preference for heavier female figures with decreasing SES in Britain and Malaysia (column 5). In addition, they found that the ideal female figure became more tubular (higher WHR) with decreasing SES (column 6). Finally, BMI was found to account for the greater variance in judgements of women's attractiveness than WHR in all study sites (columns 3 and 4; adapted from Swami and Tovée 2005b)

Study site		Variance accounted for by BMI (%)	Variance accounted for by WHR (%)	Most preferred or 'peak' BMI for attractiveness	WHR gradient
Description	Site				
High SES	British	84.1	7.4	20.85	−6.54
	British-Malaysian	82.3	8.9	21.25	−7.07
	Kuala Lumpur (Malays)	80.8	8.2	20.93	−7.29
	Kuala Lumpur (Chinese)	81.2	7.1	21.09	−7.23
	Kuala Lumpur (Indian)	77.0	6.9	20.79	−8.18
Medium SES	Kota Kinabalu	81.1	4.5	21.57	−6.75
Low SES	Rural Sabah	76.9	1.6	22.78	−3.95

compared with urban Samoans (Swami *et al.* 2007g) and when rural Thais were compared with urban Thais (Swami and Tovée in press, a). These studies lend credence to the view that the attractiveness of body weight may be linked less to ethnicity than modernity or SES (Lee and Lee 2000; Sobal and Stunkard 1989). However, the process by which preferences change as a function of SES remains unclear, and many researchers stress the role of media images and the profusion of a 'Western' notion of health in this process (Nasser 1988; Swami *et al.* 2007g, in press, b).

A related argument highlights the point that SES is likely to covary with food supplies (Marlowe and Wetsman 2001), and that, because a primary function of adipose tissue is to store calories, body fat is a reliable predictor of food availability. As fat represents stored calories, ancestral human populations will have preferred to be relatively overweight, especially as food supplies would likely have been unreliable or variable during such periods (Brown and Konner 1987; Sobal and Stunkard 1989). Moreover, among ancestral populations – just as among contemporary foragers – women who were too thin and energetically stressed would reach menarche later, ovulate less regularly, and would have had less capacity to support pregnancy and lactation (Ellisson 1990; Frisch 1987; Wood 2006). In the evolutionary past, therefore, men should have been selected to find heavier women attractive (not average weight women, as argued by Singh), as indeed they do in many societies (Marlowe and Wetsman 2001; Tovée *et al.* 2007).

This hypothesis, however, does not necessarily predict that a thin ideal will become the standard of women's beauty with a constant and reliable food supply. One attempt to justify a prediction of a thin ideal of beauty in cultures with plentiful food was put forward by Sobal and Stunkard (1989), who argued that the rich display their ability to purchase low-calorie diets and live healthily (for example, by exercising) by being thin. Low-status people, in turn, want to emulate them (Furnham and Baguma 1994; Polivy *et al.* 1986), because in most situations it pays to be of higher status. In other words, a preference for lighter body weights may begin among upper strata men and spread to lower strata men. Brown and Konner (1987) made a similar argument when they wrote that by being thin, the rich are signalling that they do not need to worry about where their next meal is coming from. While these explanations seem plausible, they do not explain the whole story, and it is likely that SES will also vary with other cultural factors, including media diffusion and cultural conformity. We return to some of these key issues in the subsequent chapter, having first considered cross-cultural differences in men's attractiveness.

Men's attractiveness across cultures

Earlier, in Chapter 5, we saw that both men and women are likely to consider a V-shaped male body within a normal BMI range as being highly attractive, at least in most socioeconomically developed settings (Maisey *et al.* 1999; Swami and Tovée in press b). In opposition to the preponderance of evolutionary psychological theories explaining women's attractiveness, however, the dominant paradigm through which men's body shape ideals have been explained is a social constructionist one. In brief, this suggests that society has certain expectations for ideal male body shapes (Hesse-Biber 1996; Leit *et al.* 2001; Murray *et al.* 1996; Peixoto Labre 2002) and that men increasingly compare their bodies to such idealised media and cultural images (Davis and Katzman 1999; Heinberg *et al.* 1995; McCreary and Sasse 2000). Women too are likely to endorse such ideals when they define what is a physically attractive male body.

In most developed settings, sociocultural pressures concerning men's body image seem to be on the increase (Andersen and DiDomenico 1992; Pope *et al.* 1999). For example, one study found a consistency in the V-shaped standard of men's bodily attractiveness presented in American men's magazines between 1960 and 1992 (Petrie *et al.* 1996). Indeed, an investigation of popular men's magazines revealed that the ideal male body marketed to men is more muscular than the ideal male body marketed to women (Frederick *et al.* 2005). Similarly, Leit and colleagues (2001) examined centrefold models in *Playgirl* from 1973 to 1997 and found that the cultural norm for the ideal male body has become increasingly muscular, especially in the 1990s. For Pope *et al.* (2000: 36), the contemporary muscular male ideal featured in the media represents a hypermale or 'more male than male' look, characterised by a disproportionate amount of muscularity in the shoulders and upper arms.

The preference for large, muscular and mesomorphic body types in settings of high SES appears to develop at a very young age (Staffieri 1967), and in men reaches its peak during early adolescence and early adulthood (Collins and Plahn 1988; Lerner 1969; McCreary and Sasse 2000). Importantly, the development of such preferences and ideals has been linked with media use and exposure (Botta 2003; Morry and Staska 2001): Thompson and colleagues (1999), for instance, report that after viewing images of idealised male physique, men's body image satisfaction decreased. One question that seems pertinent, therefore, is whether the preference for muscular, V-shaped men's bodies is found in all cultures. In other words, do all cultures and historical epochs share the same conception of men's attractiveness?

Swami (2007) has reviewed the available evidence and answered in the negative. For one thing, he notes that there has been substantial variability in the dominant notion of men's bodily attractiveness across time. Just as there was a tendency to perceive plump women as attractive during Renaissance Europe, for example, so rotund and heavyset men during the period were similarly considered highly attractive. Nevertheless the ideal of a muscular male is a relatively consistent theme throughout the ages; the point, however, was that different epochs also had male ideals that diverged from the muscular epitome (Swami 2007).

Second, the available psychological and ethnographic record suggests that contemporary cross-cultural differences in what is considered an attractive male body do exist. The muscular male ideal is less prevalent in Taiwan, for example, where magazine advertisements appear to place less emphasis on Asian male bodies than American magazines using Caucasian male models (Pope *et al.* 2001). Such images are also consistent with traditional Chinese ideals of masculinity that emphasise intelligence or wisdom, rather than body size or muscularity (Louie 2002; Yang *et al.* 2005).

While such studies emphasise the importance of ethno-cultural factors in understanding men's attractiveness, some recent evidence suggests that perceptions of an attractive body size may be linked with SES. Swami and Tovée (2005a) reported that, while upper-body shape (WCR) was the primary component of attractiveness ratings in high SES societies in Britain and Malaysia, women of low SES in Malaysia placed a greater importance on overall body weight (BMI) in making judgements of men's attractiveness. In short, while upper-body muscularity and a slender body were considered attractive in high SES settings, a more tubular, heavier body was considered attractive by low SES women (see Table 6.4).

Table 6.4 Swami and Tovée (2005a) found that, while WCR was the primary predictor of men's physical attractiveness in settings of high SES, BMI was a better predictor in settings of low SES (columns 3–5). In addition, the ideal WCR was high in the latter setting decreasing SES in Britain and Malaysia (column 7). Finally, the 'peak' or optimal BMI was significantly higher in the setting of low SES than it was in the settings of high SES (column 6) (adapted from Swami and Tovée 2005a)

Study site		Variance			Peak attractiveness	WCR gradient
Description	Site	WCR	BMI	WHR		
High SES	Britain	67.4	37.8	12.3	20.86	−27.30
	Kuala Lumpur	67.2	31.8	9.7	20.62	−26.68
Low SES	Rural Sabah	30.5	73.7	4.8	24.09	+15.73

In addition, some contemporary cultures appear to idealise the muscular ideal to a greater degree than others. Swami *et al.* (2007i) found that Greek women preferred a significantly lower WCR (indicating a more muscular body shape) than did British women, a result attributed to the different cultural and historical development of southern Europe. For example, the tradition of depicting muscular men in Greek art and sculpture is one potential explanation for this finding. In short, then, cross-cultural differences do exist in the male ideal, and sociocultural explanations are best poised to explain these.

Conclusion

The debates between those who insist on cultural similarities and those who stress cultural relativity in human behaviours have been fiercely contested. On the one hand are some evolutionary psychologists who, despite acknowledging the existence of some behavioural divergence, are keen to show that much of human behaviour is actually similar, because it derives from the same underlying process of evolution. On the other hand are anthropologists, cultural relativists and some psychologists, who believe that human behaviour, at least in relation to mate choice, is much more variable, malleable and flexible than evolutionary psychologists have allowed.

Such debates go far beyond disciplinary or academic differences of opinion. For some, they get to the heart of one of the most debated topics in human history: whether human behaviour can ultimately be explained by recourse to biology or culture, the genes or learning. Our own opinion, which we expand upon in the next chapter, is that such debates should be considered redundant. All human behaviours are a result of the interaction between biology and culture, and it is for this reason that we should expect both differences and similarities in human behaviours across cultures. Still, an interest in cultural differences has led to a better understanding of the processes that lead, in this instance, to preferences for body size in both men and women. Further studies from around the world will likely provide a better understanding both of how the human mind works and also how situational influences have the potential to affect certain behaviours.

7   Welcome to the mating market

I'm tired of all this nonsense about beauty being only skin-deep. That's deep enough. What do you want – an adorable pancreas?
    Jean Kerr, American author and playwright (*The Snake has all the Lines*, 1960)

Beauty is all very well at first sight; but who ever looks at it when it has been in the house three days?
    George Bernard Shaw, playwright (*Man and Superman*, 1903)

Beauty is worse than wine; it intoxicates both the holder and the beholder.
    Aldous Huxley, writer (1894–1963)

In previous chapters, we followed a trail of issues that, at its core, relates to the application of evolutionary principles to human behaviour and functioning. An important aspect of this approach centres around the concepts of the environment of evolutionary adaptedness and the monomorphic mind thesis (see Chapter 3). For evolutionary psychologists, the psychological modules or mechanisms that govern contemporary human behaviour were selected for in our past environment of evolutionary adaptedness, and insufficient time has lapsed for human brains to adapt to recent cultural changes. Consequently, some evolutionary psychologists propose that modern human beings may sometimes behave as though responding to situations in the environment of evolutionary adaptedness, resulting in behaviour that no longer produces reproductively successful outcomes.

While such an approach is entirely possible, in this chapter we discuss the more likely scenario that human behaviour, far from being ancestrally constrained, is in fact remarkably well adapted to current environments. The latter supposition is not alien to evolutionary psychologists, especially those who posit that evolved mental modules are highly dependent upon contextual triggers (Buss 2001; Buss and Greiling 1999; Gangestad *et al.* 2006), but it does sit uncomfortably with those authors who argue that some traits are highly 'canalised' (that is, behaviours are invariant across cultural contexts).

More generally, this view is encouraged by those critics of evolutionary psychology who do not agree that the human mind consists of 'hundreds or thousands' of domain-specific mental modules (Barrett *et al.* 2002; Buller 2005; Fodor 2000; Gray *et al.* 2003; Griffiths 2001; Stolz and Griffiths 2002; Swami in press).

The reason why this debate is of interest to us here stems from the fact that some evolutionary psychologists have argued that criteria for judging physical attractiveness are correlated positively with fitness in past environments. And because no significant evolution is said to have taken place since the end of the environment of evolutionary adaptedness, people living today use the same criteria of attractiveness that would have existed in those ancestral environments (Singh 1993a). But the available evidence would seem to go against such ancestrally constrained theories of physical attractiveness. Insofar as universality of behaviour is taken as evidence of a common environment of evolutionary adaptedness, for example, it would appear that there is little evidence of ancestrally constrained preferences, given findings of cross-cultural variability in attractiveness judgements (see Chapter 6).

An alternative evolutionary view might propose that human beings hold ancestrally unconstrained criteria of attractiveness and that mate choice is directed by general mechanisms rather than specific adaptationist modules (Sterelny and Griffiths 1999). For example, evolution might have led to human beings attempting to learn what cues in our environments are associated with health, social status, reproductive success and other relevant factors, and then to find those cues attractive (Buss and Greiling 1999; Buss and Reeve 2003; Gangestad *et al.* 2004; Haselton and Gangestad 2006; Sugiyama 2005). As this perspective suggests, there is a great deal of culture-specific learning that must take place, and ultimately social and developmental factors will impinge on any evolved criteria (Björklund and Pellegrini 2002). Our basic point is that it is possible to argue for active mate choice criteria, 'adapted' to contemporary conditions and not those of past evolutionary history. A central question that arises, therefore, is: can prevailing conditions change our notions of physical attractiveness?

The 'mating market'

In earlier chapters, we considered physical attractiveness preferences as absolutes, a perspective that derives from the notion of 'objective' beauty. While such objective ideals are perfectly reasonable, in reality there is a host of factors that serve to influence, and even change, our ideals under certain circumstances. In choosing a potential mate, for example, not everyone ends up with the most attractive individuals: attractive people do not want to be with us average-looking folk, and we in turn do not want to mate with those 'beneath' us. But more than our ideal partners having their own preferences, we also have to compete with other potential suitors in the 'mating market'.

Because the mating market is a two-way process of negotiation between ourselves and the object of our desires, and because mate choice will likely involve a great deal of competition, individuals can be expected to adjust their demands and preferences based on a realistic evaluation of what they are able to offer. As a result, mate choice and attractiveness ideals are likely to involve a conditional strategy that is dependent on what we are looking for in a potential mate, what we bring to the mating market (or, more precisely, our 'market position'), and our particular circumstances, whether environmental or biological (see Figure 7.1). In this section, we consider the first of these criteria, focusing on the influence of mating strategies on body shape preferences.

Most studies of attractiveness preferences have tended to examine such preferences in the absence of a broader framework of motivations and the situational context which gives rise to both motivations and preferences. But motives, or the disposition to strive for certain goals (McClelland 1985), are known to exert a powerful influence on sexual relationships and attractiveness ideals (Buss and Schmitt 1993). One important factor in evaluating a potential partner's attractiveness is the mating strategy of the observer, which is typically described as being either short term or long term. Individuals who follow a short-term mating strategy tend to pursue low-commitment, transient sexual relationships with multiple partners. By contrast, individuals who follow a long-term mating strategy tend to pursue a single, high-investment relationship (Buss and Schmitt 1993).

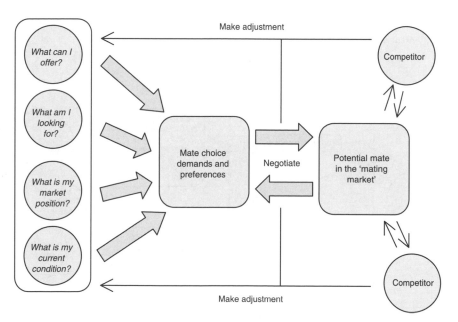

Figure 7.1 Individuals adjust their mate choice demands and preferences based on a realistic evaluation of what they can offer in the mating market.

Of course, these strategies are not mutually exclusive (Gangestad and Simpson 2000), although the pursuit of one strategy tends to make the alternative much less likely to enact. Moreover, when asked, people are capable of evaluating potential partner traits from the point of view of either short-term or long-term mating strategies, and their responses change in significant and predictable ways (Buss and Schmitt 1993). A robust finding in the literature is that men's standards for a short-term mate are generally much lower for a number of traits than their standards for a long-term mate (Kenrick *et al.* 1990). For example, Regan (1998) reported that individuals were more willing to compromise on some aspects of a potential partner, depending on the type of relationship being considered. Both women and men were unwilling to compromise on physical attractiveness when considering a casual sex partner. By contrast, when considering a long-term, romantic partner they were unwilling to compromise on interpersonal responsiveness (see Figure 7.2).

In terms of body shape ideals, some early studies did not find a difference in preferences for WHR depending on the observer's mating strategy. Singh and Young (1995), for example, report that a low WHR was the most attractive for both long- and short-term relationships. Indeed, there was a high correlation between short- and long-term relationship ratings of attractiveness for figures with varying WHRs. Furnham *et al.* (2002) found a much lower correlation, but there was still no difference between long- and short-term relationship preferences. More recently, Brase and Walker (2004) used the Sociosexual Orientation Inventory (Simpson and Gangestad 1991), a measure of the extent to which individuals place restrictions on sexual activity, but still failed to find major differences in preferences for WHR between long- and short-term relationships.

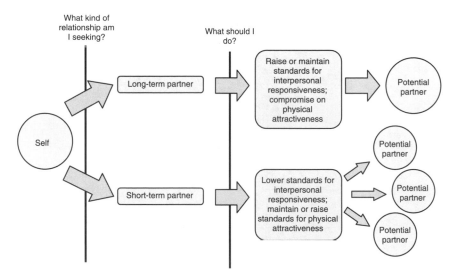

Figure 7.2 The effects of pursuing short- or long-term mating strategies.

Plate 1 In many species of animal, males have evolved elaborate 'ornaments' to seduce members of the opposite sex. For Darwin, males tend to court, while females tend to choose.

Plate 2 Due to their exaggerated nature, mate-attracting signals – such as the large tails of peacocks, deer antlers, the bright colouration of some species of fish, or the horns of a stag beetle – can prove to be a hindrance to an organism. Why, then, do such ornaments evolve?

Plate 3 Hair colour and style is an important individual marker and treated fetishistically in many cultures.

Plate 4 In almost all cultures, men and women differ in their complexions: in general, women are fairer, while men tend to be darker.

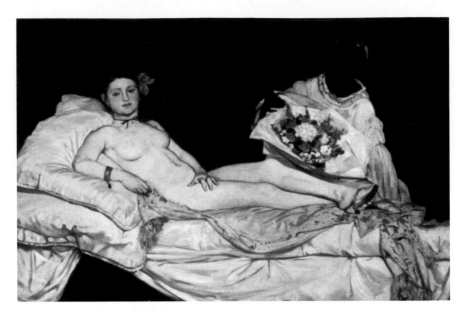

Plate 5 Many European paintings of the eighteenth and nineteenth centuries, including Édouard Manet's *Olympia*, show a white woman with one or more black servants. Both the servants and their offerings are signs in the social construction that marked the women as fair and beautiful.

Plate 6 The women in paintings by Pieter Pauwel Rubens often depict stylised plump figures that defined exuberant sensuality in Renaissance Europe: the 'ideal' woman in seventeenth- and eighteenth-century Europe was plump, even overweight, by today's standards.

Nevertheless, Brase and Walker (2004) did find a consistent pattern in what little difference did exist. Specifically, ratings appeared to be more conservative when evaluating a potential long-term relationship partner. In addition, men's own desirability had an influence on the ratings of female models. Men who had lower than average WHRs themselves, higher than average BMI, or rated themselves as lower in desirability tended to be less discriminating in some of their ratings. The authors also found that men's sociosexuality had a differential effect on approach likelihood: sociosexually restricted men were less likely to approach women rated as most attractive (with low WHRs), as compared with unrestricted men.

Schmalt (2006) has similarly made the point that the preference for a low WHR may be moderated by a 'power motive' as well as by short- and long-term mating contexts. The power motive refers to the predisposition to strive for status and power, which some studies have shown provides men with access to fertile women as well as making them more attractive to women (Kenrick *et al.* 2003; Li *et al.* 2002; Simpson and Oriña 2003). Thus, Schmalt (2006) found that a preference for a low WHR was moderated by individual differences as well as by situational contexts. Specifically, he found a stronger preference profile for individuals high in power motivation and for individuals looking for a short-term partner. While studies such as these are currently still in their infancy, they nevertheless provide preliminary evidence that the kind of relationship we are looking for can have an effect on our attractiveness ideals.

Assortative mating

What we are able to bring to the mating market – be it in relation to physical appearance, personality or resources – can also have a profound effect on what we consider to be, and not to be, physically attractive. Specifically, individuals are more likely to be attracted to, and end up in, a relationship with others who are similar to them in terms of physical, social and psychological traits. This effect is strongest for social and demographic traits (such as age, political orientation and religious attitudes), moderate for psychological characteristics like general intelligence and physical attributes, and weakest for personality characteristics (Epstein and Guttman 1984; Ho 1986; Jaffe and Chaconpuignau 1995; Klohnen and Mendelsohn 1998; Luo and Klohnen 2005; Watson *et al.* 2004).

Indeed, assortative mating appears to be the norm for human beings, with spouses tending to be similar to each other on a range of traits, including physical traits such as overall attractiveness (Berscheid *et al.* 1973), height (Ahmad *et al.* 1985; Susanne and Lepage 1988; Pawłowski 2003) and facial attractiveness (Penton-Voak *et al.* 1999a, 1999b). Moreover, physical features are typically positively correlated within couples (Spuhler 1968), and married partners tend to resemble each other to the extent that their faces can be correctly matched by strangers (Bereczkei *et al.* 2002; Griffiths and Kunz 1973; Hinsz 1989).

Some studies suggest that there are fitness benefits as a result of assortative mating, and theoretical studies have highlighted the possibility that assortative mating may be highly adaptive (Davis 1995; Thiessen and Gregg 1980). Assortative mating may maximise outbreeding while optimising inbreeding (Jaffe, 2002), which has a stabilising effect on genetic variance (Jaffe 1999, 2000). That is, assortative mating such that 'like prefers like' facilitates reproduction between genetically similar mates, which favours the stabilisation of genes supporting social behaviour, with no kin relationship between them (Jaffe 2001). Certainly, studies have shown that assortative mating affects the genetic structure of populations, influencing the evolutionary dynamics of sexual organisms (Dieckmann and Doebeli 1999; Kondrashov and Kondrashov 1999), which would suggest that it should have an important influence on psychological behaviours.

Moreover, it has been suggested that imprinting – memorising in early development the visual image of parents and then using these images of mate choice – may guide assortative mating in humans (Bereczkei *et al.* 2002; Little *et al.* 2003; Penton-Voak and Perrett 2000; Todd and Miller 1993). Children tend to resemble their parents (McLain *et al.* 2000; Nesse *et al.* 1990; Oda *et al.* 2002) and there is some evidence of mechanisms that allow humans to 'imprint' the faces of their parents at an early age (Le Grand *et al.* 2001). The visual memory created by this imprinting process may then be used to establish criteria for beauty, which in turn are used to select a mate, producing assortative mating as a consequence (Todd and Miller 1993).

While assortative mating can be interpreted as evidence of active mate choice, Barrett *et al.* (2002) have argued that it could also be interpreted as a best-of-a-bad-job strategy (see Figure 7.3). That is, having failed to entice better mates, we seek alternative strategies of mate choice which eventually lead to relationships with people who are similar to us. One such strategy is to lower one's standards, which widens the range of potential mates (Barrett *et al.* 2002; Pawłowski and Dunbar 1999). For example, in a study of American personal advertisements, Waynforth and Dunbar (1995) found that men who lacked resources were more willing to accept a woman's children from a previous marriage compared to men who did offer resources. These authors suggest that this represents a trade-off: men who recognise that they have little to offer in the way of resources attempt to make up for this by seeking alternatives that they hope will make them appear more attractive to the opposite sex.

A similar study by Cashdan (1993) asked participants to rate their agreement with a series of statements about mate attraction tactics. This study found that women who did not expect much parental investment from a potential mate were more likely to flaunt their sexuality in order to get pre-reproductive resources from men. Draper and Harpending (1982) have further suggested that such women reproduce 'fast and early' since they may 'maximise reproductive success by minimising time loss' and thus aim to increase their number of offspring per se. By contrast, women who expected

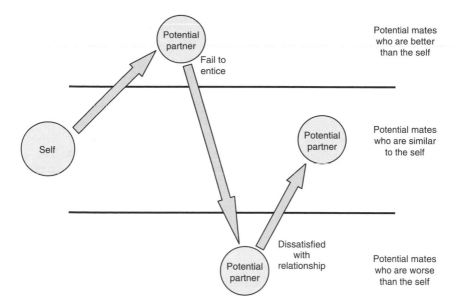

Figure 7.3 Is assortative mating a reflection of a best-of-a-bad-job strategy?

parental care from prospective mates were more likely to agree with statements extolling chastity and fidelity. Men too showed a corresponding tendency: those who were unlikely to invest favoured flaunting their sexuality to women, while those were likely to invest emphasised chastity and fidelity (Cashdan 1993).

Pawłowski and Dunbar (1999) have also considered how an individual's market value affects her or his willingness to make demands of a preferred partner. Based on British population data, they calculated that the best determinant of a woman's market value was her fecundity, whereas that for a man was a combination of his income and probability that he would still be married to a woman 20 years later. On the basis of these calculations, Pawłowski and Dunbar (1999) then examined whether individuals were sensitive to their standing in the mating market in terms of how demanding they were of potential mates (quantified as the number of traits they believed a partner should possess). In general, they found that there was a significant correlation between market value and how demanding both women and men were, suggesting that we adjust our demands based on self-evaluations of our standing in the mating market.

Social exchanges

While studies such as that by Pawłowski and Dunbar (1999) are helping to push the science of attraction forward, it is possible to extend their hypotheses even further, with the help of social psychological theories. For one thing, social psychologists have emphasised that, for attraction to be of evolution-ary significance, it must ultimately be a two-way process. In other words, attraction is useless (in an evolutionary sense) if it does not lead to the forma-tion of romantic relationships, and more than this, social situations impact upon people's interactions and the social outcomes of those interactions (Kelley *et al.* 2003).

One important social psychological theory in this respect is that of 'social exchange', a general theory of interpersonal relationships that highlights the interaction between two people. The key question for proponents of social exchange theory is: what will it cost to get a positive reward (such as having a nice time, developing a relationship) from a potential partner? The answer, quite clearly, will be dependent on both participants in the attraction process, through the joint social interactions that take place between them. The power of this theory lies in its ability to explain not just the attraction between potential romantic couples, but also our everyday interactions with people we have just met, our colleagues, friends and close companions. In all such inter-actions, we seek to obtain, preserve or exchange those things we value. Of course, some of these exchanges are brief and meaningless, but others may be brief and all-important – underscoring some people's belief in love at first sight (Averill and Boothroyd 1977) – ongoing, even long-term.

When such interactions take place over time, we enter into social relation-ships in which we try to obtain and give things that are mutually beneficial. Hogg and Vaughan (2005) have likened this to a business exchange: the attraction process is a give and take relationship between people, one in which both parties bring to the table what the other needs. Those needs, of course, can encompass a whole range of things from goods to affection, money to status, companionship to physical closeness (Foa and Foa 1975). Any of these resources can be exchanged in a relationship, and the manner in which they are exchanged will depend not just on the individuals concerned and their affection for one another, but also on structural constraints such as gender roles stereotypes, cultural conventions and so on (see Chapter 8).

At the societal level, for example, Walster and colleagues (1978) have pro-posed that social exchanges in the West are predicted on a system of equit-able relationships. That is, people in the West generally believe that social exchanges should be fair and just, and this belief is reinforced by societal norms and laws. The more inequitably (whether we receive less, or sometimes even more, than we expect) we are treated by our partners, the more distress we feel and the more we come to view our partners as unattractive (Lane and Messé 1971). Even deciding what is a fair relationship may be governed by societal norms: in societies in which the position of women is relatively undervalued compared to that of men, social exchanges may be skewed in favour of the latter.

At the level of the individual, Rusbult and colleagues (Rusbult and Buunk 1993; Rusbult *et al.* 1991, 1994) have noted that an important part of the social exchange process is a person's 'comparison level', or the standard against which we judge our relationships. Such comparison levels are the products of a lifetime of experience, encompassing everything from the outcome of past relationships to current social exchanges, our self-esteem and what we expect in future relationships (Thibaut and Kelley 1959). The reason why a person's comparison level is important is because, if the result of an exchange is positive (for example, we feel satisfied, gratified or pleasured), the relationship will be perceived as satisfying and the other person in the exchange will seem attractive. But if the result is negative (for example, what we receive from the exchange falls below our comparison level), then we begin to find our exchange partner unattractive.

Quite clearly, our comparison levels are not static – they can change with time, gender, experience, personality, culture, status and a whole host of other factors (see Figure 7.4). For instance, some research suggests that while both women and men prefer to date and mate with physically attractive individuals, women appear willing to 'trade off' attractiveness for cues to resources (Li *et al.* 2002). In one study, Waynforth (2001) had participants assign a limited number of 'points' to different qualities in a potential partner, with greater number of points indicating that a quality is more important than others. In a second task, participants were told to assume that all potential partners were of equivalently high status, and to make a second series of point assignments. Waynforth (2001) showed that when all potential partners were of high status, women increase the points the assigned to physical attractiveness proportionately more than to other qualities, suggesting they originally 'traded off' attractiveness for resources.

There may even be a comparison level for alternatives, as Hogg and Vaughan (2005) put it: that is, we may have expectations for future partners while currently involved with someone. The key point of all this, social

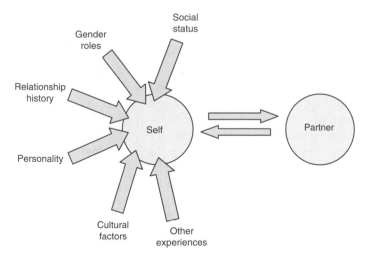

Figure 7.4 The many factors that affect social exchanges.

exchange theorists argue, is that to understand the nature of attraction, it is first necessary to understand the structure of the relationship between two people, as this structure determines the resources people bring to the mating market. While myriad factors that need to be accounted for make attraction an inherently difficult process to study scientifically, there is no getting away from the fact that such an approach more accurately approximates how things occur in everyday life.

Body weight preferences and hunger

The theory of social exchange makes it clear that physical attractiveness ideals are far from static, despite the proposals of some evolutionary psychologists. Other important considerations in this view include local socioeconomic and demographic conditions, which undoubtedly affect such judgements as body size preferences, as we saw in Chapter 6. Earlier, we examined how body weight ideals differ markedly with changing socioeconomic status (SES), with low SES observers preferring a significantly heavier body weight than high SES observers (Ford and Beach 1952; Swami and Tovée 2005b, 2007b; Tovée *et al.* 2006). Until recently, this pattern linking resource availability (as indicated by SES) and female body weight lacked an obvious psychological mechanism.

To rectify this oversight, Nelson and Morrison (2005) proposed an implicit psychological mechanism based on the situational influence of environmental conditions, which does not require the invoking of any specific evolved mechanism. They argued that collective resource scarcity has consequences for individual resources, as individual members of a society in which resources are scarce are likely to lack resources themselves. They further argued that the affective and physiological states associated with individual-level resource availability provide implicit information about collective resource availability, and that this information then plays a role in the construction of body weight preferences. In this view, it is believed that affective states can have a powerful influence on the thoughts and beliefs associated with psychological behaviours.

In a series of inventive studies, Nelson and Morrison (2005) tested this hypothesis by manipulating people's financial satisfaction or hunger (both these being proxies for personal resources in industrialised societies) and measuring their preferences for potential romantic partners. In the first study, participants reported whether or not they were carrying any money and what body weight they considered ideal in a potential partner. As predicted, men who did not have any money on them preferred significantly heavier women than men carrying money. A second study sought to remove the potential confound of money possession by using a randomly assigned manipulation of financial satisfaction. Again, participants who were more satisfied with their personal resources preferred a lighter female partner than men who felt financially poor.

In a third study, participants reported their ideal partner's body weight either before or after eating dinner. The results of this study were similar to those that manipulated financial satisfaction: hungry men preferred heavier women than did satiated men. Nelson and Morrison (2005) proposed that the construct of hunger is more universal than financial satisfaction, and suggest that their findings, therefore, lend support to the idea that implicit cues are used when stating preferences for potential partners. Moreover, when Swami and Tovée (2006a) replicated their study using photographic stimuli, using hunger as a proxy for personal resources, they found the same result: hungry men found a slightly heavier female body weight more attractive than satiated men.

One alternative explanation for these findings is that feelings of hunger or financial satisfaction were associated with different psychological variables like self-esteem. However, a separate set of findings replicated the central conclusions of Nelson and Morrison (2005), but showed that there were no changes in self-esteem (Nelson *et al.* 2007). A different concern has to do with the specificity of the effect: for instance, do hungry men prefer heavier objects in general or are the effects restricted to preferences for human beings? Research suggests that it is a very specific effect, as hungrier men do not prefer larger sport utility vehicles (Nelson *et al.* 2007), milk bottles or anvils (Swami *et al.* 2006d).

These studies provide evidence that temporary affective states can produce individual variation in physical attractiveness preferences that mirror patterns of cultural differences. In this sense, ratings of attractiveness vary over time: the mood or state of the observer can subtly, but significantly, influence his or her ratings of the physical attractiveness of a potential mate. This helps explain why preferences for body weight should vary according to SES, as individual preferences depend on situational feelings of resource scarcity. In rural contexts, where resource scarcity is more likely to be prevalent, affective and physiological states associated with individual-level resource availability provide implicit information about collective resource availability, and this information then plays a role in the construction of preferences for a heavier body weight. This hypothesis appears to have firm grounding in the psychological literature: feelings, states and psychological experiences not only often serve as 'information' about the environment, but can also influence behaviour without the engagement of complex cognitive processes (Nelson and Morrison 2005; Swami and Tovée 2006a).

Changing preferences with environment

To see how these findings apply to actual environmental contexts, consider the findings of Tovée *et al.* (2006, 2007). These authors asked four groups of participants to rate a series of photographic images of the female body: South African Zulus of low SES, Zulu migrants to Britain, Britons of African descent and British Caucasians. The results showed no difference between the body weight preferences expressed by the Caucasians and Britons of African descent. By contrast, there were large differences between these two groups and the Zulus of low SES, with the latter preferring significantly heavier (overweight and obese) women. Finally, the preferences of the Zulus who had moved to Britain seemed to be intermediate between the two previous positions. For Tovée *et al.* (2006, 2007), the fact that there were differences between the groups were explicable in terms of active adaptations to different environmental pressures.

Most people in rural South Africa live in a low resource, economically deprived society; more than half the rural population report going hungry, and most households do not have electricity, running water or significant amounts of household durable goods (which are useful proxies of SES). Among people living in rural South Africa, therefore, a higher female body weight may be perceived as reflecting affluence, high status and good health (Clark *et al.* 1999; Mvo *et al.* 1999), whereas thinness may be associated with starvation (Brown 1991; Treloar *et al.* 1999). These preferences may be further reinforced by current health problems prevalent in South Africa: there are longstanding problems with infectious diseases such as diarrhoea, tuberculosis, HIV and AIDS, which makes potential infection a serious possibility. The health consequences linked to these serious diseases include significant weight loss, and this may be reflected in the perception that a lower body mass signals potential parasitic infection or disease (Clark *et al.* 1999; Mvo *et al.* 1999).

In such a situation, a lower body weight may signal disease infection, and could reinforce a mate strategy that favours heavier bodies. Additionally, a higher preconceptual maternal BMI is correlated with a higher birth weight for the resulting child (Mohanty *et al.* 2006), and this may convey an important advantage for rural South African women. Although a higher BMI is also linked to a range of health problems (Manson *et al.* 1995), in rural South Africa the positive features of a higher female BMI may outweigh the potential dangers, which helps explain the pattern of attractiveness ratings by the South African Zulus.

In contrast, the situation in Britain is very different: the prevalence of infectious diseases like diarrhoea and HIV or AIDS is comparatively low, whereas a high BMI is strongly associated with various health risks (Calle *et al.* 2003). A low BMI is also associated with general long-term health and fertility, for both Caucasians and British Africans. Furthermore, BMI may be an indicator of SES: for a given age group, BMI is inversely proportional to nutrition and SES; that is, a higher BMI is correlated with poorer nutrition and lower SES. Taken together, there appear to be a number of ecological, environmental and demographic factors that influence Britons (and migrants to Britain) to favour a lower body weight when judging women's attractiveness.

Environmental Security Hypothesis

The examples of active attractiveness preferences that we have considered in this chapter have a common underlying theme: when faced with environmental insecurity, individuals appear to be making attractiveness judgements that, in theory, would help balance that insecurity. To explain this pattern, Pettijohn and Tesser (1999) proposed an overarching theoretical framework, known as the Environmental Security Hypothesis, to explain how cultural pressures operate on evolutionarily derived preferences. This is a context-dependent theory of attraction and attractiveness judgements that draws on both evolutionary theory and behavioural ecology, such that our perceptions of environmental security influence what we find most attractive and desirable at different times.

The theory suggests that when socioeconomic conditions are threatening or uncertain, individuals will prefer others with more mature characteristics compared to non-threatening conditions. This is primarily because maturity is associated with the ability to handle threatening situations (Pettijohn and Tesser 1999). Mature features may also communicate attributes such as strength, control and independence during a period when such qualities would have been most desired. In less threatening and environmentally secure periods, the need for mature themes and attributes becomes less important and, consequently, less mature themes are preferred.

Consistent with the Environmental Security Hypothesis, it might be predicted that when men are hungry (environmentally threatened), they should show a relatively greater preference for more mature female partners compared with satiated men. This is because hunger is a good indicator of physiological threat and reminder of resource availability (Swami and Tovée 2006a). Moreover, because body weight tends to increase with age, the Environmental Security Hypothesis would predict that hungry men should prefer heavier potential partners than satiated men, which is in fact what has been found (Nelson and Morrison 2005; Swami and Tovée 2006a).

But the Environmental Security Hypothesis does not simply predict preferences for body weight; rather, any perceived characteristic that varies along a mature-neotenous gradient might be predicted to vary with changing environmental security. For example, archival research on the facial features of American actresses appears to support the Environmental Security Hypothesis, with a greater preference for mature facial features (small eye size, thin cheeks and large chins) during periods of socioeconomic hardship (Pettijohn and Tesser 1999). By contrast, when social and economic conditions were good, actresses with neonate facial features (large eye size, round cheeks and small chins) were more popular. Similarly, Pettijohn and Yerkes (2004, 2005) examined the bodily characteristics of Miss America and Miss Hong Kong pageant winners, and report cross-cultural findings that are consistent with the Environmental Security Hypothesis.

Looking beyond archival findings, Pettijohn and Tesser (2004) designed a set of experimental manipulations to extend the utility of the Environmental Security Hypothesis. Participants were threatened with the possibility of receiving a mild or strong electric shock in the context of a learning exercise, and had to choose a partner to work with from a set of female facial photographs. Pettijohn and Tesser (2004) found that when people experienced high threat, they showed a relatively greater preference for women with smaller eyes. These and other results raise interesting questions about the influence of social and economic conditions on attractiveness preferences, and highlight the necessity of future research to examine these issues in greater detail.

Conclusion

As a final example of active attractiveness preferences, consider what has come to be known as the 'closing time effect'. Pennebaker (1979) asked individuals in three singles bars to rate the members of their own sex and the opposite sex present at three different times during the evening. While attractiveness ratings of same-sex individuals did not change as the evening progressed, members of the opposite sex were judged to be increasingly attractive with time. Pennebaker (1979) argued individuals were 'downgrading' their criteria for attractiveness as time passed and the risk of going home alone increased. While this study highlights another instance of circumstance influencing judgements of attractiveness, it should be pointed out that other studies of the 'closing time effect' have been more equivocal (Gladue and Delaney 1990; Jones *et al.* 2003; Krusse and Fromme 2005).

In conclusion, the studies reviewed in this chapter suggest that, far from being static and unchanging, judgements of physical attractiveness are actually quite variable. Not surprisingly, given this variability, many critics of evolutionary psychology have been uneasy with the ancestrally constrained, adaptationist framework evident in such research. It is unlikely that such a perspective will turn out to be a sufficient explanation for physical attractiveness preferences, in the absence of a more careful understanding of the context in which attractiveness preferences are formed and expressed. What cross-cultural and social psychologists have shown is that individual physiology and macroeconomic factors all exert predictable effects on attractiveness ideals.

8   No one is an island

Everything has its beauty, but not everyone sees it.
                Confucius, Chinese philosopher and reformer (551–479 BC)

Beauty is not in the face;
beauty is a light in the heart.
   Khalil Gibran, writer (1883–1931)

What is beauty? Not the show
Of shapely limbs and features. No.
These are but flowers
That have their dated hours
To breathe their momentary sweets, then go.
'Tis the stainless soul within
That outshines the fairest skin.
   Aubrey Thomas de Vere, Irish poet and critic (1814–1902)

Whatever we conclude about the utility of evolutionary psychological theories of physical attractiveness, it should be clear that the biological determinants of beauty do not occur in a vacuum. Rather, they occur within social and cultural contexts that have a tremendous impact on what is considered physically attractive and unattractive (Hogg and Vaughan, 2005; Sarwer *et al.* 2002). Not surprisingly, therefore, social psychologists have had much to say about human beauty, and indeed they have generated a vast body of research in the area, beginning at least in the late 1960s (Hogg and Vaughan 2005; Taylor 1998). In general, social psychologists have made two important contributions to the science of human beauty. First, social psychologists have pointed out that judgements of attractiveness are not formed in isolation from the social, cultural and developmental contexts that form our everyday being (Taylor *et al.* 1997). In this sense, our attractiveness ideals depend a great deal upon our perceived place within sociocultural environments, as well as upon information that we learn within those environments. Second, social psychological research on attraction has emphasised the importance of the process of attraction, which includes such aspects as proximity, body language and other non-physical traits (Hogg and Vaughan 2005; Huston 1974; Myers 1996). In this chapter, we consider the first of these contributions, leaving the latter to Chapter 9.

No one is an island

The phrase 'no one is an island' neatly sums up a core assumption of social psychological research, namely that human beings are inherently social creatures, for whom social isolation can be detrimental (Perlman and Peplau 1998). Taken to its logical conclusion, this view suggests our attitudes and behaviours are, in part at least, formed through our interactions with those around us (Moscovici 1961, 1981). Such learning is an integral part of the socialisation process that all individuals experience either through direct experiences or vicariously through interactions with others. But those interactions, in turn, are predicated upon a wealth of cultural knowledge and societal constructs that attempt to explain the world around us. In other words, individuals come to hold certain attitudes and ideals as a result of their everyday social interactions, which represent and promote societal constructs (Farr and Moscovici 1984; Lorenzi-Cioldi and Clémence 2001; Moscovici 1981, 1988).

More than this, social contexts do not just influence the social interactions that take place, but are also a product of social psychological processes. In this view, there is a deep interaction between the individual and the collective social context, a notion central to the 'theory of mutual constitution' (Fiske *et al.* 1998; Kim and Markus 1999; Kitayama *et al.* 1997). According to this theory, psychological and sociocultural structures constitute each other in a feedback loop between the individual and the collective social context. A comprehensive understanding of a particular psychological tendency or behaviour, such as ideals of attractiveness, therefore requires some analysis of the collective reality which grounds those ideals (see Figure 8.1).

The collective reality that grounds and enables attitudes and behaviours includes socioculturally and historically rooted ideas and values, institutions and social practices. In any society or culture, Kim and Markus (1999) suggest, it is possible to identify core values that are expressed in many aspects of social life. These values are conveyed to the individual through culture-specific practices, which involve institutions like educational systems, religious practices, and mass media products (Kim and Markus 1999). By participating in particular cultural processes, individuals form an understanding of cultural norms, which regulate their feelings and behaviours. As Moscovici (1983: 5) put it: 'Our reactions to events, our responses to stimuli, are related to a given definition, common to all members of the community to which we belong.'

This view is heavily influenced by the sociological work of Durkheim (1912/1995) on 'collective representation'. For both Moscovici and Durkheim, individuals who share similar beliefs interact in social episodes in local

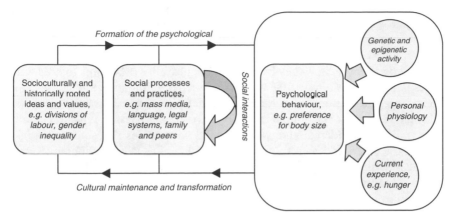

Formation of the psychological

Socioculturally and historically rooted ideas and values, e.g. divisions of labour, gender inequality

Social processes and practices, e.g. mass media, language, legal systems, family and peers

Social interactions

Psychological behaviour, e.g. preference for body size

Genetic and epigenetic activity

Personal physiology

Current experience, e.g. hunger

Cultural maintenance and transformation

Figure 8.1 The dynamic process of the mutual constitution of culture and the individual (adapted from Kim and Markus 1999).

worlds, and these interactions (along with cultural institutions) shape the individual's psychological experience (Farr and Moscovici 1984; Purkhardt 1995). As a consequence, core cultural values become internalised and represented in the behaviours, preferences and actions of individuals (Kim and Markus 1999). From this perspective, specific attitudes and behavioural dispositions are framed by, embedded in and take place within wider representational structures, which are in turn formed by social groups (Moscovici 1981, 1988).

This is why it is important to consider sociocultural factors in studies of physical attraction. The difficulty, of course, is that there is a whole host of sociocultural factors that should be considered, many of which cannot be reduced to simple quantitative constructs. To continue with our earlier example of preferences for body weight, for example, we have seen how there is an idealisation of heavier body weights in settings of low socioeconomic status (SES). Most studies have typically assumed that SES is correlated with food availability (Swami and Tovée 2006a), which presumably explains why heavier bodies should be idealised in contexts of low SES, given that only a certain class of individuals would have been able to put on body fat.

But SES is also related to many other factors that may influence preferences of body weight; nor does SES alone explain why a slim ideal should be considered attractive in contexts of high SES. Rather, for some authors, such preferences should rightly be embedded in a 'gendered complex of hegemonic forces that accompany global economic change' (Lee and Lee 2000: 324). That is, to fully understand body weight preferences, it is first necessary to recognise the role played by gendered forces that take place within sociocultural contexts. As Lee and Lee (2000) point out, socioeconomic development often means new opportunities for women, particularly in terms of self-advancement, education potential, employment opportunities and mate choice. These changes create conflicting demands on young women: on the one hand they must strive for career success, while on the other they must maintain their physical attractiveness (Malson 1998).

In this view, the gendered social roles held by women and men can have a very strong effect on how they behave and the attitudes they come to hold. Of course, as we see in Figure 8.1, women and men are not passive actors within social and cultural contexts; rather, they actively construct those contexts through various social interactions that are nevertheless predicated upon their individual understandings of gendered social roles. These interactions may lead women and men to experience their bodies in very different ways, and also help to explain why ideals of body weight can vary depending on where an individual is born and resides. For urban women who experience education opportunities, career development and mate choice, slimness is synonymous with idealised beauty (Lee 1996, 1998). By contrast, rural women's lives are still under substantial patriarchal influence, and in such rural contexts, bodily fullness still symbolises fertility and wealth (Swami 2006c; Swami and Tovée 2005b).

Gender and attractiveness

Thus far, we have considered the impact of gender on behaviour in very general terms, as it relates to core sociocultural influences. In this section, we consider some of the more direct ways in which gendered interactions and social roles can have an influence on physical attractiveness judgements. But first it is important to make clear the distinction between 'sex' and 'gender'. While many evolutionary psychologists are happy to base their conclusions about human nature based on sex differences (that is, biological sex, as ascribed at birth according to external genitalia), social psychologists and sociologists view gender as something that is learned and 'done' within social contexts (Pleck *et al.* 1994; West and Zimmerman 1987).

A key notion is that gender, or more precisely gender-role norms or stereo-types, is learned within particular 'collective realities' through a process of socialisation (Cialdini and Trost 1998). For example, social agents such as parents, teachers, peers and the media teach women and men the 'rules' and standards of femininity and masculinity, respectively (Lauer and Lauer 1994; Lytton and Romney 1991; Santrock 1994). Research confirms that this learning occurs very early in life, as evidenced by the finding that by age five children have already developed clearly defined notions of what constitutes appropriate behaviour for men and women (Lytton and Romney 1991). But more than this, women and men also use various everyday activities in their construction and reconstruction of gender, including work, language and sex (Connell 1995; Messner and Sabo 1994; Vance 1995), and through such interactions, individuals learn specific meanings of gender and gendered behaviour (Pleck 1987).

Gender roles are known to be related to a variety of behaviours and attitudes, including health-related behaviours such as smoking, drinking and help-seeking behaviour (Courtenay 2000). More pertinently as it relates to physical attractiveness, gender roles are also known to be related to eating disorders and satisfaction with body shape (Parsons 1980; Weitz 1977; Williams 1979). There is also evidence that gender roles are correlated with the perception of bodies of the opposite sex (Maier and Lavrakas 1984; Pleck 1979), although much of this literature is several decades old and requires urgent contemporary work (McCreary and Sasse 2002).

In one early study, for instance, Wiggins *et al.* (1968) found that men who were very 'masculine' according to the traditional sense (that is, had a high need for independence and dated frequently) showed a greater preference for large-breasted women than did less masculine men. Similarly, Beck *et al.* (1976) showed that women who preferred a large bust had an interest pattern which could be considered as traditionally feminine. Unfortunately, such studies have used definitions of gender roles that are today considered quite imprecise.

In another study, Lavrakas (1975) reported that women who adopted a traditionally feminine gender role had a greater preference for masculine male physiques (a tapering V-shape) than did less 'traditional' women. In conjunction with more recent work (Swami *et al.* 2007i), this study suggests that individuals adopting traditional (that is, more strongly masculine or feminine) gender roles tend to have preferences for body shapes that are defined as attractive in the 'traditional' sense, namely hourglass shapes for women and muscular V-shapes for men. In contrast, individuals adopting 'liberated' gender roles have less stereotyped preferences (Furnham and Greaves 1994; Maier and Lavrakas 1984).

Other studies have examined differences in preferences between the cultures that are defined as more or less gender-role stereotyped (after Hofstede 1983). For example, Furnham and Nordling (1998) compared the perception of body shapes in two culturally distinct samples, namely Denmark (a less gender-role stereotyped country) and Portugal (a more gender-role stereo-typed European country), finding that Portuguese participants displayed a stronger preference for traditional 'curvaceous' women and V-shaped male body shapes than did Danish participants. By contrast, Danish participants showed a stronger preference for the 'angular' shapes (with small hips) for both women and men.

In a more recent study, Swami *et al.* (2006a) found that Greek men, who were considered to inhabit a culture that was considered more strongly gender-role stereotyping than British men, showed a preferences for more curvaceous women (stronger preference for a low WHR). Similarly, Greek women appear to have a stronger preference for greater upper-body build in men than their British counterparts (stronger preference for a low WCR; Swami *et al.* in press, b). These studies would seem to suggest that gender roles have an important influence on how we perceive the bodies of potential partners. For the moment, it remains unclear to what extent individual gender-role stereotyped preferences mirror those of cultural gender roles, although it might be expected that these will be highly related. Studies are currently under way to examine the way individual and cultural gender-role stereotypes interact to influence overall preferences (McCreary *et al.* 2005).

The influence of 'subcultures'

Markus and Kitayama's (1991) theory of mutual constitution also helps to explain the initiation and perpetuation of attractiveness ideals within particular cultures or subcultures; ideals that might be considered unattractive, even repellent by others. In earlier chapters, we came across a number of such preferences that appear to be limited to particular societies. Other examples include the ancient tradition of *ohaguro* in Japan (which involved the ink-dying of teeth), the popularity of the male codpiece and the emphasis on men's thighs during Renaissance Europe and the facial scarring still practised among some African communities (see Figure 8.2). Indeed, Darwin's *Descent of Man* (1871) is full of examples of cross-cultural differences in features considered attractive, many of which were collected and passed on to him by missionaries in 'exotic locations' (Swami 2007).

Perhaps the most well-developed body of research concerning subcultural differences in contemporary settings concerns judgements of attractiveness by women and men who are attracted to others of the same sex. For example, several studies have found lesbians to hold different preferences from hetero-sexual men and women. In one study of age preferences, for example, lesbians were reported to differ from both heterosexual men and women, in that when they were older they began to be interested in younger women while continuing to be interested in women their own ages and older (Kenrick *et al.* 1995). Others have found that lesbians are less concerned than heterosexual women with a partner's financial status, and are more interested in visual sexual stimuli than heterosexual women (Bailey *et al.* 1994).

In terms of bodily attractiveness, the possible influence of lesbianism has not occupied the attention of researchers to the same degree, and until very recently few studies have considered lesbians' attitudes towards bodily attractiveness and appearance (Brand *et al.* 1992; Siever 1994). Nevertheless, many theorists now acknowledge that the lesbian community appears to possess more 'flexible' norms of the female body (Ojerholm and Rothblum 1999; Share and Mintz 2002), which may serve as a buffer against the effects of mainstream society's pressure on women to be thin.

A study by Gettelman and Thompson (1993) offers support for this suggestion. When compared with heterosexual women, lesbians expressed less concern with weight, dieting and body image issues. By contrast, heterosexual women reported more disturbed eating patterns and were also found to be more appearance oriented (Epel *et al.* 1996; Gettelman and Thompson 1993; Schneider *et al.* 1995). Similar findings have been reported by more recent studies (Bergeron and Senn 1998; Herzog *et al.* 1991; Lakkis *et al.* 1999) and a

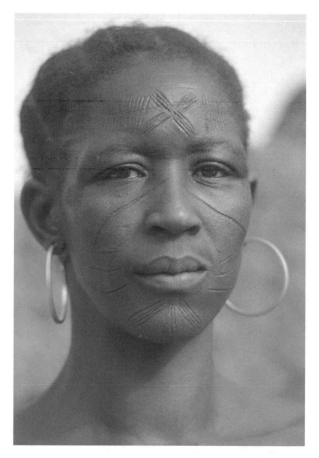

Figure 8.2 Facial scarring remains popular among some African communities.
Copyright © Charles and Josette Lenars/CORBIS.

meta-analysis (Morrison *et al.* 2004), which found that lesbians scored significantly lower than heterosexual women on a range of disordered eating,
body dissatisfaction, drive for thinness and bulimia measures.

In one study examining preferences of attractiveness, lesbians and bisexual
women were found to prefer heavier figures than heterosexual women (Cohen
and Tannenbaum 2001), which the authors proposed could be explained by
one of two conjectures: first, that lesbians on average are heavier than heterosexual women, and so may be choosing figures that more closely resembled
their own body types; or second, that their preferences reflect a rejection of
what may be seen as an inappropriate fixation on thinness. Swami and Tovée
(2006b) asked lesbians and heterosexual women to rate a series of photographs for physical attractiveness, and found that lesbians preferred a significantly heavier body weight than heterosexuals. In this study, lesbians were not
on average heavier than heterosexual woman, which lends credence to the

view that lesbians' different preferences result from a rejection of societal norms (Swami and Tovée 2006b).

To explain such findings, Brown (1987) suggested that, although all women are subjected to cultural prescriptions of the 'ideal', lesbians appear less affected. She proposed that the denigration of overweight women mirrors that of lesbians, as both are violating certain 'rules' and pushing the limits of patriarchal control. Moreover, 'lesbians appear to be over represented among fat activists . . . [who see] the stigmatisation of fat people as political oppression' (Brown 1987: 295). This, she suggested, may translate into pressure not to succumb to sociocultural norms, that is, not to define normal variations in body size or shape as deviant or pathological.

While it appears that lesbians are likely to reject what they see as societal pressure to be thin, gay men on the other hand strive to achieve stringent ideals of muscularity and body size (Russell and Keel 2002; Siever 1994). Indeed, the extant literature suggests that gay men report greater body image dissatisfaction and more disordered eating than heterosexual men (Beren *et al.* 1996; French *et al.* 1996; Morrison *et al.* 2004). Several reasons have been posited to account for this disparity, including that aspects of gay male culture emphasise physical appearance more than heterosexual male culture (Epel *et al.* 1996; Siever 1994).

Several studies have examined whether gay men hold different preferences for male attractiveness than heterosexual men and women. Herzog *et al.* (1991) suggested that gay men idealise an underweight body and are more likely to endorse a thin ideal than heterosexual men. However, more recent studies have suggested that gay men may place a greater importance on upper-body muscularity rather than overall body weight, when compared with heterosexual men (Levesque and Vichesky 2006). Swami and Tovée (in press b), for example, compared the attractiveness preferences of gay and heterosexual men, finding that, while both groups showed a similar preference for body weight, gay men preferred a lower waist-to-chest ratio, which is consistent with a more developed upper-body musculature.

A number of explanations were postulated to explain this finding. First, as suggested by Levesque and Vichesky (2006), the idealised media image of the muscular male appears to be the dominant ideal among gay men. This may be further enhanced by the strong emphasis within gay culture on physical appearance (Epel *et al.* 1994; Silberstein *et al.* 1989). In fact, Levesque and Vichesky (2006) found that involvement in the gay community was associated with desiring a more muscular body ideal, although acceptance within the gay community may also buffer gay men from pressure to look a certain way.

Second, the value of muscularity may reflect the tendency to associate muscularity with masculinity (Halkitis *et al.* 2004; Mishkind *et al.* 1986). Within the gay community, it may be that gay men are left with only their bodies as a distinguishing source of masculinity, and images of muscular and fit bodies thus represent men seeking to embody physical strength, hardness and power associated with muscular ideal, while signalling distance from ideas about femininity (Feingold 1990; Leit *et al.* 2001). The heightened value of the muscular ideal is also reflected in the tendency of gay men to integrate such ideals into their self-concepts (Silberstein *et al.* 1989). Muscularity may also be an important signal of health within the gay community, which may be especially pertinent as the community deals with the impact of HIV and AIDS (Levesque and Vichesky 2006).

Sources of learning

A theme central to the social psychological theories considered thus far is that physical attractiveness ideals involve a great deal of learning as part of the socialisation process (see Figure 8.3; Fishbein and Azjen 1975; Oskamp 1977). One of the most important sources of our attitudes and preferences is predicated upon the actions and behaviours of people around us, especially our parents when we are still young. For example, some research suggests that there is a positive correlation between high school children's preferences for particular political parties and their parents' choices (Jennings and Niemi 1968), which may also generalise to other attitudinal dispositions. Indeed, parents are known to influence the attitudes that their children hold about overweight peers (Field *et al.* 2001; Irving *et al.* 2002), and parental influences

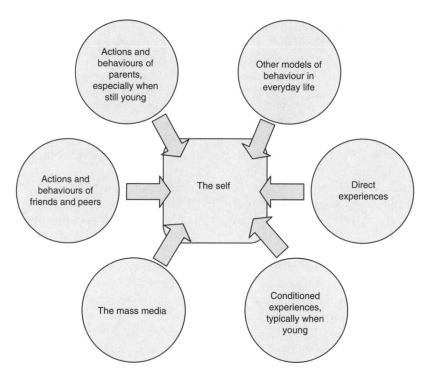

Figure 8.3 Sources of learning attractiveness ideals.

have also been implicated in children's development of ideas concerning what constitutes the 'ideal' female image (Gordon 2000; Stice 1998).

Surprisingly, few experimental studies of mate choice have considered parental preferences, even though parents in many cultures have historically had, or continue to have, influence over the long-term mate choices of their children (Beckerman 2000). In one recent study, Yu *et al.* (2007) found that, in a population of Matsigenka Amerindians, where parents influence the daughter's choice of long-term partner, women found feminine male faces to be more attractive but prefer masculine faces as sons-in-law. The authors suggest that this gives masculine males an advantage when it comes to marriage, which highlights the role of parental judgements in mate choice. Other studies have highlighted the critical role of mothers in engendering body size preferences, by encouraging their children to gain or lose weight (Rguibi and Belahsen 2006). In brief, studies such as these suggest that future research should take into account kinship and marriage systems, inheritance rules, social class and other sociocultural factors, all of which influence mate choice (McGraw 2002).

Researchers who study attractiveness ideals have also suggested that the mass media, which reflects and promotes cultural beliefs and values, plays a significant role in influencing judgements of physical attraction (Becker and Hamburg 1996; Bryant and Zhilman 2002; Fallon 1990; Harrison 1997; Heinberg and Thompson 1995; Polivy and Herman 1985; Wolf 1990). Much of this research has focused on the propagation of a thin ideal in contemporary Western cultures. Guillen and Barr (1994), for instance, have suggested that the content of magazines targeted at adolescent girls supports the perception that female happiness and success are tied to physical appearance, with ultra-slim being the preferred state of health and beauty. Such magazines promote thinness and associate attractiveness with a low body weight by presenting models who are below average in weight, and by promoting products and articles that tell readers how to become thin (Bordo 1993; Boyd and Fouts 1999; Franzoi 1995; Malkin *et al.* 1999; Shaw 1995; Snow and Harris 1986).

There seems little doubt that the mass media plays a pervasive role in communicating societal ideals of attractiveness (Levine and Smolak 1996; Owen and Laurel-Seller 2000). It has been proposed that this results in mass dissatisfaction with body weight, especially among women (Tiggemann and Rothblum 1988). Numerous studies and reviews of the literature (Abramson and Valene 1991; Baker *et al.* 1998; Cash *et al.* 1983; Posavac *et al.* 2001) have examined body satisfaction and eating disorder symptamology as correlates of using mass media, and almost all suggest an insidious role. Men have been less likely to develop body image disturbances and eating disorders (Pingitore *et al.* 1997; Walsh 1997), which is consistent with the lower level of social emphasis on male body weight and shape (Rolls *et al.* 1991), although there is evidence that this too is changing (Morry and Staska 2001; Petrie *et al.* 1996).

The fact that the propagation of Western forms of media is associated with increasing SES further pinpoints the mass media as a source of learning of what constitutes the ideal body size across cultures. That is, as previously isolated cultures experience the effects of globalisation and the import of Western media, the notion of thinness as being emblematic of feminine attractiveness becomes embedded within popular culture (Becker 2004; Swami *et al.* 2007g), and erodes any veneration of larger body sizes that may have existed previously. Indeed, Becker *et al.* (2005) have discussed how the introduction of Western-based television in Fiji was associated with Fijian girls' increased desire to be thinner.

How does learning occur?

There are, of course, other sources of learning that may be important when it comes to physical attractiveness ideals, including one's peers and social networks (Gordon 2000). But while studies have highlighted the various sources of learning, they nevertheless leave open the question of how learning occurs. Bandura (1973) believed that learning occurred by modelling our behaviour on another person, typically someone important to us. In this view, individuals learn new responses by observing significant others and the outcomes of their behaviour. For instance, objectifying women or prejudicial attitudes toward overweight individuals could be instilled in otherwise naive children if the models are significant adults (such as parents) in their lives.

Another way in which learning can take place is through the effects of direct experience: we may encounter someone and have a positive experience with her or him, which partly shapes our attraction to that person (and other similar persons). Of course, the same principle could also work in the opposite direction: having a negative experience with someone may lead us to find that individual (and other similar individuals) unattractive. Fishbein and Azjen (1975) argued that direct experiences affect our beliefs toward a person by providing us with information about that particular person, and that this information subsequently leads to beliefs that will influence our liking or disliking.

An extension of the idea of repeated association is 'classical conditioning' – of which Pavlov's experiments are probably the most well known. In classical conditioning, a formerly neutral stimulus (for example, Pavlov's bell) is 'conditioned' to elicit a reaction that was previously elicited only by another stimulus (food). Some authors have suggested that classical conditioning underlies the formation of all kinds of attitudes and behaviours (Staats and Staats 1957; Zanna *et al.* 1970). Indeed, many contemporary theories of sexual fetishes are based on some conceptual ideas of conditioning.

Fetishes

The wide range of human sexual fetishes is truly remarkable, and belies any simple explanation as to its origin (see Table 8.1). Consider, for example, that

Table 8.1 A selected list of known human fetishes

Fetish	Description
Breast fetishism	A pronounced sexual interest in the female breasts, their shape, movement, and size.
Podophilia or foot fetishism	A pronounced sexual interest in feet, which may be one of the most common male fetishes.
Trichophilia or hair fetishism	Sexual arousal in response to human hair, whether for different hairstyles or colours. Arousal may also occur from imagery or physical contact with hair, including cranial hair and pubic hair.
Navel fetishism	A fetish where an individual is strongly attracted to the human navel, often related to stomach fetishism (alvinolagnia).
Fat fetishism	Sexual pleasure derived from oneself or one's parter being overweight or obese.
Nasophilia or nose fetishism	Sexual arousal in response to the sight, touch, or sometimes the erotic sucking of human noses.
Muscle fetishism	An extreme liking for muscles and/or strength.
Abasiophilia	An attraction to disabled people who use orthopaedic appliances such as leg braces, orthopedic casts or wheelchairs.
Retifism or shoe fetihism	A sexual fixation on shoes or other footwear.
Doraphilia or fur fetishism	An attraction to people wearing fur, or in certain cases, to the garments themselves.
Latex or PVC fetishism	Sometimes known as rubber fetishism, this is an attraction to people wearing latex clothing, or in certain cases, to the bodywear itself.
Scuba fetishism	Sexual arousal by scuba diving, snorkelling, or the wearing of diving equipment. It is a type of fetish that falls under the broader category of aquaphilia, arousal involving water in some form.
Eyeglasses fetishism	An attraction to people wearing prescription eyeglasses or sunglasses, or in certain cases, to the act of wearing eyeglasses or the eyeglasses themselves.
Glove fetishism	A fetish where an individual is obsessed and fixated by another or oneself wearing gloves, sometimes enhanced by the material of the glove.
Smoking fetishism	A fetish consisting of the fetishisation of the smoking of tobacco, including cigarettes, cigars, pipes, even ash trays.
Balloon fetishism	A fascination for, or pertaining to, balloons, which provides sexual arousal or stimulation.
Necrophilia	A sexual attraction to corpses.
Sadism and masochism (S&M)	Sexual pleasure or gratification derived from the infliction of pain and suffering upon another person.

some individuals are 'fat fetishists', that is, they find sexual pleasure from themselves or their partner's being overweight or obese (Love 1994; Monaghan 2005; Swami and Furnham in press a). A strict adaptationist framework will find it difficult to explain such a fetish, especially given the negative health risks of being overweight or obese. Yet, for some individuals, the sight of 'pannus' – hanging flaps of adipose tissue of an overweight or obese person – can be both sexually arousing and physically attractive. Indeed, a large number of internet websites are dedicated to fat fetishism and feature women who are barely overweight to those who are morbidly obese (Swami and Furnham in press a).

There also exists a subculture of 'fat admirers', where a large woman is referred to as Big Beautiful Woman (BBW) and a large man as Big Handsome Man (BHM). Fat admirers can be fetishists, only being aroused if fat is involved, or just have a preference for a large partner (like the preference for thinness in others). Many within the fat admirer community consider mainstream culture to be dominated by a pro-thin bias, and many are also involved with the fat acceptance movement, which seeks to change societal opinion about overweight and obese individuals (Swami and Furnham in press a).

There is a range of other human fetishes too (Love 1994; Steele 1995). Breast fetishism, for example, involves a pronounced sexual interest in the female breasts, their shape, movement and size. In much of the Western world, a woman's breasts are perceived as symbols of sexuality and attractiveness, and the size of breasts can be particularly important in sexual arousal. In popular media, the breast size of women is relatively large (Harrison 2003), and this is sometimes said to have fuelled the market for breast enlargement surgery. Indeed, many adult actresses have capitalised on the male obsession with large breasts by having their breasts enlarged to implausible (that is, biologically unlikely) sizes. However, other individuals seem to have a fetishistic preference for large natural breasts (without implants), while others are small breast fetishists. Moreover, not all breast fetishism involves size; there are also fetishes concerned with lactation and breast firmness (with some preferring firm breasts and others preferring saggy breasts).

Aside from fat and breast fetishism, tricophilia or hair fetishism is another common fetish, involving either a fetishistic preference for certain hair colours (for example, red hair), different hairstyles or physical contact with head, pubic or axilliary hair (Love 1994). Yet other fetishes include foot fetishism, and of course fetishes that involve non-human characteristics such as shoes, leather, lingerie, body art or piercings, clothing and desks (a strangely common fetish!). The point is that, given the range of fetishes that human beings indulge in, it is unlikely that there will be a single explanation to explain all such behaviours and preferences. Still, part of the explanation for fetishes, as we suggested earlier, is likely predicated on some form of conditioned learning. Freud, for example, described sexual fetishes as the result of a childhood trauma regarding castration anxiety. According to his theory, a boy curious to see his mother's penis averts his eyes when he discovers his mother has no penis. The inanimate object on which the boy focuses when he averts his eyes becomes the fetishised object. Within this framework, men but not women are capable of having sexual fetishes, something which makes this a falsifiable theory (specifically, women are just as likely as men to have fetishes).

Freud's theory, needless to say, was based on anecdotal rather than empirical evidence, but some modern theories of fetishes still highlight the relationship between human orgasms and conditioning. In such theories, a sexual stimulus and the fetish object are presented simultaneously, which causes them to be connected in the conditioning process (the psychologist Alfred Binet, who introduced the term 'fetishism', had in fact made a similar prediction in the late nineteenth century, though he also made judgements about its pathogeneity). Some theories also stress that fetishes could be the result of generalisation: it may only be small feet that arouse a person at first, for example, but in time stimuli associated with, or that accentuate small feet (such as high-heeled shoes), may have the same effect.

One problem with such theories is that classical conditioning in the Pavlovian sense needs many repetitions, but the predicted outcome here requires only one. Some behaviourists have, therefore, argued that fetishism is the result of imprinting, which occurs during a specific time in childhood when a sexual association is imprinted on to the child's mind. Another theory based on the principles of behavioural imprinting argues that as young men masturbate frequently and as they develop a frequent pattern, the objects that are often nearby at the time of masturbation become likely objects of arousal in the future. It is theorised that because the brain is recording all sensory input during masturbation and orgasm including vision, smell, hearing and even taste, this simultaneous information can become neuronally linked with the pleasure of the activity. If nearly identical conditions are experienced during repeated masturbation sessions, the brain may learn to strongly associate any object, clothing or even the surrounding environment with impending pleasure and eventual orgasm.

Some authors have extended this idea to suggest that simple reinforcement may underlie why we are attracted to particular individuals, rather than just as an explanation of fetishes. For example, Lott and Lott (1972, 1974) proposed that we like people who happen to be present when we receive an award, even if their presence is merely incidental. Griffiths and Guay (1969) tested this idea by having a non-involved bystander present while participants were either given a reward or a punishment. They found that the bystander – who did not actually intervene in the process – was liked better when participants were given an award than when they were punished. In short, studies such as these have highlighted the important role that conditioning may play in the attraction process.

Conclusion

The evidence we have reviewed in this chapter points to the undeniable conclusion that ideas and constructs learned in social contexts have a substantial
influence on the process of attraction. Let us be clear: we are not advocating a
view in which the mind is viewed as a 'blank slate' – the infamous *tabula rasa*
– which merely 'soaks up' experiences in social worlds (in fact, we know of no
social psychologist advocating such a view). Rather, our point in this chapter
was to redress what we feel is an important oversight within the literature on
physical attraction.

To be sure, some evolutionary psychologists have pointed out that they are
keenly aware of the role that social contexts play in influencing ideals of
attractiveness. More often that not, however, such theorising appears cursory
and has (in our minds) failed to appreciate the sheer magnitude and intricacy
of social processes. Indeed, there is still a tendency among some evolutionary
psychologists to view social influences as mere 'triggers' of genetic endowments. Our argument, by contrast, is that a clearer understanding of 'culture'
does not require evolutionary psychologists to jettison their other beliefs.
Rather, it simply means that evolutionary psychologists need to be more
careful in their predictions, as we will see in the next chapter.

9   Getting to know you

A beauty is a woman you notice; a charmer is one who notices you.
                    Adlai Stevenson, American statesman (1900–1965)

The definition of a beautiful woman is one who loves me.
                    Sloan Wilson, American novelist (1920–2003)

In the preceding chapter, we suggested that social psychologists had contributed two important bodies of work to the science of physical attraction, the second of which emphasises the process of attraction. In this sense, the social psychological study of physical attraction provides new dimensions to understand the processes involved in partner choice. For social psychologists, who we find attractive is in large part a consequence of where and when we encounter potential partners, and as such may be determined by a range of non-physical variables, such as demographic and lifestyle factors (Spuhler 1968). These variables makes it clear that there will be a great deal of individual difference in who is considered physically attractive, a theme that social psychologists have been keen to stress. In this chapter, we consider some of the variables that have been highlighted in this literature.

Proximity

One of the most important factors that facilitates attraction is the proximity of one person to another (Sprecher 1998). Perhaps the most famous study to examine the influence of proximity variable was conducted by Festinger *et al.* as early as 1950: they examined the effect of physical proximity on friendship formation and interaction in a housing complex. What they found was that individuals were more likely to be friends with their neighbours than with others living on the same floor; individuals were also more likely to be friends with people on the same floor as themselves than with those on different floors, or with people living in different buildings. Even subtle architectural features, such as the location of a staircase, affected the process of making acquaintances.

Other studies have found similar results on a much larger scale (for a review, see Katz and Hill 1958). Brossard (1932) used the addresses on some 5000 marriage licences in North America to show that one-sixth of the couples lived within a block of one another, one-third lived within five blocks, and just over half lived within 20 blocks of each other. Other research showed that married couples lived within one mile of each other at the time of their first date (Clarke 1952). Finally, Spuhler (1968) reported that people are most likely to marry someone who is born within 177 kilometres of themselves.

Proximity may be an important factor in attraction for two related reasons. First, it leads to greater exposure and familiarity, which in turn enhances liking. Zajonc (1968) termed this the 'mere exposure effect': repetitive presentation of a stimulus, he reported, tends to increase liking for it. This phenomenon can be particularly effective when it comes to strangers: Jorgensen and Cervone (1978) found that the faces of strangers were liked more when they were seen more often. Similarly, Moreland and Beach (1992) found that students rated as most likeable those tutors that they saw most often. But crucially, the effects of repeated exposure do not work unendingly: Bornstein (1989) found that increased liking for photos of people levelled off after about ten exposures.

Second, proximity may facilitate liking because of the effects of 'differential association': not only do we tend to live near our potential partners, but we also have a tendency to live near people who are like ourselves (Urdy 1971). For instance, neighbourhoods are often demarcated along socioeconomic, racial, religious and educational lines. Thus, to the extent that we seek partners who have similar interests and backgrounds, we are more likely to find attractive people who live near us. Indeed, in a study of New Haven in the United States, Davie and Reeves (1939: 517) stated:

> Nearly three-quarters (73.6 per cent) of all persons marrying within the city chose mates residing in the same type of neighborhood. Nearly no intermarriage (3.9 per cent) occurred between areas far removed in social, economic and cultural traits.

Of course, these studies of the effects of proximity are somewhat dated: in the present age, mate seekers have the means to go far beyond their neighbourhoods and, therefore, to encounter more diverse potential partners. In such a scenario, proximity may not play the same role in mate choice as it did in the past (Urdy 1971).

Reciprocity

Another important factor in our interpersonal interactions is reciprocity: we tend to like those who like us and dislike those who dislike us (Sprecher 1998). At an even more basic level, we find attractive people who pay us attention – a fact recognised by artists and poets, including Hartley Coleridge (1875: 175):

> She is not fair to outward view
> As many maidens be;
> Her loveliness I never knew
> Until she smiled on me:
> Oh! then I saw her eye was bright,
> A well of love, a spring of light.

In a classic study of this effect, Dittes and Kelley (1956) led discussion groups in which participants were led to believe that other group members either liked or disliked them. Their results showed that group members who believed they were liked were more attracted to the group than those who believed they were disliked. But the effects of reciprocity may not be the same for everyone: positive interpersonal feedback may be more important for those individuals who have a higher need for interpersonal security (Sperling and Borgaro 1995). Similarly, Dittes (1959) found that people with low self-esteem showed stronger positive and negative reactions to group feedback; by contrast, people with high self-esteem did not seem to be affected by acceptance or rejection.

Situational factors can also interact with reciprocity to influence the outcome of any social interaction. For example, whether or not we positively accept praise from someone can depend on our relationship with the person doing the praising and his or her motives in doing so. Specifically, we are more likely to value praise from someone who we know is honest, compared with someone we know has ulterior motives. We also attach lower value to praise from friends than a stranger, possibly because we come to expect praise from a friend (Hogg and Vaughan 2005). The pattern in which praise is received is also important: Aronson and Linder (1965) found that we tend to like most those who initially dislike us but then warm to us, and we dislike most those people who like us at first but then turn cold.

Similarity

While proximity and reciprocity may be important during the initial stages of interpersonal attraction, similarity of attitudes and values becomes more important as the relationship progresses (Newcomb 1961). Earlier, in Chapter 7, we saw how mate choice decisions may be assortative; that is, we tend to be attracted to people who are similar to us in terms of physical attractiveness. Social psychologists have stressed that similarity of values may be one of the most important variables that affects interpersonal attraction (Sprecher 1998). Indeed, Clore and Byrne (1974) found that the effects of similarity on attraction were so strong and consistent that they formulated a 'law of attraction' – attraction to a person has a linear relationship to the proportion of attitudes shared with that person (Byrne 1971). Conversely, differences in attitudes can lead to dislike and avoidance (Singh and Ho 2000; Tan and Singh 1995), especially if such differences make us feel uncomfortable.

In one early study, Newcomb (1961) provided students with rent-free accommodation in return for filling in questionnaires about their attitudes and values. The results of this study showed that, while proximity predicted attraction in the first week after moving in, similarity of attitudes was the best predictor of attraction as the semester progressed. Cross-cultural research has further highlighted the importance of similarity: in her study of some 30 tribal groups in East Africa, Brewer (1968) found that perceived similarity of attitudes was one of a number of factors that predicted inter-tribal liking (other factors included physical distance between tribes and perceived educational and economic development). Intimate contact between tribes tended to be facilitated when the groups had similar attitudes and beliefs.

Other studies have shown that attraction is stronger between people who are similar or evenly matched in terms of social background and personality (Sprecher 1998; Stevens *et al.* 1990), sociability (Joiner 1994) and leisure activities or hobbies (Sprecher 1998). Similarity in age, education, religion and political orientation may also be important, as was highlighted in a longitudinal study of married couples (Gruber-Baldini *et al.* 1995). Indeed, the study by Gruber and colleagues (1995) found that spouses actually became *more* similar on measures of mental abilities and attitudes over time, which suggests that individuals were 'taking on' the characteristics of their partners as the relationship progressed.

A great deal of sociological work has discussed religious and ethnic 'endogamy' (that is, a group preference that its members select mates from within the group). Gordon (1964), for instance, described how many of the world's major religions emphasise the unique, if not the superior, qualities of their respective beliefs. Members of the same religion, therefore, share a belief in the superiority of their religion, and this affords an attraction to others of the same religion. The same idea is apparent as ethnocentrism when applied to racial or ethnic groups (Boas 1928). For some people, racially mixed marriages will result in the elimination of unique or distinct racial groups, and therefore the loss of identity and security.

Certainly, studies of inter-ethnic and cross-cultural relationships have revealed the importance of similarity of race. Liu *et al.* (1995), for instance, found that participants from four ethnic groups in the United States preferred to date others from their own ethnic group. Social network approval was the strongest predictor of partner preferences, suggesting that we are more likely to date someone whom our peers and family find 'acceptable', particularly in terms of ethnicity. Similarly, Warren (1970) reported that seven out of every ten men who change their religious affiliation when they get married change to the same religion as their wife. Of course, societal rules and law also deeply influence perceptions of other ethnic groups: in the United States, for instance, anti-miscegenation laws – prohibiting the union of people from different ethnicities – existed until the late 1960s.

More than just skin deep?

An age-old aphorism that retains some popularity is that beauty 'is more than just skin deep', a view which suggests that physical attraction can be influenced by other non-physical factors such as personality, feelings and thoughts. This is a view which finds a deep resonance within the arts. Edmund Spenser (1715/1936) once extolled the virtues of a sound mind:

> Ye tradeful Merchants, that with wary Toil
> Do seek most precious things to make your Gain:
> And both the Indias of their Treasure spoil,
> What needeth you to seek so far in vain?
> For lo! my Love doth in her self contain
> All this World's Riches that may far be found;
> If Saphyrs, lo! her Eyes be Saphyrs plain;
> If Rubies, lo! her Lips be Rubies found:
> If Pearls, her Teeth be Pearls, both pure and round
> If Ivory, her Forehead Ivory ween;
> If Gold, her Locks are finest Gold on ground;
> If Silver, her fair Hands are Silver sheen:
> But that which fairest is, but few behold,
> Her Mind adorn'd with Vertues manifold.

Not surprisingly, then, some social psychologists have proposed that physical attractiveness should be represented as a multifaceted feature, and that its definition should be expanded to include variables of dynamic attractiveness (Riggio *et al.* 1991). For example, the dynamic components of physical attractiveness could include an individual's conversational skills, personality, sense of humour, receptiveness and responsiveness to others (or prosocial behaviour) and his or her ability to engage in reciprocal self-disclosure (Jensen-Campbell *et al.* 1995; Lundy *et al.* 1998; Miller *et al.* 1983; Purvis *et al.* 1984; Townsend and Levy 1990).

Traditionally, experimental psychologists have tended not to examine non-physical attributes because they are difficult to measure. For example, dynamic attractiveness usually involves qualities and quantities of movement, in the form of both general expressive behaviour and social communication behaviours. This makes dynamic attractiveness more difficult to isolate and measure than static attractiveness, which can be manipulated using photographs or line-drawn stimuli. Moreover, it is almost impossible to measure dynamic attractiveness without also exposing raters to the static qualities of attractiveness. One attempt to overcome this was a study by Frable (1987), who used a 'point-light display', a procedure that involves attaching light sources to the joints of a person who moves about in darkened room, to measure expressive movement. While this procedure eliminates virtually all cues of static attractiveness, it also eliminates other cues of dynamic attractiveness (for example, speech, voice tone).

Another way to approach the measurement of dynamic attractiveness involves assessing some of the individual difference dimensions that are linked to dynamic expressive displays. Certain personality dimensions, most notably extraversion and exhibition, have been shown to be positively related to both increased display of expressive behaviour and attraction ratings in initial encounters (Friedman *et al.* 1988; Riggio *et al.* 1981; Riggio and Friedman 1986). For instance, Paunonen (2006) has shown that targets perceived as honest are rated as having faces that were more kind, feminine and attractive. What is honest, then, is beautiful.

In a recent study of non-physical attractiveness, participants were presented with line drawings that varied in WHR and body weight, but also in two levels of personality (Swami *et al.* 2007). Specifically, participants had described to them fictional personality types (extraversion and introversion) in a fictional female character named Rozie. The findings of the study showed that, while there was an independent effect of each of the three variables (with a preference for low WHRs and body weights, and for extraversion), the variables also interacted to determine Rozie's overall physical attractiveness.

Another important non-physical trait that may influence perceived physical attractiveness, especially in close-knit social groups, is reputation. In many societies, a person's reputation may mediate access to resources (Gurven *et al.* 2000a), reciprocal partners (Brown and Moore 2002; Gurven *et al.* 2000b), and may even provide useful information about health (Henderson and Anglin 2003) and promiscuity (Hess and Hagen 2002). Moreover, a person's reputation can also affect his or her physical attractiveness: in a study of Tsimane women in Bolivia, Rucas *et al.* (2006) found that positive or negative information about group members predicted rankings of attractiveness assigned to those group members. Specifically, information about motherhood, trustworthiness, housekeeping abilities, social intelligence and wealth were the most influential reputational reports on attractiveness.

Other studies have found that participants' skill in the spontaneous expression of non-verbal affect is related to the favourability of observers' impression ratings in initial encounters (Friedman *et al.* 1988; Sabatelli and Rubin 1986). Similarly, some studies have uncovered a link between possession of social and emotional role-playing skills and the favourability of impression ratings (Riggio 1986; Riggio and Friedman 1986; Riggio and Throckmorton 1988). Moreover, the influence of non-physical attributes on physical attractiveness appears to remain powerful even after a great deal of time has elapsed (Kniffin and Wilson 2004). In the latter study, it was found that women were more strongly influenced by non-physical factors than men, but there were also large individual differences within each gender. Thus, it appears that such variables as personality, expressiveness and social skills combine with static qualities of physical attractiveness in creating an overall judgement of an individual's attractiveness.

Riggio *et al.* (1991) have proposed a hypothetical model of the various components of physical attractiveness, which may lead to different outcomes (relationships, friendships, etc.). Their model consists of various components that determine overall attractiveness, including 'dynamic expressive style', facial and body attractiveness, dress sense, cosmetic use, hairstyles, and so on (Cash *et al.* 1985). The construct of 'dynamic expressive style' represents a set of individual difference variables involving such things as expressive skills, communication abilities and self-presentation skills. In their model, each of these components is represented as making a unique contribution to overall perceptions of attractiveness (see Figure 9.1).

Dressing to impress

One important factor highlighted in Figure 9.1, which we have not yet touched upon, is the influence that a person's 'ornamentation' (in the non-biological sense of the word) has on her or his physical attractiveness. Regardless of our physical appearance, there are myriad ways in which a person's physical attractiveness can be enhanced. From a person's dress sense to perfumes, make-up to jewellery, almost every culture in existence has sought artificial ways of enhancing physical beauty. Tattooing, for instance, dates back over 5000 years

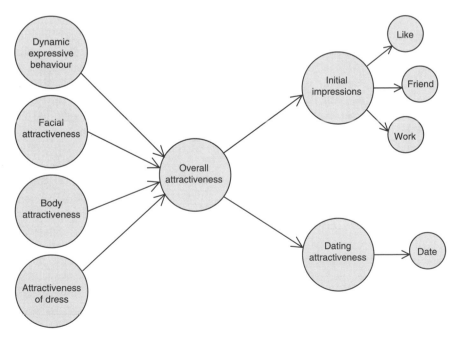

Figure 9.1 Hypothetical model of relationships among various components of attractiveness (adapted from Riggio *et al.* 1991).

(Caplan 2000; Dorfer and Moser 1998) and was practised by cultures in almost every region of the world (Rubin 1988).

In a sense, the power of ornamentation seems obvious: with very few exceptions, no one 'dresses down' unless they have to; rather, most people 'dress to impress', especially when trying to entice a potential partner. But given the sheer range of ways in which a person can ornament themselves, it makes sense to think of ornaments – cosmetics, fashions, hairstyles and colours, body modifications, scents – not just as partner enticers, but also as a means of expressing one's self (Wohlrab *et al.* 2007). By dressing in a certain way, for example, a person can express solidarity with certain others: Pitts (2003) describes the way in which the punk and gay movements of the 1980s used tattooing and piercing as a means of protesting against middle-class norms of society (see Figure 9.2). Indeed, the way a person chooses to look can reflect that individual's personality, social class, even something of how they see themselves. Certainly, in the West, a person's dress is a primary means of differentiating or ingratiating one's self with the crowd.

But of course fashions may vary significantly from one society to another; even within a single community. Fashions may vary according to age, social class, occupation, even geography and time (see Figure 9.3). In this sense, fashions become a tricky act to get right: consider, for instance, an older person who dresses in the fashions of younger age groups – get it wrong and she or he ends up looking ludicrous. Or again, while some people consider body art (piercings, tattoos, and so on) to be aesthetically pleasing and fashionable (Atkinson and Young 2001; Millner and Eichold 2001; Stirn 2004), others may not feel the same way. Indeed, in a study using line drawings of the female figure that varied in levels of tattooing, Swami and Furnham (in press b) found that British undergraduates perceived women with a greater number of tattoos as promiscuous, unattractive and heavy drinkers. They argued that this probably reflects cultural associations of tattooing, and body art more generally, with certain out-groups ('ladette' culture, for instance).

Still, most of the research that has examined the effect of non-physical attributes on physical attractiveness has dealt with attraction in brief encounters in laboratory settings. Clearly, when an interaction moves beyond the initial 'snap judgements' made about people on first meeting them (Schneider *et al.* 1979), the effects of static physical characteristics may diminish. Other variables – the dynamic components of physical attractiveness – begin to play a more important role in determining attraction in new or continuing relationships. Here, non-physical characteristics emerge as important factors in determining liking and eventual relationship formation (Byrne 1971).

Reciprocal self-disclosure

One of the most important variables that influences social interactions is reciprocal self-disclosure, which refers to the likelihood of sharing intimate topics (Altman and Taylor 1973; Vittengl and Holt 2000). A number of

Figure 9.2 By dressing in a certain way, a person can express solidarity with others who share their interests.

Figure 9.3 Fashions may vary significantly from one society to another, as is clear from the sheer variety of traditional costumes across the globe.

studies have found that people not only tend to reveal more to people they like, but also tend to like people who reveal more about their feelings (Collins and Miller 1994). This may be because disclosing personal information and being sensitive to our partner's disclosures are important for the development of relationships (Laurenceau *et al.* 1998), and therefore serve to strengthen the bond between individuals (Collins and Miller 1994).

Another reason why self-disclosure may be important in relationships is because disclosing personal matters requires trust, and trust sustains relationships. Being in a relationship is risky, not least because we risk getting on an emotional roller-coaster and making ourselves vulnerable in the hands of our partners. To manage this risk, we need to build interpersonal trust (Cvetkovich and Löfstedt 1999), and self-disclosure plays an important role in this regard. That is, the more our partner discloses to us, the safer we feel in the relationship and, in turn, the more trust we are likely to show her or him

(Boon and Holmes 1999; Holmes 2002; Rempel *et al.* 2001). Indeed, relationships tend to go sour when we feel we can no longer trust our partners, and especially when we feel she or he is no longer disclosing matters of their heart to us.

An extension of the idea that self-disclosure increases liking is the notion that 'playing hard to get' (that is, a lack of initial self-disclosure) will help attract a desirable partner. Walster *et al.* (1973) conducted a number of experiments to test this hypothesis, and concluded that playing hard to get may not be as productive as it seems. In one study, college men were recruited ostensibly to improve a computer dating service: they were asked to call their prospective date from the office so that their initial impressions could be gauged. To those in the 'easy to get' condition, the date (a confederate) responded with delight at the phone call and being asked out, whereas in the 'hard to get' condition the confederate responded with reluctance and giving the impression that she had many other dates. The participants' evaluations of the confederate were uniformly high across conditions and, thus, do not appear to support the hypothesis that playing hard to get is productive.

Walster *et al.* (1973) therefore proposed that the maximally rewarding date is one that is easy for us to get, but difficult for anyone else to get. They used the same computer dating system to test their hypothesis: participants were told that the computer had identified five possible dates for them, and participants were able to read brief biographies of the five women before making their choices. In addition to the biographies was a supposed evaluation made by the women (actually written by the experimenters) of the dates the computer had chosen for her. For one, these evaluations made the woman appear easy to get, as she rated all her dates highly; for another, it made her appear hard to get, as she rated all her dates poorly; a third woman appeared selectively hard to get, in that she only rated the participant highly. The results showed that women in all conditions were likely equally, except for the selectively hard to get woman, who was the most popular among all participants.

Non-verbal communication

Having a conversation with someone is not merely about the words we utter; rather social interactions also involve a wealth of non-verbal cues, which can serve to enhance, decrease or even confuse liking for a person (Bugental *et al.* 1971; Patterson 1983). Within social psychology, non-verbal communication is perhaps one of the most well-studied fields of research (Argyle 1988; Burgoon *et al.* 1989; DePaulo and Friedman 1998; Rimé 1983), though in truth many such studies are plagued by the difficulty of reducing non-verbal communication to a few expressions that can be studied systematically. Indeed, most people can produce countless thousands of facial expressions (Birdwhistell 1970) and about a thousand paralanguages (Hewes 1957), which says nothing yet of physical gestures, body language, hand movements, eye contact and touch (Pei 1965) – all of which have an influence on our attraction towards a person (and of course, a person's attraction towards us).

Most people tend not to be aware of the non-verbal cues they use or that they are being influenced by others' use of such cues. Having said that, a consistent finding in the literature, which highlights the influence of gender roles, is that women are more adept than men at detecting and using non-verbal communications (Brown 1986; Eagly 1987; Hall 1984). On the other hand, men may be better at recognising 'covert messages' such as deceptive communications and may also be more likely to use non-verbal messages that contradict the verbal message (for example, sarcasm accompanied by a smile; Noller 1984). Eagly (1987) has explained these differences as being related to child-rearing strategies, in which girls are encouraged to be more emotionally expressive, attentive and communicative than boys.

Perhaps the most important and information-rich of all non-verbal cues are gaze and eye contact, the latter usually referring to mutual gaze (Argyle and Ingham 1972; Kleinke 1986). 'The eyes say it all' sums up the importance of this form of non-verbal communication; or as the poet Robert Green put it in *Philomela* (1592/2005):

> On women nature did bestow two eyes
> Like hemian's [sic] bright lamps in matchless beauty shining,
> Whose beams do soonest captivate the wise
> And wary heads made rare by art's refining.
> But why did nature in her choice combining
> Plant two fair eyes within a beauteous face?
> That they might favour two with equal grace.

As various authors have pointed out, the amount and pattern of gazing provides a wealth of information about a person's current emotions (Kleinke 1986), their relative status (Dovidio and Ellyson 1985; Dovidio *et al.* 1988), their credibility, honesty and competence (Kleinke 1986), and of course their attractiveness (Kleinke *et al.* 1973). In general, people tend to gaze longer at people they like, and similarly, intimacy is communicated by greater gaze. So powerful is this effect that false information about gaze can affect our liking for a person: in one study, couples who had engaged in a ten-minute conversation were given false feedback on gaze (Kleinke *et al.* 1973). Participants who were told that they had been gazed at less than average were less attracted to their partners; by contrast, above-average gaze increased men's, but not women's, attraction for their partners.

Gaze can also serve to regulate interactions, both in terms of initiating a conversation, regulating the course of a conversation, and ending or avoiding being drawn into a conversation (Argyle 1971; Argyle and Ingham 1972; Cary 1978). But there may also be cross-cultural or cross-ethnic differences in this pattern of communication. For example, while Caucasian adults tend to gaze more when listening than when talking (Argyle and Ingham 1972), African Americans gaze more when they are speaking than when listening (LaFrance and Mayo 1976). Clearly, this can complicate matters in interracial communications, as can a lack of eye contact during some conversations (Hogg and Vaughan 2005).

Another important form of non-verbal communication that can serve to enhance or decrease liking is touch, although as always there are many different types of touch to many different parts of the body, by different people and in different contexts (Jones and Yarbrough 1985). In terms of positive affect, a number of studies have shown that even the most fleeting of touches can enhance liking. In one early study, Crusco and Wetzel (1984) found that both men and women left larger tips at a restaurant if they had been touched incidentally by their waitress on the hand. Similarly, women who had been briefly touched on the hand while checking out books at a library indicated greater liking for the librarian doing the touching, and even for the library, than those who had not been touched (Fisher *et al.* 1976). Whitcher and Fisher (1979) also showed that being touched by a nurse before an operation had a positive effect on post-operative physiology (less fear and anxiety) for women.

But there are gender differences in these effects: women derive greater positive affect from being touched than do men (indeed, in the study by Whitcher and Fisher, men who were touched in the pre-operative condition actually reported being *more* anxious post-operation), although the circumstances of the touch are important. For example, Heslin (1978) showed that women do not enjoy being 'squeezed and patted' by strange men, but men enjoyed being touched by strange women; men were also more likely than women to read sexual connotations into touch (Heslin and Alper 1983). Moreover, there are cross-cultural differences in touch (Jourard 1966): people in northern Europe, North America, Australia and Asia tend not to touch, whereas those in Latin America, the Mediterranean and Arab countries tend to touch a great deal (Argyle 1975).

Touch is also related to interpersonal distance, or proxemics, which can be used to communicate intimacy and liking (Hayduk 1983). For example, Hall (1966) identified four interpersonal distance zones (see Table 9.1), the second of which (personal distance) is the transitional area between intimate contact and formal behaviour, and is also the form of interpersonal distance most expressive of liking. In one study, Rosenfeld (1965) asked participants to talk with a confederate, with the goal of either appearing friendly or unfriendly. The 'friendly' participants placed their chairs on average 1.5 metres from the confederate, while the 'unfriendly' participants placed their chairs 2.25 metres away. Here too there may be sex and cultural differences in the patterns of interpersonal distance (or lack of it) that are tolerated (Aiello and Jones 1971).

The take-home message of this section is that physical attraction does not

Table 9.1 The four zones of space in social interactions (adapted from Hall 1966)

Zone	Distance	Description	Perceivable cues
Intimate distance	Up to 0.5 metres	Intimate exposure to a person, which may include physical contact	Sight, voice, smell, body temperature, pace of breathing
Personal distance	0.5–1.25 metres	Transitional area between intimate contact and formal behaviour	Some touch, voice, smell
Social distance	1.25–4 metres	Typical distance for casual interactions with strangers	Verbal contact
Public distance	4–8 metres	Common for lectures, public speakers and celebrities	No reliable cues

take place in a vacuum; rather, individuals are remarkably adept at enticing, tempting, charming and influencing potential partners' perceptions of them (DePaulo 1992). This includes a host of non-verbal cues, such as body language and gaze, but also the use of cosmetics, clothing, and so on. We are also able to deceive others into thinking that we are somehow better than we really are – a tactic that has provided the crux of more than one romantic comedy. And, of course, once we begin to have a conversation with a person, we are able to draw on a wealth of verbal ploys to entice her or him, whether this is the clichéd 'chat-up line' or regaling stories about our 'good side'. More than this, language communicates not only by what we say but also by how we say it – the latter can include volume, speed, tone, pauses, stress, accent, and so on (Knapp 1978), all of which have an effect on interpersonal attraction.

Love is blind

The point of the various 'tools' that human beings employ in partner attraction is to get those potential partners to fall 'head over heels' for us and, with a little luck, to form lasting relationships with us (Dion and Dion 1996). But what happens then? Does physical attraction still matter once we have 'roped in' our ideal partner, or do we rest easy (that is, no longer bother with our looks) knowing that our partners would never leave us? Conversely, do we still find our partners attractive once we get to know them better? Unfortunately, very little research has examined these questions in any detail, although this is now a popular focus for research.

At a basic level, it seems intuitive that individuals entering a relationship are not blank slates; rather, they bring to the relationship various ideals or images that can impact the way they develop as individuals and also the way their relationship grows. Indeed, being in love seems to be tied up with fantasy and 'positive illusion'; that is, when we are in love with someone, we hold an 'ideal image' of our partner that we have formed throughout the relationship. In general, this ideal is positively biased in favour of our partners, which may serve to create better relationships (Martz *et al.* 1998; Murray and Holmes 1997).

One such illusion is what Swami *et al.* (2007b) have termed the 'love is blind bias'. The authors asked participants to provide ratings of overall physical attractiveness and the attractiveness of various body parts, such as the eyes, neck, arms, and so on. Based on a normally distributed curve of 'attractiveness ratings', participants provided self-ratings and ratings of opposite-sex romantic partners. The results of the study showed that both women and men rated their partners as being significantly more attractive than themselves, a finding that appears to be somewhat robust (Murstein 1972). To explain this finding, Swami *et al.* (2007b) argued that a positive illusion in the physical attractiveness of one's partner may serve to enhance self-esteem. That is, believing that our partners are more physically attractive than ourselves may serve to enhance subjective self-appraisals, which in turn may result in improved well-being (Taylor and Brown 1994).

This seems to fit with the notion that being in a relationship is good for us, both physically and mentally (Argyle 1992; Myers 1996). For example, being in a positive relationship – including marriage – has been correlated with a lower incidence of cardiovascular problems, better mental health and longevity (Myers 1996). Indeed, several studies have found that people who were involved in a romantic relationship or marriage reported a higher sense of overall well-being than romantically uninvolved or unmarried people (Campbell *et al.* 1994; Diener *et al.* 1999). In short, then, being in love has a positive effect on our well-being, even if it means having to work hard for love in the short term.

Conclusion

What the studies in this chapter show is that social psychologists have much to say about interpersonal attraction. Yet, it is only recently that there has been a willingness on the part of evolutionary psychologists to return to some of the key concepts introduced by a generation of social psychologists. This body of work has the potential to better illuminate the interaction between biological, cultural and individual factors in determining who we find physically attractive and why. The task of combining these different perspectives will not be easy: the myriad of social forces, cues and factors alone testify to the difficulty of reaching a unified theory of attraction. Still, any evolutionary approach to physical attraction must eventually recognise both the influence of individual agency as well as the fact that, as human beings, we find ourselves 'ensnared' within social, political and cultural worlds. It makes little sense to downplay, caricature or even ignore the influence of social worlds, as many evolutionary psychologists have done. Rather, a true evolutionary approach to psychology must embrace diversity, both at the individual and cultural levels (Swami and Furnham 2007).

10 What future for physical attraction research?

Beauty is in the eye of the beholder.

Margaret Wolfe Hungerford, novelist (1855–1897)

Beauty is in the heart of the beholder.

H. G. Wells, English writer (1866–1946)

Beauty is in the imagination of the beholder.

David Newell, television actor (1938–   )

Beauty is such a fleeting blossom, how can wisdom rely upon its momentary delight?

Lucius Annaeus Seneca, Roman philosopher (3 BC–65 AD)

Not so long ago, human beauty was not considered a topic worth studying scientifically; rather, it was seen as the preserve of those 'in the know' – such as artists, philosophers and lovers – who could admire beauty from afar and thus preserve its mystery. And admire beauty they did: from the paintings that fill museums like the Louvre to the covers of glamour magazines to Shakespeare's memorable sonnets, human beauty has been a consistent thread stretching through the ages. Follow this thread far back in time and one meets such luminaries as Leonardo da Vinci (whose two most instantly recognisable works, the *Mona Lisa* and *Vitruvius Man*, stand as epitomes of feminine and masculine beauty respectively), before finally chancing upon the ancient Greeks.

It was the ancient Greeks – Pythagoras and his followers in particular – who first attempted an overarching explanation of beauty that would encompass all things from buildings to music to human beings (Armstrong 2004; Swami 2007). A peculiar aspect of the Grecian view of beauty, certainly after Plato had had his say, was that there exists an 'ideal' or absolute beauty. For all things, there is a perfect form that embodies beauty and goodness; all existing bodies are copies after this 'perfect' Platonic body. Taken to its logical conclusion, this view states that there is an objective beauty, which all humans beings can discern and appreciate.

In a sense, the Platonic view of an absolute or objective beauty finds it apogee in evolutionary psychological thinking about human physical attractiveness. Indeed, some evolutionary psychologists have not been shy in proclaiming an ideal WHR, or the perfect facial configuration, or a skin tone that is 'just right' for the ideal woman or man. For example, in defining a waist-to-hip of 0.70 as the ideal for a woman, and any deviation from this 'golden ratio' as being detrimental to her physical attractiveness, evolutionary psychologists are in fact making very similar arguments to that made by Pythagoras and other ancient Greeks. This is no accident: the view that there is an objective beauty has been a dominant strand of Western aesthetic thought, and continues to colour the way in which debates about human beauty take place today (Swami 2007).

Importantly, however, the objective view of beauty has not gone unchallenged: beginning in the late eighteenth century, philosophical debates about beauty began to jettison any clinging to its objective nature. For philosophers like Edmund Burke and David Hume, an objective notion of beauty was both impossible and pointless – and so was born the subjective concept of beauty, marked by the belief that beauty can only be understood as the response of our individual feeling, emotions or minds. Instead of seeking some absolute property of objects or individuals, we should think about the response of the beholder, as this famous statement by Hume (1757) suggests:

> Beauty is no quality in things themselves; it exists merely in the mind which contemplates them; and each mind perceives a different beauty. One person may even perceive deformity, where another is sensible to beauty ... To seek in the real beauty, or deformity, is as fruitless an enquiry, as to pretend to ascertain the real sweet or real bitter. According to the disposition of the organs, the same object may be both sweet and bitter; and the proverb has justly determined it to be fruitless to dispute concerning tastes.

This view – epitomised ever since by the maxim that 'beauty is in the eye of the beholder' – has become an important view in philosophy and art. Yet, many scientists have tended to view these pronouncements with derision, because it implies a certain generalisation: if each of us has different ideas about what is beautiful, and hence do not agree about who is, and who is not, beautiful, then what is there left to measure? But this actually obscures the point that social psychologists have been making for decades: to fully understand the perception of human beauty will require a careful analysis and description of our aesthetic feelings and the way that effect is achieved. This view does not imply that there is nothing outside our minds which corresponds to the effect produced; rather, a complete understanding of beauty must ultimately combine both the objective and subjective accounts of beauty.

Combining perspectives

Neither an evolutionary nor a social psychological approach in isolation is sufficient to understand the science of human beauty. Evolutionary psychological models of attractiveness have tended to rely on an adaptationist framework, which sees attractiveness judgements as an adaptation to our ancestral past. By downplaying the contemporary social context in which attraction takes place, however, evolutionary psychological theories tend to objectify beauty, and in doing so commit what Hume might have termed a 'fruitless enquiry'. That is, in the absence of an appreciation of contemporary ecological factors (among other things), the evolutionary psychological framework is liable to miss important facets of human decision-making and attitude formation processes.

On the other hand, social psychological theories have tended to emphasise the process of attraction, while generally being inattentive to possible evolutionary origins of at least some physical attraction phenomena. The most celebrated social psychological theories of attraction – such as those concerning the effects of proximity and reciprocity – have tended to emphasise various factors in the attraction process, rather than taking a specific look at what it means to be physically attractive. Of course, the different paths taken by social and evolutionary psychologists stem from their different perspectives. The point remains, however, that in isolation neither perspective can account for the myriad of different factors that affect our attraction to others.

In combination, however, these different strands of psychological thinking have the ability to more fully account for our attractiveness preferences, and hence do away with much of the 'mystery' of human beauty (which, truth be told, is not so much mystery as an infantile longing for ambiguity and inscrutability). The central question for such a combined perspective is how to bring the different strands together. In this book, we have tried to provide some examples of how this might happen. More practically, future research will almost certainly need to develop and extend the interdisciplinary work that has become a keystone of the science of attraction.

One theoretical model which we believe offers a useful means of combining biological and cultural models of physical attractiveness was proposed by Osborn (2004, 2006). His model is a two-part process involving various stages of the attraction process. The first part of the model consists of three filters called 'biological attractiveness', 'judged attractiveness' and 'love style'. As the name suggests, the first filter involves judging (either subconsciously or otherwise) potential partners based on the evolutionary psychological predictions we discussed in early chapters of this book (see Figure 10.1). Osborn (2004) suggests that as long as a target is judged as 'not unattractive', the observer remains interested and makes more of an effort to approach the target. In this sense, our evolutionary predispositions act as an initial filter, determining whether or not we take an interest, and find attractive, another individual.

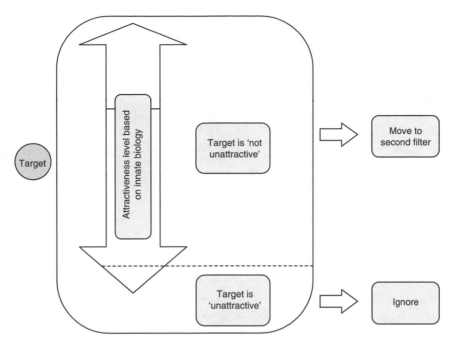

Figure 10.1 The first filter of Osborn's (2004) model: targets are filtered based on innate, biological attractiveness levels (adapted from Osborn 2004).

Moving to the second filter, a potential partner's attractiveness is judged based upon the ideas and values we learn in our respective cultural communities, as well as our own personal preferences (see Figure 10.2). Both cultural and individual factors combine to determine more specifically how we rate a particular individual's attractiveness. More than this, there may be different 'beauties' that we look for (Ashmore *et al.* 1996) – the trendy, the sexy, the cute, the intellectual are all different types of beauty that an individual may chase after at a particular time. Of course, the specifics of this filter can change, since it is subjective to our own personality and reference group values.

Filter three places the objective judgements of filter one and the subjective judgements of filter two into a secondary role, and focuses on the compatability of the target and the judge (see Figure 10.2). As this suggests, filter three can really only begin once two individuals have got to know each other, at least a little. Depending on what kind of relationship we are looking for (friendship, passion, possessive love, game-playing love, and so on), a potential partner is 'critiqued' based on our personal proclivities. The relationship can only progress if two individuals are compatible in their desires. In this sense, filter three is even more personally subjective than the preceding filter because it is based on an individual's love style preferences (Osborn 2004).

The second part of the filter is more concerned with the life experiences of two individuals in a romantic relationship, though judgements of physical

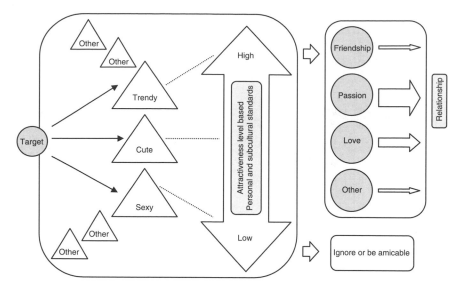

Figure 10.2 The first and third filters of Osborn's (2004) model: targets are filtered (a) personal and subcultural standards (in this case the judge is looking for a trendy partner); (b) love style compatability (the judge is looking for passion).

attraction can still fluctuate dramatically. For example, positive experiences in a relationship can lead to us perceiving our partners as 'growing' in attractiveness, whereas negative experiences may lead to a dislike for our partners, and consequently finding them unattractive. In this sense, perceptions of our partner's attractiveness are continuously modified, but for very different reasons than those in the first part of the filter. Indeed, the importance of biological and physical attractiveness in perceptions of our partner will likely have diminished by this stage of the attraction process, and our liking for him or her may be more centrally based on shared experiences (Osborn 2004).

Osborn (2006) argues that, rather than viewing the attraction process as the result of a specific biological discrimination process in which mates are selected on the basis of health or fertility, it should rightly be seen as a relatively volatile, culturally and historically variable process. In this sense, Osborn (2004) proposes, the attraction process may be more akin to fashion, designed to produce some degree of choice where potential partners are perceived as attractive if they pass a minimal threshold. In short, Osborn's (2004, 2006) model provides a useful way of combining the effects of personal taste (operating through individual psychosexual interests, personality compatibilities and love styles) and shared taste (operating through biological predispositions and subcultural beauty ideals).

While more research is certainly needed to test some of Osborn's (2004) specific predictions, all the evidence suggests that a combined perspective will push forward the science of attraction. Indeed, this body of work is now firmly at the centre of a diverse psychological programme, spanning cross-cultural, evolutionary, cognitive and social psychology, as well as related fields like anthropology and aesthetics. The science of physical attraction has also attracted such strange bedfellows as denticians, cosmetic surgeons and philosophers of mind, all of whom see some utility in discussing and debating human physical attractiveness. This combination of perspectives can only enhance our understanding of the influence of physical attractiveness on our lives.

Lookism

The key point we are trying to make is that there is no reason why scientists should not take a keen interest in the science of human beauty. Left in the hands of well-meaning, but methodologically ill-equipped, enthusiasts (artists, philosophers, lovers, and so on), human beauty is liable to be transformed into an enigma, the effects of which are poorly understood. Specifically, beauty in the eye of the aficionado suffers from the fact that it is imprecise, an amorphous construct that remains beyond rationale comprehension. But as we have shown in this book, human beauty is not beyond the realm of scientific understanding; more than this, understanding beauty from a scientific point of view will enable us better to deal with some of the effects of beauty, especially where the excessive pursuit of beauty becomes detrimental, damaging, even pathological.

One such effect is summed up by the old adage that we should not 'judge a book by its cover', as such judgements are more often than not misinformative and sometimes hurtful. Indeed, prejudice, discrimination or even just differential treatment on the basis of appearance have been receiving increased attention within academic circles (Puhl and Brownell 2001, 2003), and are sometimes referred to as 'lookism', 'beauty prejudice' or 'appearance discrimination' (Tietje and Cresap 2005). These different terms all refer to the same issue, namely that attractive individuals are given preferential treatment and (more importantly) unattractive people are denied opportunities. In recent years, a great deal of psychological work has both documented such discrimination, as well as initiating a systematic programme to combat such prejudice.

Recent reports, for instance, suggest that attractiveness receives a 'premium' and unattractiveness is penalised within employment settings (Loh 1993; Pagan and Davila 1997; Register and Williams 1990): for both men and women, there is a 7–9 per cent penalty for being in the lowest 9 per cent of looks among all workers, and a 5 per cent premium for being in the top 33 per cent (Hamermesh and Biddle 1994). Such a premium might be justified on the grounds that attractive people are actually better skilled, but there is little evidence for this. Mobius and Roseblatt (2006) found that attractive individuals were no better at solving a maze task than unattractive individuals, although the former were more confident in their ability to do so. It seems, therefore, that being attractive is related to self-confidence, a trait that may be attractive to employers (Mobius and Rosenblatt 2006). In any case, employers believe that good looks contribute to the success of their company, because many still hire on the basis of looks even though they risk charges of illegal discrimination by doing so (Greenhouse 2003).

Other research suggests that medical and mental health professionals, who most people expect to be immune to such biases, treat attractive and unattractive patients differently. For example, psychotherapists tend to attribute greater psychopathology to their unattractive patients and prefer working with 'young, attractive, verbal, interesting and successful' patients (Schofield 1964). This relationship also works with patients, who prefer to work with attractive psychotherapists (Cash and Kehr 1978). Physical appearance can also influence everyday interactions outside professional settings, including decisions about who we help and who we ask for help. For instance, several studies have shown that men are more likely to help an attractive woman than an unattractive woman, with tasks ranging from mailing letters to providing directions (Benson *et al.* 1976).

One particular aspect of lookism concerns prejudice and discrimination against people of a certain body weight, typically those who are overweight or obese (Puhl and Brownell 2001, 2003). The issue has become a major concern, so much so that some researchers have argued that weight-based discrimination is the last 'acceptable' form of discrimination (Falkner *et al.* 1999; Kilbourne 1994; O'Hara 1996; Stunkard and Sorensen 1993). That is, within Euro-American culture (and increasingly elsewhere), where the message that it is good to be thin and bad to be fat is so widespread, expressing negative attitudes toward obese people has become an accepted form of prejudice (Falkner *et al.* 1999).

The stigma of obesity is very strong indeed: Garner's (1997) survey reported that almost a quarter of women and a fifth of men said they would give up three or more years of their lives to be the weight they want. Another indication of the severity of obesity stigma is the young age at which negative attitudes become evident. In a classic study conducted in the early 1960s, schoolchildren were asked to rank six pictures of children varying in physical characteristics and disabilities in order of who they would like most for a friend (Richardson *et al.* 1961). Most children ranked a picture of an obese child last among children with crutches, in a wheelchair, with an amputated hand, and with a facial disfigurement. Latner and Stunkard (2003) recently replicated this study and found that the bias in children was even stronger than reported in the original study, which supports other recent work with children (Brylinsky and Moore 1994; Cramer and Steinwert 1998; Kraig and Keel 2001).

But obesity stigma is not restricted to the interactions of children. In their exhaustive review of the literature, Puhl and Brownell (2001) identified numerous aspects of everyday life in which obese and overweight individuals are stigmatised and discriminated against, ranging from employment and hiring to college entry, seating on public transport to treatment by professionals. The effects of such prejudice on victims can range from relatively minor inconvenience to enormous suffering, but in general is harmful because it stigmatises groups and people who belong to those groups (Crocker *et al.* 1998; Swim and Stangor, 1998).

For example, Puhl and Brownell (2003) have speculated that those exposed to weight-based stigma may be vulnerable to psychological effects such as depression and low self-esteem. This, in turn, could contribute to the exacerbation of obesity through psychological vulnerabilities that increase the likelihood of overeating and sedentary activity. Moreover, obesity stigma can have social effects such as economic hardship and isolation. Both anecdotal and experimental evidence suggest that peer rejection, especially among adolescents, is an important consequence of obesity stigma. In medical settings, too, anti-fat attitudes among health-care professionals (Maroney and Golub 1992; McArthur and Ross 1997; Price *et al.* 1987) may deter obese and overweight persons from seeking care (Adams *et al.* 1993; Wadden *et al.* 2000).

An outcome of human nature?

We have broached the issues of lookism and, in particular, weight-based discrimination, because they raise important questions about the ethics of physical attraction. Clearly, being physically attractive has its advantages in a range of settings, but is differential treatment based on a person's looks ever justified, even ethical? This is a difficult question, and there can be no easy answers. For some, lookism is an unavoidable outcome of human nature, and no amount of legislation or education will change that. This, in our minds, is an overly pessimistic view, which fails to grasp the plasticity of human behaviour that we have stressed throughout this book.

Rather, lookism or appearance prejudice should rightly be seen as the latest in a long line of discriminatory acts that includes sexism and racism. Indeed, while discrimination on the basis of gender or race has generally evolved to take on more subtle forms, discrimination on the basis of a person's appearance is a growing concern for many societies. Lookism – like racism, classism, sexism and other such isms – can create unjust barriers to equal opportunity, and for this reason alone should not be left unchallenged. In our view, there is nothing in 'human nature' which makes us prejudicial towards other human beings. Rather, prejudice against individuals is a societal problem that must be dealt with through effective education, legislation and other positive steps that seek to overcome prejudicial attitudes where they exist.

A cursory glance through human history would suggest that overcoming lookism and its detrimental effects need not be an impossible task. Not so long ago, physiognomy – the belief that a person's outer appearance reflects their character or personality – enjoyed widespread popularity, and even took on a 'scientific' hue when vocational institutes used physiognomy as one of their main tools for assessing candidates. Physiognomy even appeared in the work of many of the major nineteenth-century novelists, including Charles Dickens, Balzac and Charlotte Brontë. Others put physiognomy to more dubious use: Cesare Lombroso's 'criminal anthropology' (1895), for example, declared that murderers have prominent jaws and pickpockets have long hands and scanty beards. More generally, the characterisation of others based on their outer appearance proved to be an important tool in legitimising imperialism and colonialism (Gould 1981) – a tool not unknown to today's politicians and would-be emperors.

But history – and, more importantly, sociopolitical movements that sought to stem the tide of careless 'science' – proved physiognomy to be a baseless pseudoscience (Cohen 1973; Gould 1981). The idea that we can assess the morality of a person from their appearance is fallacious and discounts the fact that appearance is socially constructed. A person may come to be understood as 'looking intelligent' or 'looking good', but this is merely down to the socially constructed association of one signifier with one signified (Finkelstein 1991). Sociologically, physiognomy – as well as lookism – is problematic because appearance is unpredictably located within an array of changeable meanings and also because what we understand as a 'good' or 'bad' character varies across time and space (Twine 2002).

This is not to say that, in our everyday social practices, we do not make judgements based on a person's appearance. As we have seen throughout this book, people do make inferences about others based on appearance (Hassin and Trope 2000), inferences that may sometimes turn out to be valid (Berry 1990; Zebrowitz *et al.* 1996). The point is, however, that we make such inferences because of socially learned schemas – the corollary being that such schemas can, and should, be altered. More practically, the issue at hand concerns the use to which such schemas are put: inferring, for instance, that someone who is physically attractive is also an extravert may be harmless, but the same cannot be said of the inference that an overweight person is lazy. In short, lookism may provide for social relations, but inferences made on the basis of appearance are more often than not of poor quality. More seriously, they encourage a perceptual filter that objectifies others in ways that are often erroneous and discriminatory.

What future for physical attraction research?

In the 1970s, a number of feminists argued that make-up and other beauty practices arose due to the pressures that women faced in a male-dominated society which caused them to feel they should diet, depilate or use make-up. Feminist authors like Dworkin (1974) and more recently Wolf (1990) rejected the 'masculine aesthetics' that cause women to feel their bodies are somehow inadequate and to engage in practices that leave them feeling they are inauthentic or unacceptable if they do not live up to idealised images of the 'perfect' woman. 'Beauty' – a misleading term in itself – was identified as being oppressive to women, and a means for masculine society to denigrate and impede the movement for women's liberation (Wolf 1990).

In her book *Woman Hating*, for example, Dworkin (1974) analysed the idea of 'beauty' as one aspect of the way women are hated in male-dominated culture. She sees beauty practices as being harmful to women's bodies and their lives, as well as being time wasting, expensive and painful:

> Standards of beauty describe in precise terms the relationship that an individual will have to her own body. They prescribe her mobility, spontaneity, posture, gait, the uses to which she can put her body. *They define precisely the dimensions of her physical freedom.*
>
> (Dworkin 1974: 112; italics in original)

For Dworkin (1974: 112), beauty standards are 'the major substance of male–female role differentiation, the most immediate physical and psychological reality of being a woman'. Male-dominated culture uses beauty practices to ensure that the domination of one sex over the other continues, and the bedrock of this domination is the treatment of women as sex objects.

Our aim here is not to contest the validity of the feminist–patriarchal view of the world, but it is worth noting that men are increasingly subject to the same pressures that women have faced for decades (Faludi 1999; Swami 2007). While the available evidence suggests that women report significantly lower body satisfaction than men (Aruguete *et al.* 2006), men are also increasingly dissatisfied with their bodies (Pope *et al.* 1999, 2000). To be sure, cultural norms for men may be more flexible and relaxed, and there are different 'types' of masculine attractiveness depicted in the media (Humphreys and Paxton 2004). Still, men today are bombarded by a plethora of images urging them to fit into prescribed categories of attractiveness that are virtually unattainable for the majority of men (Pope *et al.* 2000). In short, 'being beautiful' is no longer (if it ever was) a distinctly female oppressive phenomenon.

In the past two decades, dissatisfaction with our bodies has become almost 'normal' (Rodin *et al.* 1984; Smolak 2006), and the lengths to which both women and men will go for the sake of beauty have become ever more severe. Today's practices include extreme dieting and fasting (even the promotion of being anorexic as a lifestyle choice; Norris *et al.* 2006), cosmetic procedures that involve the spilling of blood or the amputation of body parts or the insertion of foreign objects (such as breast implants), the use of steroids and all manner of other preoccupations – all of which are dangerous for women's and men's health (Jeffreys 2005).

Hidden behind the façade of endless talk about beauty being 'natural' or innate to human psychology, it is not difficult to see the vested interests of many different parties. For radical feminists like Dworkin (1974) and Wolf (1990), this was primarily a male-dominated society looking to stifle any move towards gender equality. We would extend this critique, as others have done, to include the large 'fashion-beauty complex' (Bartky 1990), representing the corporate interests involved in the fashion and beauty industries. In this view, beauty practices should be seen as evidence of the cultural subordination of one group by another, the latter standing to gain from the other's insecurity.

By continually depreciating women's and men's bodies through the display of images of purported 'ideals', the fashion-beauty complex ensures that women and men feel their bodies to be deficient, requiring 'heroic measures' to rectify those deficiencies (Bartky 1990: 39). Of course, the best way to rectify those 'deficiencies' is to seek refuge in the products offered by the fashion-beauty complex, thus ensuring large fortunes for transnational corporations and industries. Indeed, the profitability of beauty practices to the cosmetics, sex, fashion, advertising and medical industries is beyond serious question – in the United States alone, cosmetics is a multibillion dollar industry (Reischer and Koo 2004).

Envisioning a future in which the role of physical attractiveness is minimised, even eliminated altogether, from social interactions will only emerge from sociopolitical movements that challenge widespread assumptions about beauty. In the 1970s, many thousands of women (and men) gave up beauty practices as part of a movement for women's liberation. That movement may have waned in strength, but in the new millennium the birth of strong anti-capitalist and anti-war movements has meant a return to some of the key ideas raised by radical feminists in the late 1960s and 1970s. These movements are challenging the idea that we are given any real power through consumer 'choice', and are mounting an opposition to the ideology and practices of transnational corporations that profit from encouraging, and endorsing, lookism. They may yet give birth to a future in which women and men reject beauty practices, and find the strength to seek beauty where it really matters.

References

Abitbol, J., Abitbol, P. and Abitbol, B. (1999). Sex hormones and the female voice. *Journal of Voice, 13*, 424–446.

Abitbol, M. M. (1996). The shapes of the female pelvis: Contributing factors. *Journal of Reproductive Medicine, 41*, 242–250.

Abramson, E. E. and Valene, P. (1991). Media use, dietary restraint, bulimia and attitudes toward obesity: A preliminary study. *British Review of Bulimia and Anorexia Nervosa, 5*, 73–76.

Adams, C. H., Smith, N. J., Wilbur, D. C. and Grady, K. E. (1993). The relationship of obesity to the frequency of pelvic examinations: Do physicians and patient attitudes make a difference? *Women and Health, 20*, 45–57.

Adams, G. R. (1978). Racial membership and physical attractiveness effects on preschool teachers' expectations. *Child Study Journal, 8*, 29–41.

—— (1982). Physical attractiveness. In A. G. Miller (Ed.), *In the eye of the beholder: Contemporary issues in stereotyping* (pp. 253–304). New York: Praeger.

Adams, G. R. and Crane, P. (1980). An assessment of parents' and teachers' expectations of preschool children's social preference for attractive or unattractive children and adults. *Child Development, 51*, 224–231.

Addison, W. W. (1989). Beardedness as a factor in perceived masculinity. *Perceptual and Motor Skills, 68*, 921–922.

Ahmad, M., Gilbert, R. and Naqui, A. (1985). Assortative mating for height in Pakistani arranged marriages. *Journal of Biosocial Science, 17*, 211–214.

Aiello, J. R. and Jones, S. E. (1971). Field study of the proxemic behaviour of young children in three subcultural groups. *Journal of Personality and Social Psychology, 19*, 351–356.

Akan, G. and Greilo, C. (1995). Socio-cultural influences on eating attitudes and behaviours, body image and psychological functioning: A comparison of African-American, Asian-American and Caucasian college women. *International Journal of Eating Disorders, 18*, 181–187.

Albanes, D., Jones, D. Y., Schatzkinm A., Micozzi, M. S. and Taylor, P. R. (1988). Adult stature and risk of cancer. *Cancer Research, 48*, 1658–1662.

Alley, T. R. and Hildebrandt, K. A. (1988). Determinants and consequences of facial aesthetics. In T. R. Alley (Ed.), *Social and applied aspects of perceiving faces* (pp. 101–140). Hillsdale, NJ: Lawrence Erlbaum Associates, Inc.

Altman, I. and Taylor, D. A. (1973). *Social penetration: The development of interpersonal relationships*. New York: Holt, Rinehart and Winston.

American Association of Plastic Surgeons (2005). Top five surgical cosmetic procedures in 2005. Online publication at: http://plasticsurgery.org/media/statistics.

Amnar, H. (1954). *Growing up in an Egyptian village*. London: Routledge.

Andersen, A. E. and DiDomenico, L. (1992). Diet versus shape content of popular male and female magazines: A dose–response relationship to the incidence of eating disorders? *International Journal of Eating Disorders*, *11*, 283–287.

Anderson, J. L., Crawford, C. E., Nadeau, J. and Lindberg, T. (1992). Was the Duchess of Windsor right? A cross-cultural view of the socio-biology of ideals of female body shape. *Ethology and Sociobiology*, *13*, 197–227.

Andersson, M. (1982). Female choice selects for extreme tail length in a widowbird. *Nature*, *299*, 818–820.

—— (1986). Evolution of condition-dependent sex ornaments and mating preferences: Sexual selection based on viability differences. *Evolution*, *40*, 804–820.

Aoki, K. (2002). Sexual selection as a cause of human skin colour variation: Darwin's hypothesis revisited. *Annals of Human Biology*, *29*, 589–608.

Arechiga, J., Prado, C., Canto, M. and Carmenati, H. (2001). Women in transition – menopause and body composition in different populations. *Collective Anthropology*, *25*, 443–448.

Argyle, M. (1971). *The psychology of interpersonal behavior*. Harmondsworth: Penguin.

—— (1975). *Body communication*. London: Methuen.

—— (1988). *Bodily communication* (2nd edn). London: Methuen.

—— (1992). Benefits produced by supportive social relationships. In H. Veiel and U. Baumann (Eds.), *The meaning and measurement of social support*. New York: Hemisphere.

Argyle, M. and Ingham, R. (1972). Gaze, mutual gaze and proximity. *Semiotica*, *6*, 32–49.

Argyle, M. and McHenry, R. (1971). Do spectacles really affect judgements of intelligence? *British Journal of Social and Clinical Psychology*, *10*, 27–29.

Arking, R. (1998). *The biology of aging: Observations and principles*. Sunderland: Sinauer.

Armstrong, B. K. M. and Kricker, A. (2001). The epidemiology of UV induced skin cancer. *Journal of Photochemistry and Photobiology B: Biology*, *63*, 8–18.

Armstrong, J. (2004). *The secret power of beauty*. London: Penguin.

Aronson, E. and Linder, D. (1965). Gain and loss of esteem as determinants of interpersonal attractiveness. *Journal of Experimental Social Psychology*, *1*, 156–171.

Aruguete, M. S., Yates, A. and Edman, J. L. (2006). Further validation of the self-loathing subscale as a screening tool for eating disorders. *Eating Disorders*, *15*, 55–62.

Asch, S. E. (1946). Forming impressions of personality. *Journal of Abnormal and Social Psychology*, *41*, 258–290.

Ashmore, R. D. (1981). Sex stereotypes and implicit personality theory. In D. L. Hamilton (Ed.), *Cognitive processes in stereotyping and intergroup behavior* (pp. 37–81). Hillsdale, NJ: Lawrence Erlbaum Associates, Inc.

Ashmore, R. D., Del Boca, F. K. and Wohlers, A. J. (1986). Gender stereotypes. In R. D. Ashmore and F. K. Del Boca (Eds.), *The social psychology of female–male relations: A critical analysis of central concepts* (pp. 69–119). Orlando, FL: Academic Press.

Ashmore, R., Solomon, M. and Longo, L. (1996). Thinking about fashion models' looks: A multidimensional approach to the structure of perceived physical attractiveness. *Personality and Social Psychology Bulletin*, *22*, 1083–1104.

Atkinson, M. and Young, K. (2001). Flesh journey: Neo primitives and the contemporary rediscovery of radical body modification. *Deviant Behavior*, 22, 117–146.

Averill, J. R. and Boothroyd, P. (1977). On falling in love in conformance with the romantic ideal. *Motivation and Emotion*, 1, 235–247.

Bailey, J. M., Gaulin, S., Agyei, Y. and Gladue, B. A. (1994). Effects of gender and sexual orientation on evolutionary aspects of human mating psychology. *Journal of Personality and Social Psychology*, 66, 1081–1093.

Baker, D., Sivyer, R. and Towell, T. (1998). Body image dissatisfaction and eating attitudes in visually impaired women. *International Journal of Eating Disorders*, 24, 319–322.

Baker, P. (1997). The soft underbelly of the Abdominis: Why men are obsessed with stomach muscles. In *Pictures of Lily: About men by men* (pp. 18–23). Exhibition catalogue, Underwood Gallery, London, September.

Bandura, A. (1973). *Aggression: A social learning analysis*. Englewood Cliffs, NJ: Prentice Hall.

Barber, N. (1995). The evolutionary psychology of physical attractiveness: Sexual selection and human morphology. *Ethology and Sociobiology*, 16, 395–424.

Barkow, J. H., Cosmides, L. and Tooby, J. (Eds.) (1992). *The adapted mind: Evolutionary psychology and the generation of culture*. New York: Oxford University Press.

Baron, R., Byrne, D. and Branscombe, N. (2006). *Social psychology*. Boston, MA: Pearson.

Barrett, L., Dunbar, R. and Lycett, J. (2002). *Human evolutionary psychology*. Basingstoke: Palgrave.

Bartky, S. L. (1990). *Femininity and domination: Studies in the phenomenology of oppression*. New York: Routledge.

Bassili, J. N. (1981). The attractiveness stereotype: Goodness or glamour? *Basic and Applied Social Psychology*, 2, 235–252.

Bateman, A. J. (1948). Intra-sexual selection in Drosophila. *Heredity*, 2, 349–368.

Bateson, P. (Ed.) (1983). *Mate choice*. Cambridge: Cambridge University Press.

Beck, S. P., Ward-Hull, C. I. and McLear, P. M. (1976). Variables related to women's somatic preference of the male and female body. *Journal of Personality and Social Psychology*, 34, 1200–1210.

Becker, A. E. (1995). *Body, self and society: The view from Fiji*. Philadelphia: University of Pennsylvania Press.

—— (2004). Television, disordered eating and young women in Fiji: Negotiating body image and identity during rapid social change. *Culture, Medicine and Psychiatry*, 28, 533–559.

Becker, A. E. and Hamburg, P. (1996). Culture, the media, and eating disorders. *Harvard Review of Psychiatry*, 4, 163–167.

Becker, A. E., Gilman, S. E. and Burwell, R. A. (2005). Changes in prevalence of overweight and in body image among Fijian women between 1989 and 1998. *Obesity Research*, 13, 110–117.

Beckerman, S. (2000). Mating and marriage, husbands and lovers: Commentary on Gangestad and Simpson (2000). *Behavioral and Brain Sciences*, 23, 590–591.

Benson, P. L., Karabenick, S. A. and Lerner, R. M. (1976). Pretty pleases: The effects of physical attractiveness, race, and sex on receiving help. *Journal of Experimental Psychology*, 12, 409–415.

Bereczkei, T. (2000). Evolutionary psychology: A new perspective in the behavioral sciences. *European Journal of Psychology*, 5, 175–190.

Bereczkei, T., Gyuris, P., Koves, P. and Bernath, L. (2002). Homogramy, genetic similarity and imprinting: Parental influence on mate choice preferences. *Personality and Individual Differences*, *33*, 677–690.

Beren, S. E., Hayden, H. A., Wilfley, D. E. and Grilo, C. M. (1996). The influence of sexual orientation on body dissatisfaction in adult men and women. *International Journal of Eating Disorders*, *20*, 135–141.

Berger, J. (1977). *Ways of seeing*. London: Penguin.

Bergeron, S. M. and Senn, C. Y. (1998). Body image and sociocultural norms: A comparison of heterosexual and lesbian women. *Psychology of Women Quarterly*, *22*, 385–401.

Berry, D. S. (1990). Taking people at face value: Evidence for the kernel of truth hypothesis. *Social Cognition*, *8*, 343–361.

Berscheid, E. and Walster, E. (1974). Physical attractiveness. In L. Berkowitz (Ed.), *Advances in experimental social psychology* (Vol. 7, pp. 157–215). New York: Academic Press.

Berscheid, E., Dion, K., Walster, E. and Walster, G. W. (1973). Physical attractiveness and dating choice: A test of the matching hypothesis. *Journal of Experimental Social Psychology*, *7*, 173–189.

Berscheid, E., Walster, E. and Bohrnstedt, G. (1973). The happy American body: A survey report. *Psychology Today*, *7*, 119–131.

Bigaard, J., Frederiksen, K., Tjonneland, A., Thomsen, B. L., Overvad, K., Heitmann, B. L. *et al.* (2004). Waist and hip circumferences and all-cause mortality: Usefulness of the waist-to-hip ratio? *International Journal of Obesity*, *28*, 741–747

Birdwhistell, R. (1970). *Kinesics and context: Essays on body movement communication*. Philadelphia, PA: University of Pennsylvania Press.

Björklund, D. F. and Pellegrini, A. D. (2002). *The origins of human nature: Evolutionary developmental psychology*. Washington, DC: American Psychological Association.

Björntorp, P. (1987). Fat cell distribution and metabolism. In R. J. Wurtman and J. J. Wurtman (Eds.), *Human Obesity* (pp. 66–72). New York: New York Academy of Sciences.

—— (1991). Adipose tissue distribution and function. *International Journal of Obesity*, *15*, 67–81.

—— (1997). Body fat distribution, insulin resistance and metabolic disease. *Nutrition*, *13*, 795–803.

Blum, M. S. and Blum, N. A. (Eds.) (1979). *Sexual selection and reproductive competition in insects*. New York: Academic Press.

Boas, F. (1911). *The mind of primitive man*. New York: Macmillan.

—— (1928). *Anthropology and modern life*. New York: Norton.

—— (1955). *Primitive art*. New York: Dover.

Bohannon, P. and Bohannon, L. (1969). *A source notebook on Tiv religion*. New Haven, CT: Human Relations Area File.

Bond, S. and Cash, T. F. (1992). Black beauty: Skin color and body images among African-American college women. *Journal of Applied Social Psychology*, *22*, 874–888.

Boon, S. D. and Holmes, J. G. (1999). Interpersonal risk and the evaluations of transgressions in close relationships. *Personal Relationships*, *6*, 151–168.

Bordo, S. (1993). *Unbearable weight: Feminism, western culture and the body*. Berkeley, CA: University of California Press.

Borgerhoff Mulder, M. (1988). Early maturing Kipsigis women have higher reproductive success than later maturing women and cost more to marry. *Behavioral Ecology and Sociobiology*, *24*, 145–153.

—— (1989). Reproductive consequences of sex-biased inheritance in Kipsigis. In V. Standen and R. A. Foley (Eds.), *Comparative socioecology* (pp. 405–427). Oxford: Blackwell.

Bornstein, R. F. (1989). Exposure and affect: Overview and meta-analysis of research, 1968–1987. *Psychological Bulletin*, *106*, 265–289.

Boroughs, M., Cafri, G. and Thompson, J. K. (2005). Male body depilation: Prevalence and associated features of body hair removal. *Sex Roles*, *52*, 637–644.

Botta, R. A. (2003). For your health? The relationship between magazine reading and adolescents' body image and eating disturbances. *Sex Roles*, *48*, 389–399.

Boyd, K. and Fouts, G. (1999). Young women's magazines: A content analysis. Paper presented at the meeting of the Canadian Communications Asssociation, Sherbrooke, Quebec, June.

Bradberry, T. and Greaves, J. (2005). *The emotional intelligence quickbook*. New York: Simon and Schuster.

Brain, R. (1979). *The decorated body*. New York: Harper and Row.

Brand, P. A., Rothblum, E. D. and Solomon, L. J. (1992). Comparison of lesbians, gay men, and heterosexuals on weight and restrained eating. *International Journal of Eating Disorders*, *11*, 253–259.

Brase, G. L. and Walker, G. (2004). Male sexual strategies modify ratings of female models with specific waist-to-hip ratios. *Human Nature*, *15*, 209–224.

Bray, G. A. (1998). What is the ideal body weight? *Journal of Nutritional Biochemistry*, *9*, 489–492.

Brewer, M. B. (1968). Determinants of social distance among East African tribal groups. *Journal of Personality and Social Psychology*, *10*, 279–289.

Brewis, A. A. and McGarvey, S. T. (2000). Body image, body size, and Samoan ecological and individual modernisation. *Ecology of Food and Nutrition*, *39*, 105–120.

Brewis, A. A., McGarvey, S. T., Jones, J. and Swinburn, B. (1998). Perceptions of body size in Pacific Islanders. *International Journal of Obesity*, *22*, 185–189.

Brink, P. (1995). Fertility and fat: The Annang fattening room. In I. De Gerine and N. J. Pollock (Eds.), *Social aspects of obesity* (pp. 71–87). Amsterdam: Gordon and Breach.

Broadstock, M., Borland, R. and Gason, R. (1992). Effects of suntan on judgements of healthiness and attractiveness by adolescents. *Journal of Applied Social Psychology*, *22*, 157–172.

Brossard, J. (1932). Residential propinquity as a factor in marriage selection. *American Journal of Sociology*, *4*, 792–798.

Brown, L. S. (1987). Lesbians, weight and eating: New analyses and perspectives. In Boston Lesbian Psychologies Collective (Eds.), *Lesbian psychologies: Explorations and challenges* (pp. 294–309). Chicago: University of Illinois Press.

Brown, P. (1991). Culture and the evolution of obesity. *Human Nature*, *2*, 31–57.

Brown, P. and Konner, M. J. (1987). An anthropological perspective of obesity. *Annals of the New York Academy of Science*, *499*, 29.

Brown, R. (1986). *Social psychology* (2nd edn). New York: Fress Press.

Brown, W. M. and Moore, C. (2002). Smile asymmetries and reputation as reliable indicators of likelihood to cooperate: An evolutionary analysis. In S. P. Shohov

(Ed.), *Advances in psychology research* (Vol. 11, pp. 19–36). Hauppage: Nova Science.

Bryant, J. and Zhilman, D. (2002). *Media effects: Advances in theory and research.* Mahwah, NJ: Lawrence Erlbaum Associates, Inc.

Brylinsky, J. A. and Moore, J. C. (1994). The identification of body build stereotypes in young children. *Journal of Research in Personality, 28,* 170–181.

Buck, P. H. (1932). *Ethnology of Manihiki-Rakahanga.* Honolulu: Bernice P. Bishop Museum.

Bugental, D. E., Love, L. R. and Gianetto, R. M. (1971). Perfidious feminine faces. *Journal of Personality and Social Psychology, 17,* 314–318.

Bulik, C. M., Sullivan, P. F., Pickering, A., Dawn, A. and McCullian, M. (1999). Fertility and reproduction in women with anorexia nervosa: A controlled study. *Journal of Clinical Psychiatry, 60,* 130–135.

Bull, R. and Hawkes, C. (1982). Judging politicians by their faces. *Political Studies, 30,* 95–101.

Buller, D. J. (2005). *Adapting minds: Evolutionary psychology and the persistent quest for human nature.* New York: Bradford Books.

Bunkin, H. and Williams, R. (2000). *Beards, beards, beards.* London: Hunter and Cyr.

Burgoon, J. K., Buller, D. B. and Woodall, W. G. (1989). *Nonverbal communication: The unspoken dialogue.* New York: Harper and Row.

Burnham, T. and Phelan, J. (2000). *Mean genes.* Cambridge, MA: Perseus.

Burr, D. B., van Gerven, D. P. and Gustav, B. L. (1977). Sexual dimorphism and mechanics of the human hip: A multivariate assessment. *American Journal of Physical Anthropology, 100,* 89–100.

Buss, D. (1987). Sex differences in human mate selection criteria: An evolutionary perspective. In C. Crawford, D. Krebs and M. Smith (Eds.), *Sociobiology and psychology: Ideas, issues and applications* (pp. 335–352). Hillsdale, NJ: Lawrence Erlbaum Associates, Inc.

—— (1989). Sex differences in human mate preferences: Evolutionary hypotheses tested in 37 cultures. *Behavioural and Brain Sciences, 12,* 1–49.

—— (1994). *The evolution of desire.* New York: Basic Books.

—— (1995). Evolutionary psychology: A new paradigm for psychological science. *Psychological Inquiry, 6,* 1–30.

—— (1999). *Evolutionary psychology: The new science of the mind.* Boston: Allyn and Bacon.

—— (2001). Human nature and culture: An evolutionary psychological perspective. *Journal of Personality, 69,* 955–978.

—— (Ed.). (2005). *The handbook of evolutionary psychology.* New York: Wiley.

Buss, D. and Barnes, M. F. (1986). Preferences in human mate selection. *Journal of Personality and Social Psychology, 50,* 559–570.

Buss, D. and Greiling, H. (1999). Adaptive individual differences. *Journal of Personality, 67,* 245–258.

Buss, D. and Reeve, H. K. (2003). Evolutionary psychology and developmental dynamics. *Psychological Bulletin, 129,* 848–853.

Buss, D. and Schmitt, P. (1993). Sexual strategies theory: An evolutionary perspective on human mating. *Psychological Review, 100,* 204–232.

Buss, D. M., Abbott, M., Angleitner, A., Asherian, A., Biaggio, A., Blanco-Villa Senor, A. *et al.* (1990). International preferences in selecting mates: A study of 37 cultures. *Journal of Cross-Cultural Psychology, 21,* 5–47.

Byrne, D. (1971). *The attraction paradigm*. New York: Academic Press.

Cafri, G., Thompson, J. K., Roehrig, M., van den Berg, P., Jacobsen, P. B. and Stark, S. (2006). An investigation of appearance motives for tanning: The development and evaluation of the Physical Appearance Reasons for Tanning Scale (PARTS) and its relation to sunbathing and indoor tanning intentions. *Body Image: An International Journal of Research, 3*, 199–209.

Calle, E. D., Rodriguez, C., Walker-Thurmond, K. and Thun, M. J. (2003). Overweight, obesity and mortality from cancer in a prospectively-studied cohort of US adults. *New England Journal of Obesity, 348*, 1625–1638.

Cameron, C., Oskamp, S. and Sparks, W. (1977). Courtship American style: Newspaper ads. *Family Coordinator, 26*, 27–30.

Campbell, W. K., Sedikides, C. and Bosson, J. (1994). Romantic involvement, self-discrepancy and psychological well-being: A preliminary investigation. *Personal Relationships, 1*, 399–404.

Cant, J. G. H. (1981). Hypothesis for the evolution of human breasts and buttocks. *American Naturalist, 117*, 119–204.

Caplan, J. (2000). *Written on the body: The tattoo in European and American history*. Princeton, NJ: Princeton University Press.

Cárdenas, R. A. and Harris, L. J. (2006). Symmetrical decorations enhance the attractiveness of faces and abstract designs. *Evolution and Human Behavior, 27*, 1–18.

Caro, T. and Borgerhoff Mulder, M. (1987). Problem of adaptation in the study of human behaviour. *Ethology and Sociobiology, 8*, 61–72.

Cary, M. S. (1978). The role of the gaze in the initiation of conversation. *Social Psychology, 41*, 269–271.

Cash, T. F. (1990). Losing hair, losing points? The effect of male pattern baldness on social impression formation? *Journal of Applied Social Psychology, 20*, 154–167.

Cash, T. F. and Hicks, K. L. (1990). Being fat versus thinking fat: Relationships with body image, eating behaviours and well-being. *Cognitive Therapy and Research, 14*, 327–341.

Cash, T. F. and Janda, L. H. (1984, December). The eye of the beholder. *Psychology Today*, 46–52.

Cash, T. F. and Kehr, J. (1978). The influence of nonprofessional counselors' physical attractiveness and sex on perceptions of counselor behavior. *Journal of Counseling Psychology, 25*, 336–342.

Cash, T. F. and Soloway, D. (1975). Self-disclosure and correlates of physical attractiveness: An exploratory study. *Psychological Reports, 36*, 579–586.

Cash, T. F., Cash, D. W. and Butters, J. W. (1983). 'Mirror, mirror on the wall . . .?': Contrast effects and self-evaluations of physical attractiveness. *Personality and Social Psychology Bulletin, 9*, 351–358.

Cash, T. F., Kerr, J. A., Polyson, J. and Freeman, V. (1977). Role of physical attractiveness in peer attribution of psychological disturbance. *Journal of Consulting and Clinical Psychology, 45*, 987–993.

Cash, T. F., Rissi, J. and Chapman, R. (1985). Not just another pretty face: Sex roles, locus of control and cosmetic use. *Personality and Social Psychology Bulletin, 11*, 246–257.

Cashdan, E. (1993). Attracting mates. *Ethology and Sociobiology, 14*, 1–24.

Cassidy, C. M. (1991). The good body: When big is better. *Medical Anthropology, 13*, 181–213.

Castellow, K. S., Wuensch, K. L. and Moore, C. H. (1990). Effects of physical attractiveness of plaintiff and defendant in sexual harassment judgements. *Journal of Social Behaviour and Personality*, *16*, 39–50.

Chang, K., Chan, S. and Low, W. (1963). Climate and conception rates in Hong Kong. *Human Biology*, *35*, 367.

Chen, N. Y., Shaffer, D. R. and Wu, C. (1997). On physical attractiveness stereotyping in Taiwan: A sociocultural perspective. *Journal of Social Psychology*, *137*, 117–124.

Cialdini, R. B. and Trost, M. R. (1998). Social influence: Social norms, conformity and compliance. In D. T. Gilbert, S. T. Fiske and G. Lindzey (Eds.), *The handbook of social psychology* (4th edn, Vol. 2, pp. 151–192). New York: McGraw-Hill.

Clark, R. A., Niccolai, L., Kissinger, P. J. and Bouvier, V. (1999). Ethnic differences in body image attitudes and perceptions among women infected with human immuno-deficiency virus. *Journal of the American Dietetics Association*, *99*, 735–737.

Clarke, A. C. (1952). An examination of the operation of residential propinquity as a factor in mate selection. *American Sociological Review*, *17*, 17–22.

Clifford, M. M. and Hatfield, E. (1973). Research note: The effects of physical attractiveness on teacher expectations. *Social Education*, *46*, 248–258.

Clore, G. L. and Byrne, D. (1974). A reinforcement-affect model of attraction. In T. L. Huston (Ed.), *Foundations of interpersonal attraction* (pp. 143–165). New York: Academic Press.

Cohen, A. B. and Tannenbaum, I. J. (2001). Lesbian and bisexual women's judgements of the attractiveness of different body types. *Journal of Sex Research*, *38*, 1–15.

Cohen, R. (1973). *Patterns of personality judgements*. New York: Academic Press.

Coleridge, H. (1875). She is not fair to outward view. In F. T. Palgrave (Ed.), *The golden treasury* (p. 175). London: Macmillan.

Collins, J. K. and Plahn, M. R. (1988). Recognition accuracy, stereotypic preference, aversion and subjective judgement of body appearance in adolescents and young adults. *Journal of Youth and Adolescence*, *17*, 317–332.

Collins, N. L. and Miller, L. C. (1994). Do positive illusions foster mental health? An examination of the Taylor and Brown formulation. *Psychological Bulletin*, *116*, 2–30.

Collins, S. A. (2000). Men's voices and women's choices. *Animal Behaviour*, *60*, 773–780.

Connell, R. W. (1995). *Masculinities*. Berkeley, CA: University of California Press.

Cook, M. (1971). *Interpersonal perception*. Harmondsworth: Penguin.

Corter, C., Trehub, S., Boukydis, C., Ford, L., Celhoffer, L. and Minde, K. (1978). Nurses' judgements of the attractiveness of premature infants. *Infant Behavior and Development*, *1*, 373–380.

Courtenay, R. W. (2000). Constructions of masculinity and their influence on men's well-being: A theory of gender and health. *Social Science and Medicine*, *50*, 1385–1401.

Crago, M., Shisslak, C. M. and Estes, L. S. (1996). Eating disturbances among American minority groups: A review. *International Journal of Eating Disorders*, *19*, 239–248.

Craig, P. L., Swinburn, B. A., Matenga-Smith, T., Matangi, H. and Vaughan, G. (1996). Do Polynesians still believe that big is beautiful? Comparison of body size and preferences of Cook Island Maori and Australians. *New Zealand Medical Journal*, *109*, 200–203.

Cramer, P. and Steinwert, T. (1998). Thin is good, fat is bad: How early does it begin? *Journal of Applied Developmental Psychology, 19*, 429–451.

Crawford, C. (1998). The theory of evolution in the study of human behaviour: An introduction and overview. In C. Crawford and D. L. Krebs (Eds.), *Handbook of evolutionary psychology: Ideas, issues and applications* (pp. 3–41). Hillsdale, NJ: Lawrence Erlbaum Associates, Inc.

Crocker, J., Major, B. and Steele, C. (1998). Social stigma. In D. T. Gilbert, S. T. Fiske and G. Lindzey (Eds.), *The handbook of social psychology* (4th edn, Vol. 2, pp. 504–553). New York: McGraw-Hill.

Crusco, A. H. and Wetzel, C. G. (1984). The Midas touch: The effects of interpersonal touch on restaurant tipping. *Personality and Social Psychology Bulletin, 10*, 512–517.

Cunningham, M. R. (1986). Measuring the physical in physical attractiveness: Quasi-experiments on the sociobiology of female facial beauty. *Journal of Personality and Social Psychology, 50*, 925–935.

Cunningham, M. R., Barbee, A. P. and Pike, C. L. (1990). What do women want? Facialmetric assessment of multiple motives in the perception of male facial physical attractiveness. *Journal of Personality and Social Psychology, 59*, 61–72.

Cunningham, M. R., Roberts, A. R., Wu, C. H., Barbee, A. P. and Druen, P. B. (1995). 'Their ideas of beauty are on the whole the same as ours.' Consistency and variability in the cross-cultural perception of female physical attractiveness. *Journal of Personality and Social Psychology, 68*, 261–279.

Cvetkovich, G. and Löfstedt, R. E. (Eds.) (1999). *Social trust and the management of risk*. London: Earthscan.

Dabbs, J. M. and Mallinger, A. (1999). High testosterone levels predict low voice pitch among men. *Personality and Individual Differences, 27*, 801–804.

Darby, B. W. and Jeffers, D. (1988). The effects of defendant and juror attractiveness on simulated courtroom trials and decisions. *Social Behavior and Personality, 5*, 547–562.

Darwin, C. (1871). *The descent of man, and selection in relation to sex*. London: Murray.

—— (1887/1959). *The autobiography of Charles Darwin: With original omissions restored* (Ed. N. Barlow). London: Norton.

Davey Smith, G., Greenwood, R., Gunnell, D., Sweetnam, P., Yarnell, J. and Elwood, P. (2001). Leg length, insulin resistance, and coronary heart disease risk: The Caerphilly Study. *Journal of Epidemiology and Community Health, 55*, 867–872.

Davie, M. R. and Reeves, R. J. (1939). Propinquity of residence before marriage. *American Journal of Sociology, 4*, 219–224.

Davis, C. and Katzman, M. A. (1999). Perfection as acculturation: Psychological correlates of eating problems in Chinese male and female students living in the United States. *International Journal of Eating Disorders, 25*, 65–70.

Davis, C. H. (1995). The effect of assortative mating and environmental variation on selection for sexual reproduction. *Evolutionary Theory, 11*, 51–53.

De Garine, I. (1995). Sociocultural aspects of male fattening sessions among the Massa of northern Cameroon. In I. De Gerine and N. J. Pollock (Eds.), *Social aspects of obesity* (pp. 45–70). Amsterdam: Gordon and Breach.

Dennett, D. C. (1995). *Darwin's dangerous idea: Evolution and the meaning of life*. Harmondsworth: Penguin.

DePaulo, B. M. (1992). Nonverbal behavior and self-presentation. *Psychological Bulletin, 111*, 203–243.

DePaulo, B. M. and Friedman, H. S. (1998). Nonverbal communication. In D. T. Gilbert, S. T. Fiske and G. Lindzey (Eds.), *The handbook of social psychology* (4th edn, Vol. 2, pp. 3–40). New York: McGraw-Hill.

Dermer, M. and Thiel, D. L. (1975). When beauty may fail. *Journal of Personality and Social Psychology, 31,* 1168–1176.

De Souza, M. J. and Metzger, D. A. (1991). Reproductive dysfunction in amenorrheic athletes and anorexic patients: A review. *Medicine and Science in Sports and Exercise, 56,* 20–27.

Deurenberg, P., Deurenberg-Yap, M. and Guricci, S. (2002). Asians are different from Caucasians and from each other in their body mass index/body fat percentage relationship. *Obesity Reviews, 3,* 141–146.

Deutsch, F. M., Zalenski, C. M. and Clark, M. E. (1986). Is there a double standard of aging? *Journal of Applied Social Psychology, 16,* 771–785.

De Waal, F. (1982). *Chimpanzee politics.* New York: Harper and Row.

Dieckmann, U. and Doebeli, M. (1999). On the origin of species by sympatric speciation. *Nature, 400,* 354–357.

Diener, E., Suh, E. M., Lucas, R. E. and Smith, H. L. (1999). Subjective well-being: Three decades of progress. *Psychological Bulletin, 125,* 276–302.

Diepgen, T. L. and Mahler, V. (2002). The epidemiology of skin cancer. *British Journal of Dermatology, 146,* 1–6.

Dion, K. K. (1972). Physical attractiveness and evaluation of children's transgressions. *Journal of Personality and Social Psychology, 24,* 285–290.

—— (1974). Children's physical attractiveness and sex as determinants of adult punitiveness. *Developmental Psychology, 10,* 772–778.

—— (1981). Physical attractiveness, sex roles and heterosexual attraction. In M. Cook (Ed.), *The bases of human sexual attraction* (pp. 3–22). London: Academic Press.

—— (1986). Stereotyping based on physical attractiveness: Issues and conceptual perspectives. In C. P. Herman, M. P. Zanna and E. T. Higgins (Eds.), *Physical appearance, stigma and social behavior: The Ontario Symposium* (Vol. 3, pp. 7–21). Hillsdale, NJ: Lawrence Erlbaum Associates, Inc.

Dion, K. K. and Dion, K. L. (1996). Toward understanding love. *Personal Relationships, 3,* 1–3.

Dion, K. K., Berscheid, E. and Walster, E. (1972). What is beautiful is good. *Journal of Personality and Social Psychology, 24,* 285–290.

Dion, K. K., Pak, A. W. and Dion, K. L. (1990). Stereotyping physical attractiveness: A sociocultural perspective. *Journal of Cross-Cultural Psychology, 21,* 378–398.

Dipboye, R. L., Arvey, R. D. and Terpstra, D. E. (1977). Sex and physical attractiveness of raters and applicants as determinants of resumé evaluations. *Journal of Applied Psychology, 62,* 288–294.

Dipboye, R. L., Fromkin, H. L. and Wiback, K. (1975). Relative importance of applicant sex, attractiveness and scholastic standing in evaluation of job applicant resumes. *Journal of Applied Psychology, 60,* 39–43.

Dittes, J. E. (1959). Attractiveness of group as function of self-esteem and acceptance by group. *Journal of Abnormal and Social Psychology, 59,* 77–82.

Dittes, J. E. and Kelley, H. H. (1956). Effects of different conditions of acceptance upon conformity to group norms. *Journal of Abnormal and Social Psychology, 53,* 100–107.

Dixson, A. F., Halliwell, G., East, R., Wignarajah, P. and Anderson, M. J. (2003).

Masculine somatype and hirsuteness as determinants of sexual attractiveness to women. *Archives of Sexual Behavior*, *32*, 29–39.

Dorfer, L. and Moser, M. (1998). 5200-year-old acupuncture in central Europe? *Science*, *282*, 239.

Dovidio, J. F. and Ellyson, S. L. (1985). Patterns of visual dominance behavior in humans. In S. Ellyson and J. Dovidio (Eds.), *Power, dominance and non-verbal behavior* (pp. 129–149). New York: Springer.

Dovidio, J. F., Ellyson, S. L., Keating, C. J., Heltman, K. and Brown, C. E. (1988). The relationship of social power to visual displays of dominance between men and women. *Journal of Personality and Social Psychology*, *54*, 233–242.

Downs, A. C. and Harrison, S. K. (1985). Embarassing age spots or just plain ugly? Physical attractiveness stereotyping as an instrument of sexism on American television commercials. *Sex Roles*, *13*, 9–19.

Draper, P. and Harpending, H. (1982). Father absence and reproductive strategy: An evolutionary perspective. *Journal of Anthropological Research*, *38*, 255–273.

Drewnowski, A. and Yee, D. K. (1987). Men and body image: Are males satisfied with their body weight? *Psychosomatic Medicine*, *49*, 626–634

Drury, N. E. (2000). Beauty is only skin deep. *Journal of the Royal Society of Medicine*, *93*, 89–92.

Ducille, A. (1996). *Skin trade*. Cambridge, MA: Harvard University Press.

Dunbar, M. (1988). *Primate social systems*. London: Croom Helm.

Durkheim, E. (1912/1995). *The elementary forms of the religious life*. New York: Free Press.

Dworkin, A. (1974). *Woman hating*. New York: E. P. Dutton.

Eagly, A. H. (1987). *Sex differences in social behavior: A social-role analysis*. Hillsdale, NJ: Lawrence Erlbaum Associates, Inc.

Eagly, A. H. and Wood, W. (1999). The origins of sex differences in human behaviour: Evolved dispositions versus social roles. *American Psychologist*, *54*, 408–423.

Eagly, E. H., Ashmore, R. D., Makhijani, M. G. and Longo, L. C. (1991). What is beautiful is good, but . . . A meta-analytic review of research on the physical attractiveness stereotype. *Psychological Bulletin*, *110*, 109–128.

Ebin, V. (1979). *The body decorated*. London: Thames and Hudson.

Eco, U. (2004). *On beauty: A history of a Western idea* (trans. A. McEwen). London: Secker and Warburg.

Ehrenberg, M. (1989). *Women in prehistory*. Norman, OK: University of Oklahoma Press.

Eibl-Eibesfeldt, I. (1970). *Ethology: The biology of behaviour*. New York: Holt, Rinehart and Winston.

Einon, D. (2007). The shaping of women's bodies: Men's choice of fertility or heat stress avoidance? In. V. Swami and A. Furnham (Eds.), *The body beautiful: Evolutionary and socio-cultural perspectives*. London: Macmillan.

Ekman, P., Friesen, W. V. and Scherer, K. (1976). Body movements and voice pitch in deceptive interaction. *Semiotica*, *16*, 23–27.

Ellis, D. S. (1967). Speech and social status in America. *Social Forces*, *45*, 431–437.

Ellisson, P. (1990). Human ovarian function and reproductive ecology: New hypotheses. *American Anthropologist*, *92*, 933–952.

Ember, C. R., Ember, M., Korotayev, A. and de Munck, V. (2005). Valuing thinness or fatness in women: Reevaluating the effect of resource scarcity. *Evolution and Human Behavior*, *26*, 257–270.

Epel, E. S., Spanakos, A., Kasl-Godley, J. and Brownell, K. D. (1996). Body shape ideals across gender, sexual orientation, socioeconomic status, race and age in personal advertisements. *International Journal of Eating Disorders, 19*, 265–273.

Epstein, E. and Guttman, R. (1984). Mate selection in man: Evidence, theory and outcome. *Social Biology, 31*, 243–278.

Etcoff, N. (1999). *Survival of the prettiest: The science of beauty*. New York: Doubleday.

Falkner, N. H., French, S.A., Jeffery, R. W., Neumark-Sztainer, D., Sherwood and Morton, N. (1999). Mistreatment due to weight: Prevalence and sources of perceived mistreatment in women and men. *Obesity Research, 7*, 572–576.

Fallon, A. (1990). Culture in the mirror: Socio-cultural determinants of body image. In T. Cash and T. Przwzinky (Eds.), *Body images: Development, deviance and change* (pp. 80–109). New York: Guilford Press.

Fallon, A. E. and Rozin, P. (1985). Sex differences in perceptions of desirable body shape. *Journal of Abnormal Psychology, 94*, 102–115.

Faludi, S. (1999). *Stiffed: The betrayal of the American male*. New York: HarperCollins.

Fan, J. T. (2007). The volume–height index as a body attractiveness index. In. V. Swami and A. Furnham (Eds.), *The body beautiful: Evolutionary and socio-cultural perspectives*. London: Macmillan.

Fan, J. T., Dai, W., Liu, F. and Wu, J. (2005). Visual perception of male body attractiveness. *Proceedings of the Royal Society of London B, 272*, 219–226.

Fan, J., Liu, F., Wu, J. and Dai, W. (2004). Visual perception of female physical attractiveness. *Proceedings of the Royal Society of London B, 271*, 347–352.

Farr, R. M. and Moscovici, S. (Eds.) (1984). *Social representations*. Cambridge: Cambridge University Press.

Feingold, A. (1990). Gender differences in effects of physical attractiveness on romantic attraction: A comparison across five research paradigms. *Journal of Personality and Social Psychology, 59*, 981–993.

—— (1992). Good-looking people are not what we think. *Psychological Bulletin, 111*, 304–341.

Feinman, S. and Gill, G. W. (1977). Females' response to male beardedness. *Perceptual and Motor Skills, 94*, 533–534.

Ferrario, V. F., Sforza, C., Poggio, C. E. and Tartaglia, G. (1995). Facial morphology of television actresses compared with normal women. *Journal of Oral and Maxillofacial Surgery, 53*, 1008–1014.

Fessler, D. M. T., Haley, K. J. and Lal, R. (2005a). Sexual dimorphism in foot length proportionate to stature. *Annals of Human Biology, 32*, 44–59.

Fessler, D. M. T., Nettle, D., Afshar, Y., de Andrade Pinheiro, I., Bolyanatz, A., Borgerhoff Mulder, M. *et al.* (2005b). A cross-cultural investigation of the role of foot size in physical attractiveness. *Archives of Sexual Behavior, 34*, 267–276.

Festinger, L., Schachter, S. and Back, K. (1950). *Social pressures in informal groups: A study of human factors in housing*. New York: Harper.

Field, A. E., Carmago, C. A., Taylor, C. B., Berkey, C. S., Roberts, S. B. and Coldizt, G. A. (2001). Peer, parent and media influences on the development of weight concerns and frequent dieting among preadolescent and adolescent girls and boys. *Paediatrics, 107*, 54–60.

Fink, B. and Penton-Voak, I. S. (2002). Evolutionary psychology of facial attractiveness. *Current Directions in Psychological Science, 11*, 154–158.

Finkelstein, J. (1991). *The fashioned self*. Cambridge: Polity Press.

Fishbein, M. and Azjen, I. (1975). *Belief, attitude, intention and behavior: An introduction to theory and research*. Reading, MA: Addison-Wesley.

Fisher, E., Dunn, M. and Thompson, J. K. (2002). Social comparison and body image: An investigation of body comparison processes using multidimensional scaling. *Journal of Social and Clinical Psychology*, *21*, 566–579.

Fisher, J. D., Rytting, M. and Heslin, R. (1976). Hands touching hands: Affective and evaluative effects of an interpersonal touch. *Sociometry*, *39*, 416–421.

Fisher, R. A. (1915). The evolution of sexual preference. *Eugenics Review*, *7*, 184–192.

Fisher, R. A. (1930). *The genetical theory of natural selection* (2nd edn). New York: Dover.

Fiske, A. P., Kitayama, S., Markus, H. R. and Nisbett, R. E. (1998). The cultural matrix of social psychology. In D. T. Gilbert, S. T. Fiske and G. Lindzey (Eds.), *The handbook of social psychology* (4th edn, Vol. 2, pp. 915–981). New York: McGraw-Hill.

Fitzgibbon, M.L., Spring, B., Avellone, M. E., Blackman, L. R., Pingitore, R. and Stolley, M. R. (1998). Correlates of binge eating in Hispanic, black and white women. *International Journal of Eating Disorders*, *24*, 43–52.

Foa, E. B. and Foa, U. G. (1975). *Resource theory of social exchange*. Morristown, NJ: General Learning Press.

Fodor, J. (2000). *The mind doesn't work that way*. Cambridge, MA: MIT Press.

Foley, R. (1988). Hominids, humans and hunter-gatherers: An evolutionary perspective. In T. Ingold, D. Riches and J. Woodburn (Eds.), *Hunters and gatherers: History, evolution and social change* (pp. 207–221). New York: St. Martin's Press.

—— (1996). The adaptive legacy of human evolution: A search for the environment of evolutionary adaptedness. *Evolutionary Anthropology*, *4*, 194–203.

Folsom, A. R., Kaye, S. A., Sellers, T. A., Hong, C., Cerhan, J. R., Potter, J. D. *et al.* (1993). Body fat distribution and 5-year risk of death in older women. *Journal of the American Medical Association*, *269*, 483–487.

Folstad, I. and Karter, A. (1992). Parasites, bright males, and the immunocompetence handicap. *American Naturalist*, *139*, 603–622.

Ford, C. S. and Beach, F. A. (1952). *Patterns of sexual behavior*. New York: Harper.

Forestell, C. A., Humphrey, T. M. and Stewart, S. H. (2004). Involvement of body weight and shape factors in ratings of attractiveness by women: A replication and extension of Tassinary and Hansen (1998). *Personality and Individual Differences*, *36*, 295–305.

Forgas, D. P. (1987). The role of physical attractiveness in the interpretation of facial expression cues. *Personality and Social Psychology Bulletin*, *13*, 478–479.

Frable, D. E. (1987). Sex-typed execution and perception of expressive movement. *Journal of Personality and Social Psychology*, *53*, 391–396.

Franzoi, S. L. (1995). The body-as-object versus the body-as-process: Gender differences and gender considerations. *Sex Roles*, *33*, 417–437.

Franzoi, S. L. and Herzog, M. E. (1987). Judging physical attractiveness: What body aspects do we use? *Personality and Social Psychology Bulletin*, *13*, 19–33.

Franzoi, S. L., Anderson, J. and Frommelt, S. (1990). Individual differences in men's perceptions and reactions to thinning hair. *Journal of Social Psychology*, *130*, 209–218.

Frederick, D. A., Fessler, D. M. T. and Haselton, M. G. (2005). Do representations of male muscularity differ in men's and women's magazines? *Body Image: An International Journal of Research*, *2*, 81–86.

Frederick, D. A. and Haselton, M. G. (2003). Muscularity as a communicative signal. Paper presentation at the International Communications Association, San Diego, California.

Freedman, D. G. (1969a, October). The survival value of the beard. *Psychology Today*, 36–39.

—— (1969b). *Human sociobiology*. New York: Free Press.

Freedman, R. E. K., Carter, M. M., Sbrocco, T. and Gray, J. J. (2004). Ethnic differences in preferences for female weight and waist-to-hip ratio: A comparison of African-American and White American college and community samples. *Eating Behaviors*, 5, 191–198.

Freese, J. and Meland, S. (2002). Seven tenths incorrect: Heterogeneity and change in the waist-to-hip ratios of *Playboy* centrefolds models and Miss America pageant winners. *Journal of Sex Research*, 39, 133–138.

French, S. A., Story, M., Remafedi, G., Resnick, M. D. and Blum, R. W. (1996). Sexual orientation and prevalence of body dissatisfaction and eating disordered behaviours: A population-based study of adolescents. *International Journal of Eating Disorders*, 2, 119–126.

Friedman, H. S., Riggio, R. E. and Casella, D. F. (1988). Nonverbal skill, personal charisma, and initial attraction. *Journal of Personality and Social Psychology*, 14, 203–211.

Frisby, C. M. (2006). 'Shades of beauty': Examining the relationship of skin color to perceptions of physical attractiveness. *Facial Plastic Surgery*, 22, 175–179.

Frisch, R. E. (1987). Body fat, menarche, fitness and fertility. *Human Reproduction*, 2, 521–533.

—— (1988). Fatness and fertility. *Scientific American*, 258, 88–95.

Frost, P. (1988). Human skin color: A possible relationship between its sexual dimorphism and its social perception. *Perspectives in Biology and Medicine*, 32, 38–58.

—— (1994a). Geographic distribution of human skin colour: A selective compromise between natural selection and sexual selection? *Human Evolution*, 9, 141–153.

—— (1994b). Preference for darker faces in photographs at different phases of the menstrual cycle: Preliminary assessment of evidence for a hormonal relationship. *Perceptual and Motor Skills*, 79, 507–514.

—— (2005). *Fair women, dark men: The forgotten roots of color prejudice*. Christchurch, New Zealand: Cybereditions.

—— (2006). European hair and eye color: A case of frequency-dependent sexual selection? *Evolution and Human Behavior*, 27, 85–103.

Furnham, A. (2001). Self-estimates of intelligence: Culture and gender difference in self and other estimates of both general (*g*) and multiple intelligences. *Personality and Individual Differences*, 31, 1381–1405.

Furnham, A. and Alibhai, N. (1983). Cross-cultural differences in the perception of female body-shapes. *Psychological Medicine*, 13, 829–837.

Furnham, A. and Baguma, P. (1994). Cross-cultural differences in the evaluation of male and female body shapes. *International Journal of Eating Disorders*, 15, 81–89.

Furnham, A. and Greaves, N. (1994). Gender and locus of control correlates of body image dissatisfaction. *European Journal of Personality*, 8, 183–200.

Furnham, A. and Nordling, R. (1998). Cross-cultural differences in preferences for specific male and female body shapes. *Personality and Individual Differences*, 25, 635–648.

Furnham, A. and Radley, S. (1989). Sex differences in the perceptions of male and female body shapes. *Personality and Individual Differences, 10,* 653–662.

Furnham, A. and Reeves, E. (2006). The relative influence of facial neoteny and waist-to-hip ratio on judgements of female attractiveness and fecundity. *Psychology, Health and Medicine, 11,* 129–141.

Furnham, A. and Swami, V. (2007). Perceptions of female buttocks and breast size in profile. *Social Behavior and Personality, 35,* 1–8.

Furnham, A., Dias, M. and McClelland, A. (1998). The role of body weight, waist-to-hip ratio, and breast size in judgments of female attractiveness. *Sex Roles, 34,* 311–326.

Furnham, A., Lavancy, M. and McClelland, A. (2001). Waist-to-hip ratio and facial attractiveness. *Personality and Individual Differences, 30,* 491–502.

Furnham, A., Moutafi, J. and Baguma, P. (2002). A cross-cultural study on the role of weight and waist-to-hip ratio on judgements of women's attractiveness. *Personality and Individual Differences, 32,* 729–745.

Furnham, A., Petrides, K. V. and Constantinides, A. (2005). The effects of body mass index and waist-to-hip ratio on ratings of female attractiveness, fecundity and health. *Personality and Individual Differences, 38,* 1823–1834.

Furnham, A., Swami, V. and Shah, K. (2006). Female body correlates of attractiveness and other ratings. *Personality and Individual Differences, 41,* 443–454.

Furnham, A., Tan, T., McManus, C. (1997). Waist-to-hip ratio and preferences for body shape: A replication and extension. *Personality and Individual Differences, 22,* 539–549.

Gangestad, S. and Kaplan, H. (2005). Life history theory and evolutionary psychology. In D. Buss (Ed.), *The handbook of evolutionary psychology* (pp. 68–95). New York: Wiley.

Gangestad, S. and Scheyd, G. J. (2005). The evolution of human physical attractiveness. *Annual Review of Anthropology, 34,* 523–548.

Gangestad, S. and Simpson, J. A. (2000). The evolution of human mating: Trade-offs and strategic pluralism. *Behavioral and Brain Sciences, 2,* 573–587.

Gangestad, S. and Thornhill, R. (1998). Menstrual cycle variation in women's preferences for the scent of symmetrical men. *Proceedings of the Royal Society of London B, 265,* 727–733.

Gangestad, S. and Thornhill, R. (2003). Facial masculinity and fluctuating asymmetry. *Evolution and Human Behavior, 24,* 231–241.

Gangestad, S. W., Simpson, J. A., Cousins, A. J., Garver-Apgar, C. E. and Christensen, P. N. (2004). Women's preferences for male behavioural displays change across the menstrual cycle. *Psychological Science, 15,* 203–207.

Gangestad, S. G., Haselton, M. G. and Buss, D. M. (2006). Toward an integrative understanding of evoked and transmitted culture: The importance of specialized psychological design. *Psychological Inquiry, 17,* 75–95.

Garner, D. M. (1997). The body image survey results. *Psychology Today, 30,* 30–47.

Garner, D. M., Garfinkel, P. E., Schwartz, D. and Thompson, M. (1980). Cultural expectations of thinness in women. *Psychological Reports, 47,* 483–491.

Gaut, B. and Lopes, D. M. (2001). *The Routledge companion to aesthetics.* London: Routledge.

Gettelman, T. E. and Thompson, J. K. (1993). Actual differences and stereotypical perceptions in body image and eating disturbance: A comparison of male and female heterosexual and homosexual samples. *Sex Roles, 29,* 545–562.

Ghannam, F. (1997). Fertile, plump and strong: The social construction of female body in low income Cairo. *Monographs in Reproductive Health Number 3*. Cairo: Population Council Regional Office for West Asia and North Africa.

Gillis, J. S. and Avis, W. E. (1980). The male-taller norm in mate selection. *Personality and Social Psychology Bulletin, 6*, 396–401.

Gilman, E. B. (1980). Word and image in Quarles' 'Emblemes.' *Critical Inquiry, 6*, 385–410.

Gitter, A. G., Lomranz, J. and Saxe, L. (1982). Factors affecting perceived attractiveness of male physiques by American and Israeli students. *Journal of Social Psychology, 118*, 167–175.

Gitter, A., Lomranz, J. Saxe, L. and Bar-Tal, D. (1983). Perception of female physique characteristics by American and Israeli students. *Journal of Social Psychology, 121*, 7–13.

Gladue, B. A. and Delaney, H. J. (1990). Gender differences in perception of attractiveness of men and women in bars. *Personality and Social Psychology Bulletin, 16*, 378–391.

Gordon, A. I. (1964). *Intermarriage*. Boston, MA: Beacon Press.

Gordon, R. A. (2000). *Eating disorders: Anatomy of a social epidemic* (2nd edn). Oxford: Blackwell.

Gosselin, C. (1984). Hair loss, personality and attitude. *Personality and Individual Differences, 5*, 365–369.

Gould, J. and Gould, C. G. (1989). *Sexual selection*. New York: Scientific American Library.

Gould, S. (1980). Is a new and general theory of evolution emerging? *Paleobiology, 6*, 119–130.

Gould, S. J. (1981). *The mismeasures of man*. Harmondsworth: Penguin.

Gould, S. J. and Lewontin, R. C. (1979). The spandrels of San Marco and the Panglossian Paradigm: A critique of the adaptationist programme. *Proceedings of the Royal Society of London, 205*, 581–598.

Graham, J. A. and Jouhar, A. J. (1981). The effects of cosmetics on person perception. *International Journal of Cosmetic Science, 3*, 199–210.

Grammer, K. (1989). Human courtship behaviour: Biological basis and cognitive processing. In A. E. Rasa, C. Vogel and E. Voland (Eds.), *The sociobiology of sexual and reproductive strategies* (pp. 147–169). London: Chapman and Hall.

Grammer, K. and Atzwanger, K. (1994). Der Lolita-Komplex: Sexuelle Attraktivät und Kindchenschema. In K. F. Wessel and F. Naumann (Eds.) *Kommunikation und Humanontogenese* (pp. 77–99). Bielefeld: Kleine Verlag.

Grammer, K. and Thornhill, R. (1994). Human (*Homo sapiens*) facial attractiveness and sexual selection: The role of symmetry and averageness. *Journal of Computational Psychology, 108*, 233–242.

Grammer, K., Fink, B., Møller, A. P. and Thornhill, R. (2003). Darwinian aesthetics: Sexual selection and the biology of beauty. *Biological Review, 78*, 385–407.

Gray, R. D., Heaney, M. and Fairhall, S. (2003). Evolutionary psychology and the challenge of adaptive explanation. In K. Sterelny and J. Fitness (Eds.), *From mating to mentality: Evaluating evolutionary psychology* (pp. 247–268). Hove, UK: Psychology Press.

Graziano, W., Brothen, T. and Berscheid, E. (1978). Height and attraction: Do men and women see eye-to-eye? *Journal of Personality, 46*, 128–145.

Graziosi, P. (1960). *Palaeolithic art*. New York: McGraw Hill.

Green, R. (1592/2005). *Philomela: The Lady Fitzwater's nightingale.* Online publication at: http://www.oxford-shakespeare.com. Last retrieved: February 18, 2007.

Greenberg, B. S., Eastin, M., Hofshire, L., Lachlan, K. and Brownell, K. D. (2003). The portrayal of overweight and obese persons in commercial television. *American Journal of Public Health, 93,* 1342–1348.

Greenhouse, S. (2003, July 13). Going for the look, but risking discrimination. *New York Times.*

Greenlees, I. A. and McGrew, W. C. (1994). Sex and age differences in preferences and tactics of mate attraction: Analysis of publised advertisements. *Ethology and Sociobiology, 15,* 59–72.

Griffiths, P. E. (2001). From adaptive heuristics to phylogenetic perspective: Some lessons from the evolutionary psychology of emotion. In H. R. Holcomb III (Ed.), *Conceptual challenges in evolutionary psychology* (pp. 309–325). Dordrecht: Kluwer.

Griffiths, R. W. and Kunz, P. R. (1973). Assortative mating: A study of physiognomic homogamy. *Social Biology, 20,* 448–453.

Griffiths, W. B. and Guay, P. (1969). 'Object' evaluation and conditioned affect. *Journal of Experimental Research in Psychology, 4,* 1–8.

Gruber-Baldini, A. L., Schaie, K. W. and Willis, S. L. (1995). Similarity in married couples: A longitudinal study of mental abilities and rigidity-flexibility. *Journal of Personality and Social Psychology, 69,* 191–203.

Guillen, E. O. and Barr, S. I. (1994). Nutrition, dieting and fitness messages in a magazine for adolescent women, 1970–1990. *Journal of Adolescent Health, 15,* 464–472.

Gunnell, D., May, M., Ben-Sholomo, Y., Yarnell, J. and Smith, G. D. (2003a). Height, leg length and cancer: The Caerphilly Study. *Nutrition and Cancer, 47,* 34–39.

Gunnell, D., Whitley, E., Upton, M. N., McConnachie, A., Davey Smith, G. and Watt, G. C. M. (2003b). Associations of height, leg length and lung function with cardiovascular risk factors in the Midspan Family Study. *Journal of Epidemiology and Community Health, 57,* 141–146.

Guo, S., Salisbury, S., Roche, A. F., Chumela, W. C. and Siervogel, R. M. (1994). Cardiovascular disease risk factor and body composition: A review. *Nutrition Research, 14,* 1721–1777.

Gurven, M., Allen-Arave, W., Hill, K. and Hurtado, A. M. (2000a). 'It's a wonderful life': Signalling generosity among the Ache of Paraguay. *Evolution and Human Behavior, 21,* 263–282.

Gurven, M., Hill, K., Kaplan, H., Hurtado, A. M. and Lyles, R. (2000b). Food transfer among Hiwi foragers of Venezuela: Tests of reciprocity. *Human Ecology, 28,* 171–218.

Guthrie, R. D. (1976). *Body hot spots.* New York: Van Nostrand Reinhold.

Habermas, J. (1961/1992). *The structural transformation of the public sphere: Inquiry into a category of bourgeois society.* Cambridge: Polity Press.

Halkitis, P. N., Green, K. A. and Wilton, L. (2004). Masculinity, body image, and sexual behavior in HIV-seropositive gay men: A two-phase formative behavioral investigation using the internet. *International Journal of Men's Health, 3,* 27–42.

Hall, E. T. (1966). *The hidden dimension.* New York: Doubleday.

Hall, J. A. (1984). *Nonverbal sex differences: Communication accuracy and expressive style.* Baltimore, MD: Johns Hopkins University Press.

Hall, K. (1995). *Things of darkness: Economies of race and gender in early modern England.* London: Cornell University Press.

Hamermesh, D. S. and Biddle, J. E. (1994). Beauty and the labor market. *American Economic Review, 84,* 1174–1194.

Hamilton, W. D. and Zuk, M. (1982). Heritable true fitness and bright birds: A role for parasites? *Science, 218,* 384–387.

Hankins, N. E., McKinnie, B. and Bailey, R. C. (1979). Effects of height, physique and cranial hair on job-related attributes. *Psychological Reports, 45,* 853–854.

Harms, L. S. (1963). Listener comprehension of speakers of three status groups. *Language Speech, 4,* 109–112.

Harrison, K. (1997). Does interpersonal attraction to thin media personalities promote eating disorders? *Journal of Broadcasting and Electronic Media, 41,* 478–500.

—— (2003). Television viewers' ideal body proportions: The case of the curvaceously thin woman. *Sex Roles, 48,* 255–264.

Harwood, J. and Anderson, K. (2002). The presence and portrayal of social groups on prime-time television. *Communication Reports, 15,* 81–97.

Haselton, M. G. and Gangestad, S. W. (2006). Conditional expression of women's desires and men's mate guarding across the ovulatory cycle. *Hormones and Behavior, 49,* 509–518.

Hassin, R. and Trope, Y. (2000). Facing faces: Studies on the cognitive aspects of physiognomy. *Journal of Personality and Social Psychology, 78,* 837–852.

Hatfield, E. and Sprecher, S. (1986). *Mirror, mirror . . . The importance of looks in everyday life.* Albany, NY: University of New York Press.

Hattori, K. (1995). Physique of Sumo wrestlers in relation to some cultural characteristics of Japan. In I. De Garine and N. J. Pollock (Eds.), *Social aspects of obesity* (pp. 32–39). Amsterdam: Gordon and Breach.

Hayduk, L. A. (1983). Personal space: Where we now stand. *Psychological Bulletin, 94,* 293–335.

Heaney, M. (2000). Male preference for female waist-to-hip ratio: Evolutionary adaptation, cultural confound, or methodological artefact? Honours dissertation, Department of Psychology, University of Auckland.

Heilman, M. E. and Saruwatari, L. R. (1979). When beauty is beastly: The effects of appearance and sex on evaluations of job applicants for managerial and nonmanagerial jobs. *Organizational Behavior and Human Decision Processes, 23,* 360–372.

Heinberg, L. J. and Thompson, J. K. (1995). Body image and televised images of thinness and attractiveness: A controlled laboratory investigation. *Journal of Social and Clinical Psychology, 14,* 325–338.

Heinberg, L. J., Thompson, J. K. and Stormer, S. (1995). Development and validation of the Sociocultural Attitudes Towards Appearance Questionnaire. *International Journal of Eating Disorders, 17,* 81–89.

Henderson, J. J. A. and Anglin, J. M. (2003). Facial attractiveness predicts longevity. *Evolution and Human Behavior, 24,* 351–356.

Henrich, J. and Gil-White, F. J. (2001). The evolution of prestige: Freely conferred deference as a mechanism for enhancing the benefits of cultural transmission. *Evolution and Human Behavior, 22,* 165–196.

Hensley, W. E. (1994). Height as a basis for interpersonal attraction. *Adolescence, 29,* 469–474.

Henss, R. (1995). Waist-to-hip ratio and attractiveness. Replication and extension. *Personality and Individual Differences, 19,* 479–488.

—— (2000). Waist-to-hip ratio and female attractiveness. Evidence from photographic stimuli and methodological considerations. *Personality and Individual Differences, 28*, 501–513.

—— (2001). Social perceptions of male pattern baldness. *Dermatology and Psychosomatics, 2*, 63–71.

Herbozo, S., Tantleff-Dunn, S., Gokee-Larose, J. and Thompson, J. K. (2004). Beauty and thinness messages in children's media: A content analysis. *Eating Disorders, 12*, 21–34.

Herzog, D. B., Newman, K. L. and Warshaw, M. (1991). Body image dissatisfaction in homosexual and heterosexual males. *Journal of Nervous and Mental Disease, 179*, 356–359.

Heslin, R. (1978). Responses to touching as an index of sex-role norms and attitudes. Paper presented at the annual meeting of the American Psychological Association, Toronto, August.

Heslin, R. and Alper, T. (1983). Touch: A bonding gesture. In J. M. Wiemann and R. P. Harrison (Eds.), *Nonverbal interaction* (pp. 47–75). Beverly Hills, CA: Sage.

Hess, N. C. and Hagen, E. H. (2002). *Informational warfare*. Online publication at Cogprints (http://cogprints.org/2112).

Hesse-Biber, S. (1996). *Am I thin enough yet? The cult of thinness and the commercialisation of identity*. New York: Oxford University Press.

Hewes, G. W. (1957). The anthropology of posture. *Scientific American, 196*, 123–132.

Heywood, J. S. (1989). Sexual selection by the handicap mechanism. *Evolution, 43*, 1387–1397.

Higham, P. A. and Carment, W. D. (1992). The rise and fall of politicians: The judged heights of Broadbent, Mulroney and Turner before and after the 1988 Canadian federal election. *Canadian Journal of Behavioral Science, 24*, 404–409.

Hildebrandt, K. A. and Fitzgerald, H. E. (1981). Physical appearance cues and interpersonal attraction in children. *Child Development, 45*, 305–310.

Hill, M. E. (2002). Skin color and the perception of attractiveness among African Americans: Does gender make a difference? *Social Psychology Quarterly, 65*, 77–91.

Hinsz, V. B. (1989). Facial resemblance in engaged and married couples. *Journal of Social and Personality Relationships, 6*, 223–229.

Ho, H. S. (1986). Assortative mating in unwed-birth parents? Adoptive and nonadoptive parents. *Social Biology, 33*, 77–86.

Hofstede, G. (1983). Dimensions of national cultures in fifty countries and three regions. In J. Deregowski, S. Dzuirawiec and R. Annis (Eds.), *Explications in cross-cultural psychology* (pp. 335–355). Lisse, Switzerland: Swets and Zietlinger.

Hogg, M. A. and Vaughan, G. M. (2005). *Social psychology* (4th edn). Harlow: Pearson.

Holmberg, A. R. (1946). The Siriono: A study on the effect of hunger frustration on the culture of a semi-nomadic Bolivian Indian society. PhD thesis, Yale University.

Holmes, J. G. (2002). Interpersonal expectations as the building blocks of social cognition: An interdependence theory perspective. *Personal Relationships, 9*, 1–26.

Horai, J., Naccari, N. and Fatoullan, E. (1974). The effects of expertise and physical attractiveness upon opinion agreement and liking. *Sociometry, 37*, 601–606.

Horn, M. J. and Gurel, L. M. (1981). *The second skin* (3rd edn). Boston, MA: Houghton Mifflin.

Hovath, T. (1979). Correlates of physical beauty in men and women. *Social Behaviour and Personality, 7*, 145–151.

Huang, Z., Willet, W. C. and Colditz, G. A. (1999). Waist circumference, waist:hip ratio, and risk of breast cancer in the Nurses' Health Study. *American Journal of Epidemiology, 150,* 1316–1324.

Huenemann, R. L., Shapiro, L. R., Hampton, M. C. and Mitchell, B. (1966). A longitudinal study of gross body composition and body confirmation and their association with food and activity in a teenage population. *American Journal of Clinical Nutrition, 18,* 325–338.

Hughes, K. A., Du, L., Rodd, F. H. and Reznick, D. N. (1999). Familiarity leads to female mate preference for novel males in the guppy, *Poecilia reticulata. Animal Behaviour, 58,* 907–916.

Hughes, S. M. and Gallup Jr., G. G. (2003). Sex differences in morphological predictors of sexual behavior: Shoulder-to-hip and waist-to-hip ratios. *Evolution and Human Behavior, 24,* 173–178.

Hughes, S. M., Dispenza, F. and Gallup Jr., G. G. (2004). Ratings of voice attractiveness predict sexual behavior and body configuration. *Evolution and Human Behavior, 25,* 295–304.

Hughes, S. M., Harrison, M. A. and Gallup Jr., G. G. (2002). The sound of symmetry: Voice as a marker of developmental instability. *Evolution and Human Behavior, 23,* 173–180.

Hume, D. (1757). *Four dissertations. IV: Of the standard of taste.* London: Millar.

Humphreys, P. and Paxton, S. J. (2004). Impact of exposure to idealized male images on adolescent boys' body image. *Body Image: An International Journal of Research, 1,* 253–266.

Huston, T. (1974). *Foundations of interpersonal attraction.* London: Academic Press.

Huxley, J. S. (1938). The present standing of the theory of sexual selection. In G. R. de Beer (Ed.), *Evolution: Essays on aspects of evolutionary biology* (pp. 11–42). Oxford: Clarendon Press.

Irving, L. M., Wall, M., Neumark-Sztainer, D. and Story, M. (2002). Steroid use among adolescents: Findings from Project EAT. *Journal of Adolescent Health, 30,* 243–252.

Iwasa, Y., Pomiankowski, A. and Nee, S. (1991). The evolution of costly mate preferences: the handicap principle. *Evolution, 45,* 1431–1442.

Jablonski, N. G. and Chaplin, G. (2000). The evolution of human skin coloration. *Journal of Human Evolution, 39,* 57–106.

Jackson, K. M. and Aiken, L. S. (2000). A psychosocial model of sun protection and sunbathing in young women: The impact of health beliefs, attitudes, norms and self-efficacy for sun protection. *Health Psychology, 13,* 86–90.

Jackson, L. A. (1992). *Physical appearance and gender: Sociobiological and sociocultural perspectives.* Albany, NY: State University of New York Press.

Jackson, L. A. and Ervin, K. S. (1992). Height stereotypes of women and men: The liabilities of shortness for both sexes. *Journal of Social Psychology, 132,* 433–445.

Jacobi, L. and Cash, T. F. (1994). In pursuit of the perfect appearance: Discrepancies among self-ideal perceptions of multiple physical attributes. *Journal of Applied Social Psychology, 24,* 379–396.

Jacobson, M. B. (1981). Effects of victim's and defendant's physical attractiveness on subjects' judgements in a rape case. *Sex Roles, 7,* 247–255.

Jaffe, K. (1999). On the adaptive value of some mate selection strategies. *Acta Biotheoretica, 47,* 29–40.

—— (2000). Emergence and maintenance of sex among diploid organisms aided by assortative mating. *Acta Biotheoretica*, *48*, 137–147.

—— (2001). On the relative importance of haplo-diploidy, assortative mating and social synergy on the evolutionary emergence of social behavior. *Acta Theoretica*, *49*, 29–42.

—— (2002). On sex, mate selection and evolution: An exploration. *Comments on Theoretical Biology*, *7*, 91–107.

Jaffe, K. and Chaconpuignau, G. (1995). Assortative mating: Sex-differences in mate selection for married and unmarried couples. *Human Biology*, *67*, 111–120.

Jasienka, G., Ziomkiewicz, A., Ellison, P. T., Lipson, S. F. and Thune, I. (2004). Large breasts and narrow waists indicate high reproductive potential in women. *Proceedings of the Royal Society of London B*, *271*, 1213–1217.

Jeffreys, S. (2005). *Beauty and misogyny: Harmful cultural practices in the west*. London: Routledge.

Jelínek, J. (1975). *The pictorial encyclopedia of the evolution of man*. London: Hamlyn.

Jennings, M. K. and Niemi, R. G. (1968). The transmission of political values from parent to child. *American Political Review*, *62*, 546–575.

Jensen-Campbell, L., Graziano, W. G. and West, S. G. (1995). Dominance, prosocial orientation, and female preferences: Do nice guys really finish last? *Journal of Personality and Social Psychology*, *68*, 427–440.

Johnson, K. and Tassinary, L. (2005). Perceiving sex directly and indirectly. *Psychological Science*, *16*, 890–897.

Johnson, K. L. and Tassinary, L. G. (2007). Interpersonal metaperception: The importance of compatibility in the aesthetic appreciation of bodily cues. In V. Swami and A. Furnham (Eds.), *The body beautiful: Evolutionary and socio-cultural perspectives*. London: Macmillan.

Johnston, V. S. and Franklin, M. (1993). Is beauty in the eye of the beholder? *Ethology and Sociobiology*, *14*, 183–199.

Johnston, V. S., Hagel, R., Franklin, M., Fink, B. and Grammer, K. (2001). Male facial attractiveness: Evidence for hormone medicated adaptive design. *Evolution and Human Behavior*, *21*, 251–267.

Joiner Jr., T. E., (1994). The interplay of similarity and self-verification in relationship formation. *Social Behavior and Personality*, *22*, 195–200.

Jones, B. C., Little, A. C., Feinberg, D. R. and Penton-Voak, I. S. (2004). The relationship between shape symmetry and perceived skin condition in male facial attractiveness. *Evolution and Human Behavior*, *25*, 24–30.

Jones, B. T., Jones, B. C., Thomas, A. P. and Piper, J. (2003). Alcohol consumption increases attractiveness ratings of opposite-sex faces: A possible third route to risky sex. *Addiction*, *98*, 1069–1075.

Jones, D. (1995). Sexual selection, physical attractiveness and facial neoteny. *Current Anthropology*, *36*, 723–748.

—— (1996). *Physical attractiveness and the theory of sexual selection*. Ann Arbor, MI: Museum of Anthropology, University of Michigan.

—— (1999). Evolutionary psychology. *Annual Review of Anthropology*, *28*, 553–575.

—— (2001). Social comparison and body image: Attractiveness comparisons to models and peers among adolescent boys and girls. *Sex Roles*, *45*, 645–664.

Jones, P. R. M., Hunt, M. J., Brown, T. P. and Norgan, N. G. (1986). Waist–hip circumference ratio and its relation to age and overweight in British men. *Human Nutrition: Clinical Nutrition*, *40*, 239–247.

Jones, S. E. and Yarbrough, A. E. (1985). A naturalistic study of the meanings of touch. *Communication Monographs, 52*, 19–56.

Jorgensen, B. W. and Cervone, J. C. (1978). Affect enhancement in the pseudo recognition task. *Personality and Social Psychology Bulletin, 4*, 285–288.

Jourard, S. M. (1966). An exploratory study of body-accessibility. *British Journal of Social and Clinical Psychology, 5*, 221–231.

Judge, T. A. and Cable, D. M. (2004). The effect of physical height on workplace success and income: Preliminary test of a theoretical model. *Journal of Applied Psychology, 89*, 428–441.

Junqueira, L. C., Carneiro, J. and Kelley, R. O. (1995). *Basic histology* (8th edn). Norwalk CT: Appleton and Lange.

Kaplan, H. and Gangestad, S. (2005). Life history theory and evolutionary psychology. In D. M. Buss (Ed.), *The handbook of evolutionary psychology* (pp. 68–95). New York: Wiley.

Katz, A. M. and Hill, R. (1958). Residential propinquity and marital selection. *Marriage and Family Living, 20*, 27–35.

Kaye, S. A., Folsom, A. R., Prineas, R. J. and Gapstur, S. M. (1990). The association of body fat distribution with lifestyle and reproductive factors in a population study of post-menopausal women. *International Journal of Obesity, 14*, 583–591.

Keenan, K. (1996). Skin tones and physical features of blacks in magazine advertisements. *Journalism and Mass Communication Quarterly, 73*, 905–912.

Keith, V. M. and Herring, C. (1991). Skintone and stratification in the black community. *American Journal of Sociology, 97*, 760–778.

Kelley, H. H., Holmes, J. G., Kerr, N. L., Reis, H. T., Rusbult, C. E. and van Lange, P. A. M. (2003). *An atlas of interpersonal situations*. New York: Cambridge University Press.

Kenny, C. T. and Fletcher, D. (1973). Effects of beardedness on person perception. *Perceptual and Motor Skills, 37*, 413–414.

Kenrick, D. T. and Keefe, R. C. (1992). Age preferences in mates reflect sex differences in human reproductive strategies. *Behavioral and Brain Sciences, 15*, 75–133.

Kenrick, D. T., Keefe, R. C., Bryan, A., Barr, A. and Brown, S. (1995). Age preferences and mate choice among homosexuals and heterosexuals: A case for modular psychological mechanisms. *Journal of Personality and Social Psychology, 69*, 1166–1172.

Kenrick, D. T., Li, N. P. and Butner, J. (2003). Dynamical evolutionary psychology: Individual decision rules and emergent social norms. *Psychological Review, 110*, 3–28.

Kenrick, D. T., Sadalla, E. K., Groth, G. and Trost, M. R. (1990). Evolution, traits and the stages of human courtship: Qualifying the parental investment model. *Journal of Personality, 58*, 97–117.

Kenrick, D. T., Trost, M. R. and Sheets, V. L. (1996). Power, harassment, and trophy mates: The feminist advantages of an evolutionary perspective. In D. M. Buss and N. M. Malamuth (Eds.), *Sex, power and conflict: Evolutionary and feminist perspectives* (pp. 29–53). New York: Oxford University Press.

Kilbourne, J. (1994). Still killing us softly: Advertising and the obsession with thinness. In P. Fallon, M. A. Katzman and S. C. Wooley (Eds.), *Feminist perspectives on eating disorders* (pp. 395–418). New York: Guilford Press.

Kim, H. and Markus, H. R. (1999). Deviance or uniqueness, harmony or conformity? A cultural analysis. *Journal of Personality and Social Psychology, 77*, 785–800.

Kim, M. P. and Rosenberg, S. (1989). The effects of involvement on persuasion: A meta-analysis. *Psychological Bulletin, 106*, 290–314.

Kirchengast, S. and Huber, J. (1999). Body composition characteristics, sex hormone levels and circadian gonadotrophin fluctuations in infertile young women. *Collegium Anthropologicum, 23*, 407–423.

Kirkpatrick, M. and Ryan, M. J. (1991). The evolution of mating preferences and the paradox of the lek. *Nature, 350*, 33–38.

Kirschner, M. A. and Samojlik, E. (1991). Sex hormone metabolism in upper and lower body obesity. *International Journal of Obesity, 15*, 101–108.

Kissebah, A. H. and Krakower, G. R. (1994). Regional adiposity and mortality. *Physiological Review, 74*, 761–811.

Kitayama, S., Markus, H. R., Matsumoto, H. and Norasakkunkit, U. (1997). Individual and collective processes in the construction of the self: Self-enhancement in the United States and self-criticism in Japan. *Journal of Personality and Social Psychology, 72*, 1245–1267.

Kitcher, P. (1985). *Vaulting ambition: Sociobiology and the quest for human nature.* Cambridge, MA: MIT Press.

—— (2004). Evolutionary theory and the social uses of biology. *Biology and Philosophy, 19*, 1–15.

Kleck, R. E., Richardson, S. A. and Ronald, L. (1974). Physical appearance cues and interpersonal attraction in children. *Child Development, 45*, 305–310.

Klein, H. and Shiffman, K. S. (2006). Messages about physical attractiveness in animated cartoons. *Body Image: An International Journal of Research, 3*, 353–363.

Kleinke, C. L. (1986). Gaze and eye contact: A research review. *Psychological Bulletin, 100*, 78–100.

Kleinke, C. and Staneski, R. (1980). First impressions of female bust size. *Journal of Social Psychology, 110*, 123–134.

Kleinke, C. L., Bustos, A. A., Meeker, F. B. and Staneski, R. A. (1973). Effects of self-attributed and other-attributed gaze on interpersonal evaluations between males and females. *Journal of Experimental Social Psychology, 9*, 154–163.

Klohnen, E. C. and Mendelsohn, G. A. (1998). Partner selection for personality characteristics: A couple-centred approach. *Personality and Social Psychology Bulletin, 24*, 268–278.

Knapp, M. L. (1978). *Nonverbal communication in human interaction* (2nd edn). New York: Holt, Rinehart and Winston.

Kniffin, K. M. and Wilson, D. S. (2004). The effect of non-physical traits on the perception of physical attractiveness: Three naturalistic studies. *Evolution and Human Behavior, 25*, 88–101.

Knight, D., Davies, P., Swami, V. and Tovée, M. J. (2004). The relative contributions of body-mass index (BMI) and waist-to-hip ratio (WHR) on Samoan adolescent male perceptions of female attractiveness. *Archives of Disease in Childhood, 89* (Supplement 1), A17.

Koehler, N., Rhodes, G. and Simmons, L. W. (2002). Are human female preferences for symmetrical male faces enhanced when conception is likely? *Animal Behaviour, 64*, 233–238.

Koehler, N., Simmons, L. W., Rhodes, G. and Peters, M. (2004). The relationship between sexual dimorphism in human faces and fluctuating asymmetry. *Proceedings of the Royal Society of London B, 271* (Supplement 4), S233–236.

Koff, E. and Benevage, A. (1998). Breast size perception and satisfaction, body image,

188   *References*

188   *References*

and psychological functioning in Caucasian and Asian American college women. *Sex Roles*, *38*, 655–673.

Kokko, H. (2001). Fisherian and 'good genes' benefits of mate choice: How (not) to distinguish between them. *Ecology Letters*, *4*, 159–165.

Kokko, H., Brooks, R., Jennions, M. and Morley, J. (2003). The evolution of mate choice and mating biases. *Proceedings of the Royal Society of London B*, *270*, 653–664.

Kokko, H., Jennions, M. D. and Brooks, R. (2006). Unifying and testing models of sexual selection. *Annual Reviews of Ecology, Evolution and Systematics*, *37*, 43–66.

Kondrashov, A. S. and Kondrashov, F. A. (1999). Interactions among quantitative traits in the course of symaptric speciation. *Nature*, *400*, 351–354.

Kopelman, P. G. (2000). Obesity as a medical problem. *Nature*, *404*, 635–643.

Kosambi, D. and Raghavachari, D. (1962). Seasonal variation in the Indian birth rate. *Annals of Eugenics*, *16*, 173.

Kraig, K. A. and Keel, P. K. (2001). Weight-based stigmatization in children. *International Journal of Obesity*, *25*, 1661–1666.

Krauss, R. M., Freyberg, R. and Morsella, E. (2002). Inferring speakers' physical attributes from their voices. *Journal of Experimental Social Psychology*, *38*, 618–625.

Krusse, M. I. and Fromme, K. (2005). Influence of physical attractiveness and alcohol on men's perceptions of potential sexual partners and sexual behavior intentions. *Experimental and Clinical Psychopharmacology*, *13*, 146–156.

Kulka, R. A. and Kessler, J. D. (1978). Is justice really blind? The influence of litigant physical attractiveness on juridical judgements. *Journal of Applied Social Psychology*, *8*, 366–381.

Kurtz, D. L. (1969). Physical appearance and stature: Important variables in sales recruiting. *Personnel Journal*, *48*, 981–983.

LaFrance, M. and Mayo, C. (1976). Racial differences in gaze behavior during conversations: Two systematic observational studies. *Journal of Personality and Social Psychology*, *33*, 547–552.

Lake, J. K., Power, C. and Cole, T. J. (1997). Women's reproductive health: The role of body mass index in early and adult life. *International Journal of Obesity*, *21*, 432–438.

Lakkis, J., Ricciardelli, L. A. and Williams, R. J. (1999). Role of sexual orientation and gender-related traits in disordered eating. *Sex Roles*, *41*, 1–16.

Landy, D. and Sigall, H. (1974). Beauty is talent: Task evaluation as a function of the performer's physical attractiveness. *Journal of Personality and Social Psychology*, *29*, 299–304.

Lane, I. M. and Messé, L. A. (1971). Equity and the distribution of rewards. *Journal of Personality and Social Psychology*, *20*, 1–17.

Langlois, J., Ritter, J., Casey, R. and Swain, D. (1995). Infant attractiveness predicts maternal behaviors and attitudes. *Developmental Psychology*, *31*, 464–472.

Langlois, J. H., Kalakanis, L. E., Rubenstein, A. J., Larson, A. D., Hallam, M. J. and Smoot, M. T. (2000). Maxims and myths of beauty: A meta-analytic and theoretical review. *Psychological Bulletin*, *126*, 390–423.

Langlois, J. H., Ritter, J. M., Roggman, L. A. and Vaughn, L. S. (1991). Facial diversity and infant preferences for attractive faces. *Developmental Psychology*, *27*, 79–84.

Lanska, D. J., Lanska, M. J., Hartz, A. J. and Rimm, A. A. (1985). Factors influencing anatomical location of fat tissue in 52,953 women. *International Journal of Obesity*, *9*, 29–38.

Latner, J. D. and Stunkard, A. J. (2003). Getting worse: The stigmatization of obese children. *Obesity Research, 11*, 452–456.

Lauer, R. H. and Lauer, J. C. (1994). *Marriage and family: The quest for intimacy.* Madison: Brown and Benchmark.

Laurenceau, J. P., Barrett, L. F. and Peitromonaco, P. R. (1998). Intimacy as an interpersonal process: The importance of self-disclosure, partner disclosure and perceived partner responsiveness in interpersonal exchanges. *Journal of Personality and Social Psychology, 74*, 1238–1251.

LaVelle, M. (1995). Natural selection and developmental sexual variation in the human pelvis. *American Journal of Physical Anthropology, 98*, 59–72.

Lavrakas, P. J. (1975). Female preferences for male physique. *Journal of Research in Personality, 9*, 324–334.

Lawson, E. D. (1971). Hair color, personality, and the observer. *Psychological Reports, 28*, 311–322.

Lean, M. E., Han, T. S. and Morrison, C. E. (1995). Waist circumference as a measure for indicating need for weight management. *British Medical Journal, 311*, 158–161.

Lee, K., Gray, E. and Mahler, H. I. (2004). Effects of magazine ads on mood and attitudes toward tanning. Paper presented at the Annual Meeting of the Society for Behavioural Medicine.

Lee, S. (1996). Reconsidering the status of anorexia nervosa as a western culture-bound syndrome. *Social Science and Medicine, 42*, 21–34.

—— (1998). Global modernity and eating disorders in Asia. *European Eating Disorders Review, 6*, 151–153.

Lee, S. and Lee, A. M. (2000). Disordered eating in three communities of China: A comparative study of female high school students in Hong Kong, Shenzhen, and rural Hunan. *International Journal of Eating Disorders, 27*, 317–327.

Le Grand, R., Mondloch, C. J., Maurer, D. and Brent, P. (2001). Early visual experience and face processing. *Nature, 410*, 890.

Leit, R. A., Pope, Jr., H. G. and Gray, J. J. (2001). Cultural expectations of muscularity in men: The evolution of *Playgirl* centrefolds. *International Journal of Eating Disorders, 29*, 90–93.

Leitch, I. (1951). Growth and health. *British Journal of Nutrition, 5*, 142–151.

Leong, A. (2006). Sexual dimorphism of the pelvic architecture: A struggling response to destructive and parsimonious forces by natural and mate selection. *McGill Journal of Medicine, 9*, 61–66.

Lerner, R. M. (1969). The development of stereotyped expectancies of body build–behaviour relations. *Child Development, 40*, 137–141.

Leroi-Gourhan, A. (1968). *The art of prehistoric man in western Europe.* London: Thames and Hudson.

Leslie, M. (1995). Slow fade to advertising in *Ebony* magazine, 1957–1989. *Journalism and Mass Communication Quarterly, 72*, 426–435.

Lester, D. and Sheehan, D. (1980). Attitudes of supervisor toward short police officers. *Psychological Reports, 47*, 462.

Leung, F., Lam, S. and Sze, S. (2001). Cultural expectations of thinness in Chinese women. *Eating Disorders, 9*, 339–350.

Levesque, M. J. and Vichesky, D. R. (2006). Raising the bar on the body beautiful: An analysis of the body image concerns on homosexual men. *Body Image: An International Journal of Research, 3*, 45–55.

Lévi-Strauss, C. (1963). *Structural anthropology*. New York: Basic Books.

Levine, M. P. and Smolak, L. (1996). Media as a context for the development of disordered eating. In L. Smolak, M. P. Levine and R. Strigel-Moore (Eds.), *The developmental psychopathology of eating disorders: Implications for research, prevention and treatment* (pp. 235–257). Mahwah, NJ: Lawrence Erlbaum Associates, Inc.

Lewontin, R. C. (1978). Adaptation. *Scientific American, 239*, 156–169.

Li, N. P., Bailey, J. M., Kenrick, D. T. and Linsenmeier, J. A. (2002). The necessities and luxuries of mate preferences: Testing the tradeoffs. *Journal of Personality and Social Psychology, 82*, 947–955.

Little, A. C., Burt, D. M., Penton-Voak, I. S. and Perrett, D. I. (2001). Self-perceived attractiveness influences human female preferences for sexual dimorphism and symmetry in male faces. *Proceedings of the Royal Society of London B, 268*, 39–44.

Little, A. C., Penton-Voak, I. S., Burt, D. M. and Perrett, D. I. (2003). Investigating an imprinting-like phenomenon in humans: Partners and opposite-sex parents have similar hair and eye colour. *Evolution and Human Behavior, 24*, 43–51.

Liu, J. H., Campbell, S. M. and Condie, H. (1995). Ethnocentrism in dating preferences for an American sample: The ingroup bias in social context. *European Journal of Social Psychology, 25*, 95–115.

Loh, E. S. (1993). The economic effects of physical appearance. *Social Science Quarterly, 71*, 130–141.

Lombroso, C. (1895). Criminal anthropology. *The Forum, 20*, 33–49.

Lorenzi-Cioldi, F. and Clémence, A. (2001). Group processes and the construction of social representations. In M. A. Hogg and R. S. Tindale (Eds.), *Blackwell handbook of social psychology: Group processes* (pp. 311–333). Oxford: Blackwell.

Lott, A. J. and Lott, B. E. (1972). The power of liking: Consequences of interpersonal attitudes derived from a liberalized view of secondary reinforcement. In L. Berkowitz (Ed.), *Advances in experimental social psychology* (Vol. 6, pp. 109–148). New York: Academic Press.

—— (1974). The role of reward in the formation of positive interpersonal attitudes. In T. L. Huston (Ed.), *Foundations of interpersonal attraction* (pp. 171–189). New York: Academic Press.

Louie, K (2002). *Theorising Chinese masculinity: Society and gender in China*. Cambridge: Cambridge University Press.

Love, B. (1994). *The encyclopedia of unusual sexual practises*. London: Barricade Books.

Low, B. S. (1979). Sexual selection and human ornamentation. In N. A. Chagnon and W. Irons (Eds.), *Evolutionary biology and human social behavior*. North Scituate, MA: Duxbury.

Lundy, D. E., Tan, J. and Cunningham, M. R. (1998). Heterosexual romantic preferences: The importance of humor and physical attractiveness for different types of relationships. *Personal Relationships, 5*, 311–325.

Luo, S. and Klohnen, E. C. (2005). Assortative mating and marital quality in newlyweds: A couple-centered approach. *Journal of Personality and Social Psychology, 88*, 304–326.

Luszyk, D. (2001). Gender-specific mating preferences: A contribution to the discussion between evolutionary psychology and social role theory. *Zeitschrift fuer Sozialpsychologie, 32*, 95–106.

Lynch, S. M. and Zellner, D. A. (1999). Figure preferences in two generations of men:

The use of figure drawings illustrating differences in muscle mass. *Sex Roles*, *40*, 833–843.

Lytton, H. and Romney, D. M. (1991). Parents' differential socialization of boys and girls: A meta-analysis. *Psychological Bulletin*, *109*, 267–296.

McArthur, L. and Ross, J. (1997). Attitudes of registered dietitians toward personal overweight and overweight clients. *Journal of the American Dietetic Association*, *97*, 63 66.

McBurney, D. H. and Streeter, S. A. (2007). Waist-to-hip ratios and female attractiveness: Comparing apples, oranges, and pears. In. V. Swami and A. Furnham (Eds.), *The body beautiful: Evolutionary and socio-cultural perspectives*. London: Macmillan.

McClelland, D. C. (1985). *Human motivation*. Glenview, IL: Scott, Foresman.

McCreary, D. R. and Sadava, S. W. (2001). Gender differences in relationships among perceived attractiveness, life satisfaction and health in adults as a function of body mass index and perceived weight. *Psychology of Men and Masculinity*, *2*, 108–116.

McCreary, D. R. and Sasse, D. K. (2000). Exploring the drive for muscularity in adolescent boys and girls. *Journal of American College Health*, *48*, 297–304.

—— (2002). Gender differences in high school students' dieting behavior and their correlates. *International Journal of Men's Health*, *1*, 195–213.

McCreary, D. R., Saucier, D. M. and Courtenay, W. H. (2005). The drive for muscularity and masculinity: Testing the associations among gender-role traits, behaviors, attitudes, and conflict. *Psychology of Men and Masculinity*, *6*, 83–94.

McGarvey, S. (1991). Obesity in Samoans and a perspective in its aetiology in Polynesians. *American Journal of Clinical Nutrition*, *53*, 86–94.

McGraw, K. J. (2002). Environmental predictors of geographic variation in human mating preferences. *Ethology*, *108*, 303–317.

McKeigue, P. M., Shah, B. and Marmot, M. G. (1991). Relation of central adiposity and insulin resistance with high diabetes prevalence and cardiovascular risk in South Asians. *Lancet*, *337*, 382–386.

McLain, D. K., Setters, D., Moulton, M. P. and Pratt, A. E. (2000). Ascription of resemblance of newborns by parents and non-relatives. *Evolution and Human Behavior*, *21*, 11–23.

McLellan, B. and McKelvie, S. J. (1993). Effects of age and gender on perceived facial attractiveness. *Canadian Journal of Behavioral Science*, *25*, 135–142.

Maddox, K. (2004). Perspectives on racial phenotypicality bias. *Personality and Social Psychology Review*, *8*, 383–401.

Maier, R. and Lavrakas, P. J. (1984). Attitudes towards women, personality rigidity, and idealized physique preferences in males. *Sex Roles*, *11*, 425–433.

Maisey, D. M., Vale, E. L. E., Cornelissen, P. L. and Tovée, M. J. (1999). Characteristics of male attractiveness for women. *Lancet*, *353*, 1500.

Malcom, L. W. G. (1925). Note on the seclusion of girls among the Efik at Old Calabar. *Man*, *25*, 113–114.

Malina, R. M., Katzmarzyk, P. T., Song, T. M. K., Theriault, G. and Bouchard, C. (1997). Somatype and cardiovascular risk factors of healthy adults. *American Journal of Human Biology*, *9*, 11–19.

Malkin, A. R., Wornian, K. and Chrisler, J. C. (1999). Women and weight: Gendered messages on magazine covers. *Sex Roles*, *40*, 647–655.

Malson, H. (1998). *The thin woman: Feminism, post-structuralism and the social psychology of anorexia nervosa*. London: Routledge.

Mann, J. (2003, October 26). The uncovered poll. *Observer*.

Manning, J. T., Anderton, K. and Washington, S. M. (1996). Women's waist and the sex ratio of their progeny: Evolutionary aspects of the ideal female body shape. *Journal of Human Evolution*, *31*, 41–47.

Manning, J. T., Bundred, P. E. and Mather, F. M. (2004). Second to fourth digit ratio, sexual selection, and skin colour. *Evolution and Human Behavior*, *25*, 38–50.

Manning, J. T., Trivers, R. L., Singh, D. and Thornhill, A. (1999). The mystery of female beauty. *Nature*, *399*, 214–215.

Manson, J. E., Willet, W. C., Stampfer, M. J., Colditz, G. A, Hunter, D. J., Hankinson, S. E. *et al.* (1995). Body weight and mortality among women. *New England Journal of Medicine*, *333*, 677–685.

Markus, H. and Kitayama, S. (1991). Culture and the self: Implications for cognition, emotion and motivation. *Psychological Review*, *98*, 224–253.

Marlowe, F. (1998). The nubility hypothesis: The human breast as an honest signal of residual reproductive value. *Human Nature*, *9*, 263–271.

Marlowe, F. (2005). Hunter-gatherers and human evolution. *Evolutionary Anthropology*, *14*: 54–67.

Marlowe, F. and Wetsman, A. (2001). Preferred waist-to-hip ratio and ecology. *Personality and Individual Differences*, *30*, 481–489.

Marlowe, F. W., Apicella, C. L. and Reed, D. (2005). Men's preferences for women's profile waist-hip-ratio in two societies. *Evolution and Human Behavior*, *26*, 458–468.

Maroney, D. and Golub, S. (1992). Nurses' attitudes toward obese persons and certain ethnic groups. *Perceptual and Motor Skills*, *75*, 387–391.

Martel, L. F. and Billier, H. B. (1987). *Stature and stigma*. Lexington, MA: Lexington Books.

Marti, B., Tuomilehto, J., Saloman, V., Kartovaara, H. J. and Pietinen, P. (1991). Body fat distribution in the Finnish population: Environmental determinants and predictive power for cardiovascular risk factor level. *Journal of Epidemiology and Community Health*, *45*, 131–137.

Martz, J. M., Verette, J., Arriaga, X. B., Slovic, L. F., Cox, C. L. and Rusbult, C. E. (1998). Positive illusion in close relationships. *Personal Relationships*, *5*, 159–181.

Massara, E. B. (1980). Obesity and cultural weight evaluation. *Appetite*, *1*, 291–298.

——— (1989). *Que Gordita! A study of weight among women in a Puerto Rican community*. New York: AMS Press.

Mazella, R. and Feingold, A. (1994). The effect of physical attractiveness, race, socioeconomic status, and gender of defendants and victims on judgements of mock jurors: A meta-analysis. *Journal of Applied Social Psychology*, *24*, 1315–1344.

Mazur, A. (1986). US trends in feminine beauty and overadaptation. *Journal of Sex Research*, *22*, 281–303.

Mazur, A., Mazur, J. and Keating, C. F. (1984). Military rank attainment of a West Point class: Effects of cadets' physical features. *American Journal of Sociology*, *90*, 125–150.

Messner, M. A. and Sabo, D. F. (1994). *Sex, violence and power in sports: Rethinking masculinity*. Freedom, CA: The Crossing Press.

Mikash, S. H. and Bailey, J. M. (1999). What distinguished women with high numbers of sex partners? *Evolution and Human Behavior*, *20*, 141–150.

Miller, A. G., Ashton, W. A., McHoskey, J. W. and Gimbel, J. (1990). What price attractiveness? Stereotype and risk factors in suntanning behavior. *Journal of Applied Social Psychology*, *23*, 1390–1406.

Miller, G. F. (1993). Evolution of the human brain through runaway sexual selection: The mind as a Protean courtship device. PhD thesis, Stanford University Psychology Department.

—— (1998). How mate choice shaped human nature: A review of sexual selection and human evolution. In C. Crawford and D. L. Krebs (Eds.), *Handbook of evolutionary psychology: Ideas, issues and applications* (pp. 87–129). Mahwah, NJ: Lawrence Erlbaum Associates, Inc.

Miller, L. C., Berg, J. H. and Archer, R. L. (1983). Openers: Individuals who elicit intimate self-disclosure. *Journal of Personality and Social Psychology, 44*, 1234–1244.

Millner, V. S. and Eichold, B. H. (2001). Body piercing and tattooing perspectives. *Clinical Nursing Research, 10*, 424–441.

Mishkind, M. E., Rodin, J., Silberstein, L. R. and Striegel-Moore, R. H. (1986). The embodiment of masculinity: Cultural, psychological and behavioral dimensions. *American Behavioral Scientist, 29*, 545–562.

Misra, A. and Vikram, N. (2003). Clinical and pathophysiological consequences of abdominal adiposity and abdominal adipose tissue depots. *Nutrition, 19*, 456–457.

Miyake, K. and Zuckerman, M. (1993). Beyond personality impressions: Effects of physical and vocal attractiveness on false consensus, social comparison, affiliation, and assumed and perceived similarity. *Journal of Personality, 61*, 411–437.

Mobius, M. M. and Rosenblatt, T. S. (2006). Why beauty matters. *American Economic Review, 96*, 222–235.

Mohanty, C., Prasad, R., Reddy, A. S., Ghosh, J. K., Singh, T. B. and Das, B. K. (2006). Maternal anthropometry as predictors of low birth weight. *Journal of Tropical Pediatrics, 52*, 24–29.

Molarius, A., Seidell, J. C., Sans, S., Tuomilehto, J. R. and Kuulasmaa, K. (1999). Waist and hip circumference, and waist-to-hip ratio in 19 populations of WHO MONICA Project. *International Journal of Obesity, 23*, 116–125.

Møller, A. P. (1988). Female choice selects for male sexual tail ornaments in the monogamous swallow. *Nature, 332*, 640–642.

—— (1991). Sexual selection in the monogamous barn swallow (*Hirundo rustica*): I. Determinants of tail ornament size. *Evolution, 45*, 1823–1836.

—— (1992). Female swallow preference for symmetrical male sexual ornaments. *Nature, 357*, 238–240.

—— (1996). Developmental stability of flowers, embryo abortion, and developmental stability of plants. *Proceedings of the Royal Society of London B, 263*, 53–56.

Møller, A. P. and Swaddle, J. P. (1997). *Asymmetry, developmental stability, and evolution.* Oxford: Oxford University Press.

Møller, A. P and Thornhill, R. (1998). Bilateral symmetry and sexual selection: A meta-analysis. *American Naturalist, 151*, 174–192.

Monaghan, L. F. (2005). Big handsome men, bears and others: Virtual constructions of 'fat male embodiment.' *Body and Society, 11*, 81–111.

Montagna, W. (1983). The evolution of human skin. *Journal of Human Evolution, 14*, 3–22.

Moreland, R. L. and Beach, S. R. (1992). Exposure effects in the classroom: The development of affinity among students. *Journal of Experimental Social Psychology, 28*, 255–276.

Morris, A., Cooper, T. and Cooper, P. J. (1989). The changing shape of female fashion models. *International Journal of Eating Disorders, 8*, 593–596.

Morris, D. (1978). *Manwatching*. London: Grafton Books.

—— (1987). *Bodywatching*. London: Grafton Books.

Morrison, M. A., Morrison, T. G. and Sager, C.-L. (2004). Does body satisfaction differ between gay men and lesbian women and heterosexual men and women? A meta-analytic review. *Body Image: An International Journal of Research, 1*, 127–138.

Morry, M. M. and Staska, S. L. (2001). Magazine exposure: Internalization, self-objectification, eating attitudes, and body satisfaction in male and female university students. *Canadian Journal of Behavioural Sciences, 33*, 269–279.

Moscovici, S. (1961). *La psychoanalyse: Son image et son public*. Paris: Presses Universitaires de France.

—— (1981). On social representation. In J. P. Forgas (Ed.), *Social cognition: Perspectives on everyday understanding* (pp. 181–209). London: Academic Press.

—— (1983). The phenomenon of social representations. In R. M. Farr and S. Moscovici (Eds.), *Social representations* (pp. 3–69). Cambridge: Cambridge University Press.

—— (1988). Notes towards a description of social representations. *European Journal of Social Psychology, 18*, 211–250.

Mueser, K. T., Grau, B. W., Sussman, S. and Rosen, A. J. (1984). You're only as pretty as you feel: Facial expression as a determinant of physical attractiveness. *Journal of Personality and Social Psychology, 46*, 469–478.

Murray, S. H., Touyz, S. W. and Beumont, P. J. V. (1996). Awareness and perceived influence of body ideals in the media: A comparison of eating disorder patients and the general community. *Eating Disorders: The Journal of Treatment and Prevention, 4*, 33–46.

Murray, S. L. and Holmes, J. G. (1997). A leap of faith? Positive illusions in romantic relationships. *Personality and Social Psychology Bulletin, 23*, 586–604.

Murstein, B. I. (1972). Physical attractiveness and marital choice. *Journal of Personality and Social Psychology, 22*, 8–12.

Musimeci, C. and Shahani-Denning, C. (1996). Self-monitoring: Impact on applicant attractiveness and selection decisions. Paper presented at the annual convention of the Society for Industrial and Organizational Psychology, San Diego, April.

Mvo, Z., Dick, J. and Steyn, K. (1999). Perceptions of overweight African women about acceptable body size of women and children. *Curatonis, 22*, 27–31.

Myers, D. (1996). *Social psychology*. New York: McGraw Hill.

Nasser, M. (1988). Eating disorders: The cultural dimension. *Social Psychiatry and Psychiatric Epidemiology, 23*, 184–187.

National Heart, Lung and Blood Institute (1998). *Clinical guidelines on the identification, evaluation and treatment of overweight and obesity in adults: The evidence report* (NIH Publication no. 98 – 4083). Bethesda, MD: National Institute of Health.

Nelson, L. D. and Morrison, E. L. (2005). The symptoms of resource scarcity: Judgements of food and finances influence preference for potential partners. *Psychological Science, 16*, 167–173.

Nelson, L. D., Pettijohn, T. F. and Galak, J. (2007). Mate preferences in a social cognitive context: When environmental and personal change leads to predictable cross-cultural variation. In V. Swami and A. Furnham (Eds.), *The body beautiful: Evolutionary and socio-cultural perspectives*. London: Macmillan.

Nelson, S. M. (1997). *Gender in archaeology: Analyzing power and prestige*. Walnut Creek, CA: Altamira Press.

Nesse, R. M., Silverman, A. and Bortz, A. (1990). Sex differences in ability to recognize family resemblance. *Ethology and Sociobiology, 11,* 11–21.

Nettle, D. (2002a). Height and reproductive success in a cohort of British men. *Human Nature, 13,* 473–491.

—— (2002b). Women's height, reproductive success and the evolution of sexual dimorphism in modern humans. *Proceedings of the Royal Society of London B, 269,* 1919–1923.

Newcomb, T. M. (1961). *The acquaintance process.* New York: Holt, Rinehart and Winston.

Noller, P. (1984). *Nonverbal communication and marital interaction.* Oxford: Pergamon Press.

Noor, F. and Evans, D. C. (2003). The effect of facial symmetry on perceptions of personality and attractiveness. *Journal of Research in Personality, 37,* 339–347.

Norris, M. L., Boydell, K. M., Pinhas, L. and Katzman, D. B. (2006). Ana and the internet: A review of pro-anorexia websites. *International Journal of Eating Disorders, 39,* 443–447.

Norton, K. I., Olds, T. S., Olive, S. and Dank, S. (1996). Ken and Barbie at life size. *Sex Roles, 34,* 287–294.

Oda, R., Matsumoto-Oda, A. and Kurashima, A. (2002). Facial resemblance of Japanese children to their parents. *Journal of Ethology, 20,* 81–85.

O'Dea, J. A. and Rawsthorne, P. R. (2001). Male adolescents identify their weight gain practices, reasons for desired weight gain, and sources of weight gain information. *Journal of the American Dietetic Association, 101,* 105–107.

O'Hara, M. D. (1996). Please weight to be seated: Recognizing obesity as a disability to prevent discrimination in public accommodations. *Whittier Law Review, 17,* 895–954.

Ojerholm, A. and Rothblum, E. (1999). The relationships of body image, feminism, and sexual orientation in college women. *Feminism and Psychology, 9,* 431–438.

Oliver, D. (1974). *Ancient Tahitian society.* Honolulu: University of Hawaii Press.

Osborn, D. R. (2004). A biological, cultural and interactional (BIC) model of physical attractiveness judgements. Poster presented at the 16th Annual Convention of the American Psychological Society, Chicago, May 27–30.

—— (2006). Historico-cultural factors in beauty judgments: 16th-century courtesans judged against 21st-century media ideals. Poster presented at the Annual Meeting of the Association for Psychological Science, New York, May 28–31.

Oskamp, S. (1977). *Attitudes and opinions.* Englewood Cliffs, NJ: Prentice Hall.

Owen, P. R. and Laurel-Seller, E. (2000). Weight and shape ideals: Thin is dangerously in. *Journal of Applied Social Psychology, 30,* 979–990.

Pagan, J. A. and Davila, A. (1997). Obesity, occupational attainment, and earnings. *Social Sciences Quarterly, 78,* 756–770.

Palmer, J. A. and Palmer, L. K. (2002). *Evolutionary psychology: The ultimate origins of human behavior.* Boston, MA: Allyn and Bacon.

Pancer, S. M. and Meindl, J. R. (1978). Length of hair and beardedness as determinants of personality impressions. *Perceptual and Motor Skills, 46,* 1328–1330.

Park, B. (1986). A method for studying the development of impressions of real people. *Journal of Personality and Social Psychology, 51,* 907–917.

Parsons, J. H. (Ed.) (1980). *The psychobiology of sex differences and sex roles.* Washington, DC: Hemisphere.

Pasquali, R., Gambineri, A., Anconetani, B., Vicennati, V., Colitta, D., Caramelli, E. *et al.* (1999). The natural history of the metabolic syndrome in young women with the polycystic ovary syndrome and the effect on long-term oestrogen-progestagen treatment. *Clinical Endocrinology, 50,* 517–527.

Passemard, L. (1938). *Les statuettes féminines Paléolithiques dites Vénus stéatopyges.* Nîmes: Teissier.

Patterson, M. L. (1983). *Nonverbal behavior: A functional perspective.* New York: Springer.

Patzer, G. L. (1985). *Physical attractiveness phenomena.* New York: Plenum Press.

—— (2002). *The power and paradox of physical attractiveness.* Boca Raton, FL: Brown Walker Press.

—— (2006). *The power and paradox of physical attractiveness.* Boca Raton, FL: Brown Walker Press.

Paunonen, S. V. (2006). You are honest, therefore I like you and find you attractive. *Journal of Research in Personality, 40,* 237–249.

Pawłowski, B. (2001). The evolution of gluteal/femoral fat deposits and balance during pregnancy in bipedal *Homo. Current Anthropology, 42,* 572–574.

—— (2003). Variable preferences for sexual dimorphism in height as a strategy for increasing the pool of potential partners in humans. *Proceedings of the Royal Society of London B, 270,* 709–712.

Pawłowski, B. and Dunbar, R. I. M. (1999). Impact of market value on human mate choice decisions. *Proceedings of the Royal Society of London B, 266,* 281–285.

—— (2005). Waist-to-hip ratio versus body mass index as predictors of fitness in women. *Human Nature, 16,* 164–177.

Pawłowski, B. and Grabarczyk, M. (2003). Center of body mass and the evolution of female body shape. *American Journal of Biology, 15,* 144–150.

Pawłowski, B. and Koziel, S. (2002). The impact of traits offered in personal advertisements on response rates. *Evolution and Human Behavior, 23,* 139–149.

Pawłowski, B., Dunbar, R. I. M. and Lipowicz, A. (2000). Tall men have more reproductive success. *Nature, 403,* 156.

Pei, M. (1965). *The story of language* (2nd edn). Philadelphia, PA: Lippincott.

Peixoto Labre, M. (2002). Adolescent boys and the muscular male body ideal. *Journal of Adolescent Health, 30,* 233–242.

Pellegrini, R. J. (1973). Impressions of male personality as a function of beardedness. *Psychology, 10,* 29–33.

Pennebaker, J. W. (1979). Don't the girls get prettier at closing time: A country and western application to psychology. *Personality and Social Psychology Bulletin, 5,* 122–125.

Penton-Voak, I. S. and Perrett, D. I. (2000). Consistency and individual differences in facial attractiveness judgements: An evolutionary perspective. *Social Research, 67,* 219–245.

Penton-Voak, I. S., Jones, B. C., Little, A. C., Baker, S., Tiddeman, B., Burt, D. M. *et al.* (2001) Symmetry, sexual dimorphism in facial proportions, and male facial attractiveness. *Proceedings of the Royal Society of London B, 268,* 1617–1623.

Penton-Voak, I. S., Perrett, D. I., Castles, D., Burt, M., Kobayashi, T. and Murray, L. K. (1999a). Female preference for male faces changes cyclically. *Nature, 399,* 741 742.

Penton-Voak, I. S., Perrett, D. I. and Pierce, J. (1999b). Computer graphic studies of the role of facial similarity in attractiveness judgements. *Current Psychology, 18,* 104–117.

Perez, M. and Joiner, T. E., Jr. (2003). Body image dissatisfaction and disordered eating in black and white women. *International Journal of Eating Disorders, 33*, 342–350.

Perlman, D. and Peplau, L. A. (1998). Loneliness. *Encyclopedia of mental health* (Vol. 2, pp. 571–581). New York: Academic Press.

Perrett, D. I., Burt, D. M., Penton-Voak, I. S. and Lee, K. J. (1999). Symmetry and human facial attractiveness. *Evolution and Human Behavior, 20*, 295–307.

Perret, D. I., Lee, K. J., Penton-Voak, I., Rowland, D., Yoshikawa, S., Burt, D. M. *et al.* (1998). Effects of sexual dimorphism on facial attractivenes. *Nature, 394*, 884–887.

Peterkin, A. (2001). *One thousand beards: A cultural history of facial hair.* London: Arsenal Pulp Press.

Peterson, K. and Curran, J. P. (1976). Trait attribution as a function of hair length and correlates of subjects' preference for hair style. *Perceptual and Motor Skills, 46*, 1328–1330.

Petrie, M. (1992). Peacocks with low mating success are more likely to suffer predation. *Animal Behavior, 44*, 585–586.

Petrie, M., Halliday, T. and Sanders, C. (1991). Peahens prefer peacocks with elaborate trains. *Animal Behavior, 41*, 323–331.

Petrie, T. A., Austin, L. J., Crowley, B. J., Helmcamp, A., Johnson, C. E., Lester, R. *et al.* (1996). Sociocultural expectations of attractiveness for males. *Sex Roles, 35*, 581–602.

Pettijohn II, T. F. and Tesser, A. (1999). An investigation of popularity in environmental context: Facial feature assessment of American movie actresses. *Media Psychology, 1*, 229–247.

Pettijohn II, T. F., and Yerkes, M. E. (2004). Miss America facial and body feature changes across social and economic conditions. Paper presented at the 16th Annual American Psychological Society Convention. Chicago, IL, May.

—— (2005). Miss Hong Kong facial and body feature changes across social and economic conditions and time. Paper presented at the 17th Annual American Psychological Society Convention. Los Angeles, CA, May.

Phillips, K. A. and Diaz, S. F. (1997). Gender differences in body dysmorphic disorder. *Journal of Nervous and Mental Disease, 185*, 570–577.

Pinel, J. (1993). *Biopsychology* (2nd edn). Toronto: Allyn and Bacon.

Pingitore, R., Spring, B. and Garfield, D. (1997). Gender differences in body satisfaction. *Obesity Research, 5*, 402–409.

Pinker, S. (1997). *How the mind works.* New York: Norton.

—— (2002). *The blank slate.* New York: Viking.

Pitts, V. (2003). *In the flesh: The cultural politics of body modification.* New York: Palgrave Macmillan.

Plautus, T. M. (*c.* 2 BC/1997). *Miles gloriosus.* Cambridge, MA: Harvard University Press.

Pleck, J. H. (1979). The male sex role: Definitions, problems, and sources of change. In J. H. Williams (Ed.), *Psychology of women.* New York: Norton.

—— (1987). *The myth of masculinity* (3rd edn). Cambridge, MA: MIT Press.

Pleck, J. H., Sonenstein, F. L. and Ku, L. C. (1994). Problem behaviours and masculinity ideology in adolescent males. In R. D. Ketterlinus and M. E. Lamb (Eds.), *Adolescent problem behaviours: Issues and research* (pp. 165–186). Hillsdale, NJ: Lawrence Erlbaum Associates, Inc.

198   *References*

Plotkin, H. (1994). *Darwin machines and the nature of knowledge*. Cambridge, MA: Harvard University Press.

—— (1997). *Evolution in mind: An introduction to evolutionary psychology*. London: Penguin.

Podratz, K. and Dipboye, R. L. (2002). In search of the 'beauty is beastly' effect. Paper presented at the annual convention of the Society for Industrial and Organizational Psychology, Toronto, April.

Polivy, J. and Herman, P. C. (1985). Dieting and binging. *American Psychologist, 40*, 193–201.

Polivy, J., Garner, D. M. and Garfinkel, P. E. (1986). Causes and consequences of the current preference for thin female physiques. In C. P. Herman, M. Zanna and E. T. Huggins (Eds.), *Physical appearance, stigma and social behavior* (pp. 89–112). Hillsdale, NJ: Lawrence Erlbaum Associates, Inc.

Pollock, N. J. (1995a). Social fattening patterns in the Pacific: The positive side of obesity: A Nauru case study. In I. De Gerine and N. J. Pollock (Eds.), *Social aspects of obesity* (pp. 87–110). Amsterdam: Gordon and Breach.

—— (1995b). Cultural elaborations of obesity: Fattening processes in Pacific societies. *Asia Pacific Journal of Clinical Nutrition, 4*, 357–360.

Pond, C. M. (1981). Storage. In C. R. Townsend and P. Calow (Eds.), *Physiological ecology* (pp. 190–219). Sunderland, MS: Sinauer.

Pond, C. M. and Mattachs, C. A. (1987). The anatomy of adipose tissue in captive Macaca monkeys and its implications for human biology. *Folia Primatology, 48*, 164–185.

Pope, A. (1711). *An essay on criticism*. Online publication at: http://poetry.eserver.org. Last retrieved February 17, 2007.

Pope, H. G., Gruber, A. J., Mangweth, B., Bureau, B., deCol, C., Jouvent, R. *et al.* (2000). Body image perception among men in three countries. *American Journal of Psychiatry, 157*, 1297–1301.

Pope, H. G., Olivardia, R., Borowiecki, J. B. and Cohane, G. H. (2001). The growing commercial value of the male body: A longitudinal survey of advertising in women's magazines. *Psychotherapy and Psychosomatics, 70*, 189–192.

Pope, Jr., H. G., Olivardia, R., Gruber, A. and Borowiecki, J. (1999). Evolving ideals of male body image as seen through action toys. *International Journal of Eating Disorders, 26*, 65–72.

Pope Jr., H. G., Phillips, K. A., Olivardia, R. (2000). *The Adonis complex: How to identify, treat, and prevent body obsession in men and boys*. New York: Simon and Schuster.

Popenoe, R. (2003). *Feeding desire: Fatness and beauty in the Sahara*. London: Routledge.

Poran, M. A. (2002). Denying diversity: Perceptions of beauty and social comparison processes among Latina, Black and White women. *Sex Roles, 47*, 65–81.

Posavac, H. D., Posavac, S. S. and Weigel, R. G. (2001). Reducing the impact of media images on women at risk for body image disturbance: Three targeted interventions. *Journal of Social and Clinical Psychology, 20*, 324–340.

Powdermaker, H. (1960). An anthropological approach to the problem of obesity. *Bulletin of the New York Academy of Science, 36*, 286–295.

Price, J. H., Desmond, S. M., Krol, R. A., Snyder, F. F. and O'Connell, J. K. (1987). Family practise physicians' beliefs, attitudes and practises regarding obesity. *American Journal of Preventitive Medicine, 3*, 339–345.

Puhl, R. M. and Boland, F. J. (2001). Predicting female physical attractiveness: Waist-to-hip ratio versus thinness. *Psychology, Evolution and Gender*, *3*, 27–46.

Puhl, R. M. and Brownell, K. D. (2001). Bias, discrimination and obesity. *Obesity Research*, *9*, 788–805.

—— (2003). Psychosocial origins of obesity stigma: Toward changing a powerful and pervasive bias. *Obesity Reviews*, *4*, 213–227.

Purkhardt, S. C. (1995). *Transforming social representations*. London: Routledge.

Purvis, J. A., Dabbs, J. M. and Hopper, C. H. (1984). The 'opener': Skilled user of facial expression and speech pattern. *Personality and Social Psychology Bulletin*, *10*, 61–66.

Puts, D. A. (2005). Menstrual phase and mating context affects women's preferences for male voice pitch. *Evolution and Human Behavior*, *26*, 388–397.

Puts, D. A., Gaulin, S. J. C. and Verdolini, K. (2006). Dominance and the evolution of sexual dimorphism in human voice pitch. *Evolution and Human Behavior*, *27*, 283–296.

Ramachandran, V. S. (1997). Why do gentlemen prefer blondes? *Medical Hypotheses*, *48*, 19–20.

Randall, S. (1995). Low fertility in pastoral populations: Constraints or choice? In R. I. M. Dunbar (Ed.), *Human reproductive decisions: Biological and social aspects* (pp. 279–296). London: Macmillan.

Rebuffé-Scrive, M. (1988). Metabolic differences in deposits. In C. Bouchard and F. E. Johnston (Eds.), *Fat distribution during growth and later health outcomes* (pp. 163–173). New York: Alan R. Liss.

—— (1991). Neuroregulation of adipose tissue: Molecular and hormonal mechanisms. *International Journal of Obesity*, *15*, 83–86.

Reed, J. A. and Blunk, E. M. (1990). The influence of facial hair on impression formation. *Social Behavior and Personality*, *18*, 169–175.

Regan, P. C. (1998). What if you can't get what you want? Willingness to compromise ideal mate selection standards as a function of sex, mate value, and relationship context. *Personality and Social Psychology Bulletin*, *24*, 1294–1303.

Register, C. A. and Williams, D. R. (1990). Wage effects of obesity among young workers. *Social Science Quarterly*, *71*, 130–141.

Reid, R. L. and van Vugt, D. A. (1987). Weight related changes in reproductive function. *Fertility and Sterility*, *48*, 905–913.

Reischer, E. and Koo, K. S. (2004). The body beautiful: Symbolism and agency in the social world. *Annual Review of Anthropology*, *33*, 297–317.

Rempel, J. K., Ross, M. and Holmes, J. G. (2001). Trust and communicated attributions in close relationships. *Journal of Personality and Social Psychology*, *81*, 57–64.

Rentschler, I., Jüttner, M., Unzicker, A. and Landis, A. (1998). Facial symmetry and the perception of beauty. *Psychometric Bulletin and Review*, *5*, 659–669.

Rguibi, M. and Belahsen, R. (2006). Body size preferences and sociocultural influences on attitudes towards obesity among Moroccan Sahraoui women. *Body Image: An International Journal of Research*, *3*, 395–400.

Rhodes, G., Roberts, J. and Simmons, L. (1999). Reflections on symmetry and attractiveness. *Psychology, Evolution and Gender*, *1*, 279–295.

Rhodes, G., Yoshikawa, S., Clark, A., Lee, K., McKay, R. and Akamatsu, S. (2001a). Attractiveness of facial averageness and symmetry in non-western cultures: In search of biologically-based standards of beauty. *Perception*, *30*, 611–625.

Rhodes, G., Zebrowitz, L. A., Clark, A., Kalick, S M., Hightower, A. and McKay, R. (2001b). Do facial averageness and symmetry signal health? *Evolution and Human Behavior, 22*, 31–46.

Rhodes, G., Chan, J., Zebrowitz, L. A. and Simmons, L. (2003). Does sexual dimorphism in human faces signal health? *Proceedings of the Royal Society of London B, 266*, 2089–2093.

Ricciardelli, L. A. and McCabe, M. P. (2003). A longitudinal analysis of the role of biopsychosocial factors in predicting body change strategies among adolescent boys. *Sex Roles, 48*, 349–359.

Rice, P. C. (1982). Prehistoric Venuses: Symbols of motherhood or womanhood? *Journal of Anthropological Research, 37*, 402–414.

Rich, M. K. and Cash, T. F. (1993). The American image of beauty: Media representations of hair colour for four decades. *Sex Roles, 29*, 113–122.

Richardson, S. A., Goodman, N., Hastorf, A. H. and Dornbusch, S. M. (1961). Cultural uniformity in reaction to physical disabilities. *American Sociological Review, 26*, 241–247.

Riggio, R. E. (1986). Assessment of basic social skills. *Journal of Personality and Social Psychology, 51*, 649–660.

Riggio, R. E. and Friedman, H. S. (1986). Impression formation: The role of expressive behavior. *Journal of Personality and Social Psychology, 50*, 421–427.

Riggio, R. E. and Throckmorton, B. (1988). The relative effects of verbal and nonverbal behavior, appearance and social skills on evaluations made in hiring interviews. *Journal of Applied Social Psychology, 18*, 331–348.

Riggio, R. E., Friedman, H. S. and DiMatteo, M. R. (1981). Nonverbal greetings: Effects of the situation and personality. *Personality and Social Psychology Bulletin, 7*, 682–689.

Riggio, R. E., Widaman, K. F., Tucker, J. S. and Salinas, C. (1991). Beauty is more than skin deep: Components of attractiveness. *Basic and Applied Social Psychology, 12*, 423–439.

Rimé, B. (1983). Nonverbal communication or nonverbal behavior. In W. Doise and S. Moscovici (Eds.), *Current issues in European social psychology* (Vol. 1, pp. 85–141). Cambridge: Cambridge University Press.

Rittenbaugh, C. (1982). Obesity as a culture-bound syndrome. *Culture, Medicine and Psychiatry, 6*, 347–361.

—— (1991). Body size and shape: A dialogue of culture and biology. *Medical Anthropology, 13*, 173–180.

Roberts III, T. L. and Weinfield, A. B. (2005). 'Universal' and ethnic ideals of beautiful buttocks and how to create them surgically. Paper presented at the American Society for Aesthetic Plastic Surgery, New Orleans, Louisiana, April 30.

Rodin, J., Silberstein, L. and Striegel-Moore, R. (1984). Women and weight: A normative discontent. *Nebraska Symposium on Motivation, 32*, 267–307.

Roll, S. and Verinis, J. S. (1971). Stereotypes of scalp and facial hair as measured by the semantic differential. *Psychological Reports, 28*, 975–980.

Rolls, B. J., Fedoroff, I. C. and Guthrie, J. F. (1991). Gender differences in eating behaviour and body weight regulation. *Health Psychology, 10*, 133–142.

Rosenberg, S. (1977). New approaches to the analysis of personal constructs in person perception. In A. L. Land and J. K. Cole (Eds.), *Nebraska Symposium on Motivation 1976* (Vol. 24, pp. 179–242). Lincoln: University of Nebraska Press.

Rosenblatt, P. C. (1974). Cross-cultural perspective on attraction. In T. L. Huston (Ed.), *Foundations of interpersonal attraction.* New York: Academic Press.

Rosenblatt, P. C. and Cozby, P. C. (1972). Courtship patterns associated with freedom of choice of spouse. *Journal of Marriage and the Family, 34,* 689–695.

Rosenfeld, H. M. (1965). Effect of approval-seeking induction on interpersonal proximity. *Psychological Reports, 17,* 120–122.

Ross, C. E. and Mirowsky, J. (1983). The social epidemiology of overweight: A substantive and methodological investigation. *Journal of Health and Social Behavior, 24,* 288–298.

Ross, W. D. and Ward, R. (1982). Human proportionality and sexual dimorphism. In R. L. Hall (Ed.), *Sexual dimorphism in Homo sapiens: A question of size* (pp. 317–361). New York: Praeger.

Rowe, L. and Houle, D. (1996). The lex paradox and the capture of genetic variance by condition-dependent traits. *Proceedings of the Royal Society of London B, 263,* 1415–1421.

Rozmus-Wrzesinska, M. and Pawłowski, B. (2005). Men's ratings of female attractiveness are influenced more by changes in female waist size compared with changes in hip size. *Biological Psychology, 68,* 299–308.

Rubin, A. (1988). *Marks of civilization.* Los Angeles, CA: Museum of Cultural History.

Rubinstein, S. and Caballero, B. (2000). Is Miss America an undernourished role model? *Journal of the American Medical Association, 283,* 1569.

Rucas, S., Kaplan, H., Winking, J., Gurven, M., Gangestad, S. and Crespo, M. (2006). Female intrasexual competition and reputational effects on attractiveness among the Tsimane of Bolivia. *Evolution and Human Behavior, 27,* 40–52.

Rucker III, C. E. and Cash, T. F. (1992). Body images, body-size perceptions, and eating behaviour among African-Americans and white college women. *International Journal of Eating Disorders, 12,* 291–299.

Rusbult, C. E. and Buunk, B. R. (1993). Commitment processes in close relationships: An interdependence analysis. *Journal of Social and Personal Relationships, 10,* 175–204.

Rusbult, C. E., Drigotas, S. M. and Verette, J. (1994). The investment model: An interdependence analysis of commitment processes and relationship maintenance phenomena. In D. Canary and L. Stafford (Eds.), *Communication and relational maintenance* (pp. 115–139). San Diego, CA: Sage.

Rusbult, C. E., Verette, J., Whitney, G. A., Slovik, L. F. and Lipkus, I. (1991). Accommodation processes in close relationships: Theory and preliminary empirical evidence. *Journal of Personality and Social Psychology, 60,* 53–78.

Russell, C. J. and Keel, P. K. (2002). Homosexuality as a specific risk factor for eating disorders in men. *International Journal of Eating Disorders, 31,* 300–306.

Russell, K., Wilson, M. and Hall, R. (1992). *The color complex: The politics of skin color among African Americans.* New York: Harcourt Brace Jovanovich.

Russell, P. (1998). The palaeolithic mother-goddess: Fact or fiction? In K. Hays-Giplin and D. S. Whitley (Eds.), *Reader in gender archaeology* (pp. 261–268). London: Routledge.

Sabatelli, R. M. and Rubin, M. (1986). Nonverbal expressiveness and physical attractiveness as mediators of interpersonal perceptions. *Journal of Nonverbal Behavior, 10,* 120–133.

Sahay, S. and Piran, N. (1997). Skin-color preferences and body satisfaction among

South Asian Canadian and European-Canadian female university students. *Journal of Social Psychology*, *137*, 161–171.

Salusso-Deonier, C. J., Markee, N. L. and Pedersen, E. L. (1993). Gender differences in the evaluation of physical attractiveness ideals for male and female body builds. *Perceptual and Motor Skills*, *76*, 1155–1167.

Samaras, T. T., Elrick, H. and Storms, L. H. (1999). Is attainment of greater height and body size really desirable? *Journal of the National Medical Association*, *91*, 317–321.

Sandars, N. K. (1968). *Prehistoric art in Europe*. Baltimore, MA: Penguin.

Santrock, J. (1994). *Child development* (6th edn). Madison: Brown and Benchmark.

Sarwer, D. B., Grossbart, T. A. and Didie, E. R. (2002). Beauty and society. In M. S. Kaminer, J. S. Dover and K. A. Arndt (Eds.), *Atlas of cosmetic surgery* (pp. 48–59). Philadelphia: Saunders.

Scheib, J. E., Gangestad, S. W. and Thornhill, R. (1999). Facial attractiveness, symmetry and cues of good genes. *Proceedings of the Royal Society of London B*, *266*, 1318–1321.

Schmalt, H.-D. (2006). Waist-to-hip ratio and female physical attractiveness: The moderating role of power motivation and the mating context. *Personality and Individual Differences*, *41*, 455–465.

Schneider, D. J., Hastorf, A. H. and Ellsworth, P. C. (1979). *People perception*. Reading, MA: Addison-Wesley.

Schneider, J. A., O'Leary, A. and Jenkins, S. R. (1995). Gender, sexual orientation, and disordered eating. *Psychology and Health*, *10*, 113–128.

Schofield, W. (1964). *Psychotherapy: The purchase of friendship*. New York: Prentice Hall.

Schultz, A. H. (1969). *The life of primates*. New York: University Books.

Schweder, B. I. M. (1994). The impact of the face on long-term relationships. *Homo*, *45*, 74–93.

Scrimshaw, N. S. and Dietz, W. H. (1995). Potential advantages and disadvantages of human obesity. In I. De Gerine and N. J. Pollock (Eds.), *Social aspects of obesity* (pp. 147–162). Amsterdam: Gordon and Breach.

Seidell, J. C., Perusse, L., Despres, J. P. and Bouchard, C. (2001). Waist and hip circumferences have independent and opposite effects on cardiovascular disease risk factors: The Quebec Family Study. *American Journal of Clinical Nutrition*, *74*, 315–321.

Seifert, T. (2005). Anthropomorphic characteristics of centerfold models: Trends toward slender figures over time. *International Journal of Eating Disorders*, *37*, 271–274.

Shackelford, T. K. and Larsen, R. J. (1997). Facial asymmetry as an indicator of psychological, emotional and physiological distress. *Journal of Personality and Social Psychology*, *72*, 456–466.

Shaffer, D. R., Crepaz, N. and Sun, C.-R. (2000). Physical attractiveness stereotyping in cross-cultural perspective. *Journal of Cross-Cultural Psychology*, *31*, 557–582.

Shahani-Denning, C. and Plumitallo, D. (1993). The influence of physical attractiveness and gender on disciplinary decisions. Paper presented at the fifth annual convention of the American Psychological Society, Chicago.

Shahani-Denning, C., Dipboye, R. L. and Gehrlein, T. M. (1993). Attractiveness bias in the interview: Exploring the boundaries of an effect. *Basic and Applied Social Psychology*, *14*, 317–328.

Shakespeare, W. (1596/2003). *The merchant of Venice*. Online publication at: http://www.opensourceshakespeare.org. Last retrieved on February 2, 2007.

—— (1598/2003). *The passionate pilgrim*. Online publication at: http://www.open sourceshakespeare.org. Last retrieved on February 17, 2007.

Share, T. L. and Mintz, L. B. (2002). Differences between lesbians and heterosexual women in disordered eating and related attitudes. *Journal of Homosexuality*, *42*, 89–106.

Shaw, J. (1995). Effects of fashion magazines on body dissatisfaction and eating psychopathology in adolescent and adult females. *Eating Disorders Review*, *3*, 15–23.

Sheldon, W. H., Dupertuis, C. W. and McDermott, E. (1954). *Atlas of men*. New York: Harper.

Sheldon, W. H., Stevens, S. S. and Tucker, W. B. (1940). *The varieties of the human physique*. New York: Harper.

Shennan, S. (2000). Population, culture history and the dynamics of culture change. *Current Anthropology*, *41*, 811–836.

Sheppard, J. and Strathman, A. (1989). Attractiveness and height: The role of stature in dating preference, frequency of dating and perceptions of attractiveness. *Personality and Social Psychology Bulletin*, *15*, 617–627.

Shetty, P. S. and James, W. P. T. (1994). *Body mass index: A measure of chronic energy deficiency in adults*. Rome: Food and Agriculture Organisation of the United Nations, Food and Nutrition Paper 56.

Shors, A. R., Solomon, C., McTiernan, A. and White, E. (2001). Melanoma risk in relation to height, weight and exercise (United States). *Cancer Causes and Control*, *12*, 599–606.

Siever, M. D. (1994). Sexual orientation and gender as factors in socioculturally acquired vulnerability to body dissatisfaction and eating disorders. *Journal of Consulting and Clinical Psychology*, *62*, 252–260.

Sigall, H. and Ostrove, N. (1975). Beautiful but dangerous: Effects of offender's attractiveness and nature of the crime on juridic judgements. *Journal of Personality and Social Psychology*, *31*, 410–414.

Silberstein, L. R., Mishkind, M. E., Striegel-Moore, R. H., Timko, C. and Rodin, J. (1989). Men and their bodies: A comparison of homosexual and heterosexual men. *Psychosomatic Medicine*, *51*, 337–346.

Silverstein, B., Perdue, L., Peterson, B. and Kelly, E. (1986). The role of the mass media in promoting a thin standard of bodily attractiveness for women. *Sex Roles*, *14*, 519–533.

Simchuk, A. P. (2001). Frequency-dependent sexual selection in a natural population of oak leafroller moth (*Tortrix viridana* L.). *Tsitologiya i Genetika*, *35*, 25–29.

Simmons, L. W., Rhodes, G., Peters, M. and Koehler, N. (2004). Are human preferences for facial symmetry focussed on signals of developmental instability? *Behavioral Ecology*, *15*, 864–871.

Simpson, J. A. and Gangestad, S. W. (1991). Individual differences in sociosexuality: Evidence for convergent and discriminant validity. *Journal of Personality and Social Psychology*, *60*, 870–883.

Simpson, J. A. and Oriña, M. (2003). Strategic pluralism and context-specific mate preferences in humans. In K. Sterelny and J. Fitness (Eds.), *From mating to mentality* (pp. 39–70). Hove: Psychology Press.

Singh, D. (1993a). Adaptive significance of female physical attractiveness: Role of waist-to-hip ratio. *Journal of Personality and Social Psychology*, *65*, 292–307.

204   *References*

—— (1993b). Body shape and women's attractiveness. The critical role of waist-to-hip ratio. *Human Nature, 4,* 297–321.

—— (1994a). Is thin really beautiful and good? Relationship between waist-to-hip ratio (WHR) and female attractiveness. *Personality and Individual Differences, 16,* 123–132.

—— (1994b). Waist-to-hip ratio and judgements of attractiveness and healthiness of females' figures by male and female physicians. *International Journal of Obesity, 18,* 731–737.

—— (1994c). Body fat distribution and perception of desirable female body shape by young black men and women. *International Journal of Eating Disorders, 16,* 289–294.

—— (1995a). Female health, attractiveness and desirability for relationships: Role of breast asymmetry and WHR. *Ethology and Sociobiology, 16,* 465–481.

—— (1995b). Female judgement of male attractiveness and desirability for relationships: Role of waist-to-hip ratio and financial status. *Journal of Personality and Social Psychology, 69,* 1089–1101.

—— (2002). Female mate value at a glance: Relationship of waist-to-hip ratio to health, fecundity and attractiveness. *Human Ethology and Evolutionary Psychology, 23,* 81–91.

—— (2006). Universal allure of the hourglass figure: An evolutionary theory of female physical attractiveness. *Clinics in Plastic Surgery, 33,* 359–370.

Singh, D. and Luis, S. (1995). Ethnic and gender consensus for the effect of waist-to-hip ratio on judgements of women's attractiveness. *Human Nature, 6,* 51–65.

Singh, D. and Randall, P. K. (2007). Beauty is in the eye of the plastic surgeon: Waist–hip ratio (WHR) and women's attractiveness. *Personality and Individual Differences, 43,* 329–340.

Singh, D. and Young, R. K. (1995). Body weight, waist-to-hip ratio, breasts, and hips: Role in judgements of female attractiveness and desirability for relationships. *Ethology and Sociobiology, 16,* 483–507.

Singh, D. and Zambarano, R. J. (1997). Offspring sex ratio in women with android body fat distribution. *Journal of Human Biology, 69,* 545–556.

Singh, D., Davis, M. and Randall, P. (2000). Fluctuating ovulation: Lower WHR, enhanced self-perceived attractiveness, and increased sexual desire. Paper presented at Human Evolution and Behaviour Society meeting, London, 13–17 June.

Singh, D., Renn, P. and Singh, A. (in press). Did the perils of abdominal obesity affect depiction of feminine beauty in the sixteenth to eighteenth century British literature? Exploring the health and beauty link. *Proceedings of Royal Society of London B.*

Singh, R. and Ho, S. Y. (2000). Attitudes and attraction: A new test of the attraction, repulsion and similarity-dissimilarity asymmetry hypotheses. *British Journal of Social Psychology, 39,* 197–211.

Smith, K. L., Cornelissen, P. L. and Tovée, M. J. (2007a). Color 3D bodies and judgements of human female attractiveness. *Evolution and Human Behavior, 28,* 48–54.

Smith, K. L., Tovée, M. J., Hancock, P. J. B., Bateson, M., Cox, M. A. A. and Cornelissen, P. L. (2007b). An analysis of body shape attractiveness based on image statistics: Evidence for a dissociation between expressions of preference and shape discrimination. *Visual Cognition, 15,* 1–27.

Smith, S. M., McIntosh, W. D. and Bazzini, D. G. (1999). Are the beautiful good in

Hollywood? An investigation of the beauty-and-goodness stereotype on film. *Basic and Applied Social Psychology*, *21*, 69–80.

Smolak, L. (2006). Body image. In J. Worell and C. D. Goodheart (Eds.), *Handbook of girls' and women's psychological health: Gender and well-being across the lifespan* (pp. 69–76). New York: Oxford University Press.

Snow, J. T. and Harris, M. B. (1986). An analysis of weight and diet content in five women's magazines. *Journal of Obesity and Weight Regulation*, *5*, 194–214.

Snyder, M., Tanke, E. D. and Berscheid, E. (1977). Social perception and interpersonal behavior: On the self-fulfilling nature of social stereotypes. *Journal of Personality and Social Psychology*, *35*, 656–666.

Sobal, J. and Stunkard, A. J. (1989). Socio-economic status and obesity: A review of the literature. *Psychological Bulletin*, *105*, 260–275.

Soler, J. J., Cuervo, J. J., Møller, A. P. and de Lope, F. (1998). Nest building is a sexually selected behaviour in the barn swallow. *Ecology*, *56*, 1435–1442.

Solomon, M. R. and Schopler, J. (1978). The relationship of physical attractiveness and punitiveness: Is the linearity assumption out of line? *Personality and Social Psychology Bulletin*, *4*, 483–486.

Spenser, E. (1715/1936). Amoretti, XV: Sonnet 15. In R. E. Neil Dodge (Ed.), *The complete poetical works of Spenser*. Boston: Houghton Mifflin.

Sperling, M. B. and Borgaro, S. (1995). Attachment anxiety and reciprocity as moderators of interpersonal attraction. *Psychological Reports*, *76*, 323–335.

Spitzer, B. L., Henderson, K. A. and Zivian, M. T. (1999). Gender differences in population versus media body sizes: A comparison over four decades. *Sex Roles*, *40*, 545–565.

Sprecher, S. (1998). Insiders' perspectives on reasons for attraction to a close other. *Social Psychology Quarterly*, *61*, 287–300.

Spuhler, J. (1968). Assortative mating with respect to physical characteristics. *Social Biology*, *15*, 128–140.

Staats, C. K. and Staats, A. W. (1957). Meaning established by classical conditioning. *Journal of Experimental Social Psychology*, *54*, 74–80.

Staffieri, J. R. (1967). A study of social stereotypes of body image in children. *Journal of Personality and Social Psychology*, *7*, 101–104.

Stainton Rogers, W. and Stainton Rogers, R. (2001). *The psychology of gender and sexuality*. Maidenhead, UK: Open University Press.

Steele, V. (1995). *Fetish: Fashion, sex and power*. Oxford: Oxford University Press.

Stephan, C. W. and Langlois, J. H. (1984). Baby beautiful: Adult attributions of infant competence as a function of infant attractiveness. *Child Development*, *55*, 576–585.

Sterelny, K. and Griffiths, P. E. (1999). *Sex and death: An introduction to the philosophy of biology*. Chicago: University of Chicago Press.

Stevens, G., Owens, D. and Schaefer, E. (1990). Education and attractiveness in marriage choices. *Social Psychology Quarterly*, *53*, 62–70.

Stewart, J. E. (1980). Defendant's attractiveness as a factor in the outcome of criminal trials: An observational study. *Journal of Applied Social Psychology*, *10*, 348–361.

—— (1984), Appearance and punishment: The attraction–leniency effect in the courtroom. *Journal of Social Psychology*, *125*, 373–378.

Stice, E. (1998). Modelling of eating pathology and social reinforcement of the thin-ideal predict onset of bulimic symptoms. *Behaviour Research Therapy*, *36*, 931–944.

Stirn, A. (2004). Motivationen von Tätowierten und Gepiercten für ihre Körpermodifikationen [Motivations of tattooed and pierced for their body modifications]. *Zeitschrift für Klinische Psychologie, Psychiatrie und Psychotherapie, 51,* 43–58.

Stogdill, R. M. (1948). Personal factors associated with leadership: A survey of the literature. *Journal of Psychology, 25,* 35–71.

Stolz, K. C. and Griffiths, P. E. (2002). Dancing in the dark: Evolutionary psychology and the argument from design. In S. J. Scher and F. Rauscher (Eds.), *Evolutionary psychology: Alternative approaches* (pp. 135–160). Dordrecht: Kluwer.

Streeter, L. A., Krauss, R. M., Geller, V. J., Olson, C. T. and Apple, W. (1977). Pitch changes during attempted deception. *Journal of Personality and Social Psychology, 35,* 345–350.

Streeter, S. A. and McBurney, D. (2003). Waist–hip ratio and attractiveness: New evidence and a critique for a 'critical test.' *Evolution and Human Behaviour, 24,* 88–98.

Stunkard, A. J. (2000). Factors in obesity: Current views. In M. Pena and J. Bacallo (Eds.), *Obesity and poverty* (pp. 23–29). Washington, DC: PAHO.

Stunkard, A. J. and Sorensen, T. I. A. (1993). Obesity and socioeconomic status: A complex relation. *New England Journal of Medicine, 329,* 1036–1037.

Sugiyama, L. S. (2004). Is beauty in the context-sensitive adaptations of the beholder? Shiwiar use of waist-to-hip ratio in assessments of female mate value. *Evolution and Human Behaviour, 25,* 51–62.

—— (2005). Physical attractiveness in adaptationist perspective. In D. M. Buss (Ed.), *The handbook of evolutionary psychology* (pp. 293–343). New York: Wiley.

Susanne, C. and Lepage, Y. (1988). Assortative mating for anthropometric characteristics. In C. Mascie-Taylor and A. Boyce (Eds.), *Human mating patterns* (pp. 137–159). Cambridge: Cambridge University Press.

Swaddle, J. P. and Cuthill, I. C. (1994). Preference for symmetric males by female zebra finches. *Nature, 367,* 165–166.

—— (1995). Asymmetry and human facial attractiveness: symmetry may not always be beautiful. *Proceedings of the Royal Society of London B, 261,* 111–116.

Swami, V. (2006a). Darwin's legacy: What evolution means today. Invited talk given at Marxism 2006, London, July 9.

—— (2006b). The influence of body weight and shape in determining female and male physical attractiveness. In M. V. Kindes (Ed.), *Body image: New research* (pp. 35–61). New York: Nova Biomedical Books.

—— (2006c). Female physical attractiveness and body image disorders in Malaysia. *Malaysian Journal of Psychiatry, 14,* 3–7.

—— (2007). *The missing arms of Vénus de Milo: Reflections on the science of physical attractiveness.* Brighton: Book Guild.

—— (in press). Evolutionary psychology: 'New science of the mind' or 'Darwinian fundamentalism'? *Historical Materialism.*

Swami, V. and Furnham, A. (2006). The science of attraction. *The Psychologist, 19,* 362–365.

—— (Eds.) (2007a). *The body beautiful: Evolutionary and socio-cultural perspectives.* London: Macmillan.

—— (2007b). Big and beautiful: The body weight and shape preferences of 'fat admirers.' *Archives of Sexual Behavior,* under review.

—— (2007c). Unattractive, promiscuous and heavy drinkers: Perceptions of women with tattoos. Manuscript under review.

Swami, V. and Tovée, M. J. (2005a). Male physical attractiveness in Britain and Malaysia: A cross-cultural study. *Body Image: An International Journal of Research*, 2, 383–393.

—— (2005b). Female physical attractiveness in Britain and Malaysia: A cross-cultural study. *Body Image: An International Journal of Research*, 2, 115–128.

—— (2006a). Does hunger influence judgements of female physical attractiveness? *British Journal of Psychology*, 97, 353–363.

—— (2006b). The influence of body weight on the physical attractiveness preferences of feminist and non-feminist heterosexual women and lesbians. *Psychology of Women Quarterly*, 30, 252–257.

—— (2007a). Differences in attractiveness preferences between observers in low and high resource environments in Thailand. Manuscript under review.

—— (2007b). Perceptions of female body weight and shape among indigenous and urban Europeans. *Scandinavian Journal of Psychology*, 48, 43–50.

—— (in press). The muscular male: A comparison of the physical attractiveness preferences of gay and heterosexual men. *International Journal of Men's Health*.

Swami, V., Antonakopoulos, N., Tovée, M. J. and Furnham, A. (2006a). A critical test of the waist-to-hip ratio hypothesis of female physical attractiveness in Britain and Greece. *Sex Roles*, 54, 201–211.

Swami, V., Caprario, C., Tovée, M. J. and Furnham, A. (2006b). Female physical attractiveness in Britain and Japan: A cross-cultural study. *European Journal of Personality*, 20, 69–81.

Swami, V., Einon, D. and Furnham, A. (2006c). An investigation of the leg-to-body ratio as a human aesthetic criterion. *Body Image: An International Journal of Research*, 3, 317–323.

Swami, V., Poulogianni, K. and Furnham, A. (2006d). The influence of resource availability on preferences for human body weight and non-human objects. *Journal of Articles in Support of the Null Hypothesis*, 4, 17–28.

Swami, V., Einon, D., Furnham, A. and Sung, K.-M. (2007a). Perbezaan antara budaya dalam piliphan rupa badan perempuan [Cross-cultural differences in preferences for female body shape]. Manuscript under review.

Swami, V., Furnham, A., Georgiades, C. and Pang, L. (2007b). Evaluating self and partner physical attractiveness. *Body Image: An International Journal of Research*, 4, 94–101.

Swami, V., Furnham, A., Shah, K., McClelland, A. and Baguma, P. (2007c). Body mass index, waist-to-hip ratio and breast size correlates of ratings of physical attractiveness in Britain and Uganda. Manuscript under review.

Swami, V., Gray, M. and Furnham, A. (2007d). The female nude in Rubens: Disconfirmatory evidence of the waist-to-hip ratio hypothesis of female physical attractiveness. *Imagination, Cognition and Personality*, 26, 136–147.

Swami, V., Greven, C. and Furnham, A. (2007e). More than just skin-deep? A pilot study integrating physical and non-physical factors in the perception of physical attractiveness. *Personality and Individual Differences*, 42, 563–572.

Swami, V., Jones, J., Einon, D. and Furnham, A. (2007f). Men's preferences for women's profile waist-to-hip ratio, breast size and ethnic group in Britain and South Africa. Manuscript under review.

Swami, V., Knight, D., Tovée, M. J., Davies, P. and Furnham, A. (2007g). Perceptions of female body size in Britain and the South Pacific. *Body Image: An International Journal of Research*, 4, 219–223.

Swami, V., Rozmus-Wrzesinska, M., Voracek, M., Haubner, T., Danel, D., Pawłowski, B. *et al.* (2007h). The influence of skin tone, body weight and hair colour on perceptions of women's attractiveness, health and fertility: A cross-cultural investigation. Manuscript under review.

Swami, V., Smith, J., Tsiokris, A., Georgiades, C., Sangareau, Y., Tovée, M. J., *et al.* (2007i). Male physical attractiveness in Britain and Greece: A cross-cultural study. *Journal of Social Psychology, 147,* 15–26.

Swami, V., Tovée, M. J. and Furnham, A. (2007j). The relative contributions of profile waist-to-hip ratio and body mass index to judgements of female attractiveness in three societies. Manuscript under review.

Swami, V., Chan, F., Wong, V., Furnham, A. and Tovée, M. J. (in press, a). Weight-based discrimination in occupational hiring and helping behaviour. *Journal of Applied Social Psychology.*

Swami, V., Neto, F., Tovée, M. J. and Furnham, A. (in press, b). Preference for female body weight and shape in three European countries. *European Psychologist.*

Swim, J. T. and Stangor, C. (1998). *Prejudice from the target's perspective.* Santa Barbara, CA: Academic Press.

Symons, D. (1979). *The evolution of human sexuality.* New York: Oxford University Press.

—— (1987). If we're all Darwinians, what the fuss about? In C. B. Crawford, M. S. Smith and D. L. Krevs (Eds.), *Sociobiology and psychology: Ideas, issues and applications* (pp. 121–146). Hillsdale, NJ: Lawrence Erlbaum Associates, Inc.

—— (1989). A critique of Darwinian anthropology. *Ethology and Sociobiology, 10,* 131–144.

—— (1990). Adaptiveness and adaptation. *Ethology and Sociobiology, 11,* 427–444.

—— (1992). On the use and misuse of Darwinism in the study of human behaviour. In J. H. Barkow, L. Cosmides and J. Tooby (Eds.), *The adapted mind: Evolutionary psychology and the generation of culture* (pp. 137–159). New York: Oxford University Press.

—— (1995). Beauty is the adaptations of the beholder: The evolutionary psychology of human female sexual attractiveness. In P. R. Abramhamson and S. D. Pinker (Eds.), *Sexual nature/sexual culture* (pp. 80–118). Chicago: Chicago University Press.

Sypeck, M. F., Gray, J. J. and Ahrens, A. H. (2004). No longer just a pretty face: Fashion magazines' depictions of ideal female beauty from 1959 to 1999. *International Journal of Eating Disorders, 36,* 342–347.

Sypeck, M. F., Gray, J. J., Etu, S. F., Ahrens, A. H., Mosimann, J. E. and Wiseman, C. V. (2006). Cultural representations of thinness in women, redux: *Playboy* magazine's depiction of beauty from 1979 to 1999. *Body Image: An International Journal of Research, 3,* 229–235.

Tan, D. T. Y. and Singh, R. (1995). Attitudes and attraction: A developmental study of the similarity–attraction and dissimilarity–repulsion hypotheses. *Personality and Social Psychology Bulletin, 21,* 975–986.

Tassinary, L. G. and Hansen, K. A. (1998). A critical test of the waist-to-hip ratio hypothesis of female physical attractiveness. *Psychological Science, 9,* 150–155.

Taylor, S. E. (1998). The social being in social psychology. In D. T. Gilbert, S. T. Fiske and G. Lindzey (Eds.), *The handbook of social psychology* (4th edn, Vol. 1, pp. 58–95). New York: McGraw-Hill.

Taylor, S. E. and Brown, J. D. (1994). Positive illusions and well-being revisited: Separating fact from fiction. *Psychological Bulletin, 116,* 21–27.

Taylor, S. E., Peplau, L. and Sears, D. (1997). *Social psychology*. Englewood Cliffs, NJ: Prentice Hall.

Terry, R. L. and Krantz, J. H. (1993). Dimensions of trait attributions associated with eyeglasses, men's facial hair and women's hair length. *Journal of Applied Social Psychology*, *23*, 1757–1769.

Teti, V. (1995). Food and fatness in Calabria. In I. De Garine and N. J. Pollock (Eds.), *Social aspects of obesity* (pp. 3 30). Amsterdam: Gordon and Breach.

Thelen, T. H. (1983). Minority type human mate preference. *Social Biology*, *30*, 162–180.

Thibaut, J. and Kelley, H. (1959). *The social psychology of groups*. New York: Wiley.

Thiessen, D. and Gregg, B. (1980). Human assortative mating and genetic equilibrium: An evolutionary perspective. *Ethology and Sociobiology*, *1*, 111–140.

Thompson, J. K., Heinberg, L. J., Altabe, M. and Tantleff-Dunn, S. (1999). Socio-cultural theory: The media and society. In J. K. Thompson (Ed.), *Exacting beauty: Theory, assessment and treatment of body image disturbance* (pp. 85–124). Washington, DC: American Psychological Association.

Thompson, M. S. and Keith, V. M. (2001). The blacker the berry: Gender, skin tone, self-esteem and self-efficacy. *Gender and Society*, *15*, 336–357.

Thornhill, R. (1992). Fluctuating asymmetry and the mating system of the Japanese scorpionfly, *Panorpa japonica*. *Animal Behavior*, *44*, 867–879.

Thornhill, R. and Gangestad, S. W. (1993). Human facial beauty: Averageness, symmetry and parasite resistance. *Human Nature*, *4*, 237–269.

—— (1999). Facial attractiveness. *Trends in Cognitive Science*, *3*, 452–460.

Thornhill, R. and Grammer, K. (1999). The body and face of women: One ornament that signals quality? *Evolution and Human Behavior*, *20*, 105–120.

Thornhill, R., Gangestad, S. W. and Comer, R. (1995). Human female orgasm and mate fluctuating asymmetry. *Animal Behaviour*, *50*, 1601–1615.

Tietje, L. and Cresap, S. (2005). Is lookism unjust? The ethics of aesthetics and public policy implications. *Journal of Liberterian Studies*, *19*, 31–50.

Tiggemann, M. and Rothblum, E. D. (1988). Gender differences in social consequences of perceived overweight in the United States and Australia. *Sex Roles*, *18*, 75–86.

Tinbergen, N. (1957). *The herring gulls' world*. Oxford: Oxford University Press.

Tobias, P. V. (1957). Bushmen of the Kalahari. *Man*, *36*, 33–40.

Todd, P. M. and Miller, G. F. (1993). Parental guidance suggested: How parental imprinting evolves through sexual selection as an adaptive learning mechanism. *Adaptive Behavior*, *2*, 5–47.

Tomkinson, G. R. and Olds, T. S. (2000). Physiological correlates of bilaterial symmetry in humans. *International Journal of Sports Medicine*, *21*, 545–550.

Tooby, J. and Cosmides, L. (1990a). The past explains the present: Emotional adaptations and the structure of ancestral environments. *Ethology and Sociobiology*, *11*, 375–424.

—— (1990b). On the universality of human nature and the uniqueness of the individual: The role of genetics and adaptation. *Journal of Personality*, *58*, 17–67.

—— (1992). The psychological foundations of culture. In J. H. Barkow, L. Cosmides and J. Tooby (Eds.), *The adapted mind: Evolutionary psychology and the generation of culture* (pp. 19–136). New York: Oxford University Press.

—— (1995). Foreword. In S. Baron-Cohen, *Mindblindness* (pp. xi–xviii). Cambridge, MA: MIT Press.

Tovée, M. J. and Cornelissen, P. L. (1999). The mystery of human beauty. *Nature*, *399*, 215–216.

—— (2001). Female and male perceptions of female physical attractiveness in front-view and profile. *British Journal of Psychology*, *92*, 391–402.

Tovée, M., Mason, S., Emery, J., McCluskey, S. and Cohen-Tovée, E. (1997). Super-models: Stick insects or hourglasses? *Lancet*, *350*, 1474–1475.

Tovée, M. J., Reinhardt, S., Emery, J. and Cornelissen, P. (1998). Optimum body-mass index and maximum sexual attractiveness. *Lancet*, *352*, 548.

Tovée, M. J., Maisey, D. S., Emery, J. L. and Cornelissen, P. L. (1999). Visual cues to female physical attractiveness. *Proceedings of the Royal Society of London B*, *266*, 211–218.

Tovée, M. J., Tasker, K. and Benson, P. J. (2000). Is symmetry a visual cue to attractiveness in the human female body? *Evolution and Human Behavior*, *21*, 191–200.

Tovée, M. J., Brown, J. E. and Jacobs, D. (2001). Maternal waist–hip ratio does not predict child gender. *Proceedings of the Royal Society London B*, *268*, 1007–1010.

Tovée, M. J., Hancock, P., Mahmoodi, S., Singleton, B. R. R. and Cornelissen, P. L. (2002). Human female attractiveness: Waveform analysis of body shape. *Proceedings of the Royal Society of London B*, *269*, 2205–2213.

Tovée, M. J., Benson, P. J., Emery, J. L., Mason, S. M. and Cohen-Tovée, E. M. (2003). Measurement of body size and shape perception in eating-disordered and control observers using body-shape software. *British Journal of Psychology*, *94*, 501–516.

Tovée, M. J., Swami, V., Furnham, A. and Mangalparsad, R. (2006). Changing perceptions of attractiveness as observers are exposed to a different culture. *Evolution and Human Behavior*, *27*, 443–456.

Tovée, M. J., Furnham, A. and Swami, V. (2007). Healthy body equals beautiful body? Changing perceptions of health and attractiveness with shifting socioeconomic status. In V. Swami and A. Furnham (Eds.), *The body beautiful: Evolutionary and socio-cultural perspectives*. London: Macmillan.

Townsend, J. M. and Levy, G. D. (1990). Effects of potential partners' physical attractiveness and socioeconomic status on sexuality and partner selection. *Archives of Sexual Behavior*, *19*, 149–164.

Treloar, C., Porteous, J., Hassan, F., Kasniyah, N., Lakshmandu, M., Sama, M. *et al.* (1999). The cross-cultural context of obesity: An INCLEN multicentre collaborative study. *Health and Place*, *5*, 279–286.

Trivers, R. (1972). Parental investment and sexual selection. In B. Campbell (Ed.), *Sexual selection and the descent of man* (pp. 136–179). New York: Aldine de Gruyrer.

—— (1985). *Social evolution*. Menlo Park, CA: Benjamin Cummings.

Twine, R. (2002). Physiognomy, phrenology and the temporality of the body. *Body and Society*, *8*, 67–88.

Ucko, P. J. (1962). The interpretation of prehistoric anthropomorphic figurines. *Journal of the Royal Anthropological Institute of Great Britain and Ireland*, *92*, 38–54.

Urdy, R. J. (1971). *The social context of marriage* (2nd edn). Philadelphia, PN: J. B. Lippincott.

Van den Berghe, P. L. and Frost, P. (1986). Skin color preference, sexual dimorphism and sexual selection: A case of gene-culture co-evolution? *Ethnic and Racial Studies*, *9*, 87–113.

Van Dijk, N. (1991). The Hansel and Gretel syndrome: A critique of Houghton's cold adaptation hypothesis and an alternative model. *New Zealand Journal of Archae-ology*, *13*, 65–89.

Van Hooff, M. H., Voorhorst, F. J., Kaptein, M. B., Hirasing, R. A., Koppenaal, C. and Schoemaker, J. (2000). Insulin, androgen and gonadotrophin concentration, body mass index, and waist-to-hip ratio in the first years after menarche in girls with regular menstrual cycle, irregular menstrual cycle, or oligomenorrhea. *Journal of Clinical Endocrinology and Metabolism*, *85*, 1394–1400.

Vance, C. S. (1995). Social construction theory and sexuality. In M. Berger, B. Wallis and S. Watson (Eds.), *Constructing masculinity* (pp. 37–48). New York: Routledge.

Vittengl, J. R. and Holt, C. S. (2000). Getting acquainted: The relationship of self-disclosure and social attraction to positive affect. *Journal of Social and Personal Relationships*, *17*, 53–66.

Voland, E. (1988). Differential infant and child mortality in evolutionary perspective: Data from 17th to 19th century Ostfriesland (Germany). In L. Betzig, M. Borgerhff Mulder and P. W. Turke (Eds.), *Human reproductive behaviour: A Darwinian perspective* (pp. 253–262). Cambridge: Cambridge University Press.

Voracek, M. and Fisher, M. L. (2002). Shapely centrefolds? Temporal change in body measures: Trend analysis. *British Medical Journal*, *325*, 1447–1448.

—— (2006). Success is all in the measures: Androgenousness, curvaceousness and starring frequencies in adult media actresses. *Archives of Sexual Behavior*, *35*, 297–304.

Wadden, T. A., Anderson, D. A., Foster, G. D., Bennett, A., Steinberg, C. and Sarwer, D. B. (2000). Obese women's perceptions of their physicians' weight management attitudes and practises. *Archives of Family Medicine*, *9*, 854–860.

Walrath, D. E. and Glantz, M. M. (1996). Sexual dimorphism in the pelvic midplane and its relationship to Neandertal reproductive patterns. *American Journal of Physical Anthropology*, *100*, 89–100.

Walsh, B. T. (1997). Eating disorders. In A. Tasman, J. Kay and J. A. Lieberman (Eds.), *Psychiatry* (Vol. 2, pp. 1202–1216). New York: Saunders.

Walster, E., Walster, G. W., Piliavin, J. and Schmidt, L. (1973). Playing hard-to-get: Understanding an elusive phenomenon. *Journal of Personality and Social Psychology*, *26*, 113–121.

Walster, E., Walster, G. W. and Berscheid, E. (1978). *Equity theory and research*. Boston, MA: Allyn and Bacon.

Wang, J. X., Davies, M. and Norman, R. J. (2000). Body mass and probability of pregnancy during assisted reproduction to treatment: Retrospective study. *Lancet*, *321*, 1320–1321.

Warren, B. L. (1970). Socioeconomic achievement and religion: The American case. In E. O. Laumann (Ed.), *Social stratification: Research and theory for the 1970s* (pp. 130–155). Indianapolis, IL: Bobbs-Merrill.

Washburn, D. and Humphrey, D. (2001). Symmetries in the mind: Production, per-ception and preference for seven one-dimensional patterns. *Visual Arts Research*, *70*, 57–68.

Wass, P., Waldenstrom, U., Rossner, S. and Hellberg, D. (1997). An android body fat distribution in females impairs the pregnancy rate of in-vitro fertilisation-embryo transfer. *Human Reproduction*, *12*, 2057–2060.

Watkins, L. M. and Johnston, L. (2000). Screening job applicants: The impact of physical attractiveness and application quality. *International Journal of Selection and Assessment*, *8*, 76–84.

Watson, D., Klohnen, E. C., Casillas, A., Nus Simms, E., Haig, J. and Berry, D. S. (2004). Match makers and deal breakers: Analyses of assortative mating in newly-wed couples. *Journal of Personality*, *72*, 1029–1068.

Waynforth, D. (2001). Mate choice trade-offs and women's preference for physically attractive men. *Human Nature*, *12*, 207–219.

Waynforth, D. and Dunbar, R. (1995). Conditional mate choice strategies in humans: Evidence from lonely hearts advertisements. *Behaviour*, *132*, 735–779.

Weeden, J. and Sabini, J. (2005). Physical attractiveness and health in western societies: A review. *Psychological Bulletin*, *131*, 635–653.

Weitz, S. (1977). *Sex roles: Biological, psychological and social foundations*. New York: Oxford University Press.

Wells, P. A., Wilmoth, T. and Russell, R. J. (1995). Does fortune favour the bald? Psychological correlates of hair loss in males. *British Journal of Psychology*, *86*, 337–344.

West, C. and Zimmerman, D. H. (1987). Doing gender. *Gender and Society*, *1*, 125–151.

Wetsman, A. and Marlowe, F. (1999). How universal are preferences for female waist-to-hip ratios? Evidence from the Hadza of Tanzania. *Evolution and Human Behaviour*, *20*, 219–228.

Whitcher, S. J. and Fisher, J. D. (1979). Multidimensional reaction to therapeutic touch in hospital setting. *Journal of Personality and Social Psychology*, *37*, 87–96.

Wichstrom, L. (1994). Predictors of Norwegian adolescents' sunbathing and use of sunscreen. *Health Psychology*, *13*, 412–420.

Wiederman, M. W. (1993). Evolved gender differences in mate preferences: Evidence from personal advertisements. *Ethology and Sociobiology*, *14*, 331–352.

Wiggins, J., Wiggins, N. and Conger, J. (1968). Correlates of heterosexual somatic preferences. *Journal of Personality and Social Psychology*, *10*, 82–90.

Wilkinson, J., Ben-Tovim, D. and Walker, M. (1994). An insight into the personal significance of weight and shape in large Samoan women. *International Journal of Obesity*, *18*, 602–606.

Willet, W. C., Manson, J. E., Stampfer, M. J., Colditz, G. A., Rosner, B., Speizer, F. E. *et al.* (1995). Weight, weight change and coronary heart disease in women: Risk within the 'normal' weight range. *Journal of the American Medical Association*, *273*, 461–465.

Williams, J. H. (Ed.) (1979). *Psychology of women*. New York: Norton.

Williams, S. R. P., Goodfellow, J., Davies, B., Bell, W., McDowell, I. and Jones, E. (2000). Somatypes and angiographically determined atherosclerotic coronary artery disease in men. *American Journal of Human Biology*, *12*, 128–138.

Wilson, J. M. B., Tripp, D. A. and Boland, F. J. (2005). The relative contributions of waist-to-hip ratio and body mass index to judgements of attractiveness. *Sexualities, Evolution and Gender*, *7*, 245–267.

Wiseman, C. V., Gray, J. J., Mosimann, J. E. and Ahrens, A. H. (1992). Cultural expectations of thinness in women: An update. *International Journal of Eating Disorders*, *11*, 85–89.

Wogalter, M. S. and Hosie, J. A. (1991). Effects of cranial and facial hair on perceptions of age and person. *Journal of Social Psychology*, *131*, 589–591.

Wohlrab, S., Stahl, J. and Kappeler, P. M. (2007). Modifying the body: Motivations for getting tattooed and pierced. *Body Image: An International Journal of Research*, *4*, 219–223.

Wolf, N. (1990). *The beauty myth*. London: Chatto and Windus.

Wong, B. B. M. and Candolin, U. (2005). How is female mate choice affected by male competition? *Biological Reviews of the Cambridge Philosophical Society, 80*, 1–13.

Wood, D. R. (1986). Self-perceived masculinity between bearded and non-bearded males. *Perceptual and Motor Skills, 62*, 769–770.

Wood, L. E. P. (2006). Obesity, waist–hip ratio and hunter-gatherers. *BJOG: An International Journal of Obstetrics and Gynaecology, 113*, 1110–1116.

Wuensch, K. L. and Moore, C. H. (2004). Effects of physical attractiveness on evaluations of a male employee's allegation of sexual harassment by his female employer. *Journal of Social Psychology, 144*, 207–217.

Wuensch, K. L., Castellow, W. A. and Moore, C. H. (1991). Effects of defendant attractiveness and type of crime on juridic judgement. *Journal of Social Behaviour and Personality, 5*, 547–562.

Yang, C.-F. J., Gray, P. and Pope Jr., H. G. (2005). Male body image in Taiwan versus the west: *Yanggang Zhiqi* meets the Adonis complex. *American Journal of Psychiatry, 162*, 263–269.

Yarmouk, U. (2000). The effect of presentation modality on judgements of honesty and attractiveness. *Social Behavior and Personality, 28*, 269–278.

Young, T. J. and French, L. A. (1998). Height and perceived competence of US presidents. *Perceptual and Motor Skills, 87*, 321–322.

Yu, D. W. and Shepard, G. H. (1998). Is beauty in the eye of the beholder? *Nature, 396*, 321–322.

—— (1999). The mystery of female beauty – reply. *Nature, 399*, 216.

Yu, D. W., Proulx, S. R. and Shepard, G. H. (2007). Masculinity, culture and the paradox of the leks. In. V. Swami and A. Furnham (Eds.), *The body beautiful: Evolutionary and socio-cultural perspectives*. London: Macmillan.

Zaadstra, B. M., Seidell, J. C., van Noord, P. A. H., te Velde, E. R., Habbema, J. D. F., Vrieswijk, B. *et al.* (1993). Fat and female fecundity: Prospective study of effect of body fat distribution on conception rates. *British Medical Journal, 306*, 484–487.

Zahavi, A. (1975). Mate selection – a selection for a handicap. *Journal of Theoretical Biology, 53*, 205–214.

Zajonc, R. B. (1968). Attitudinal effects of mere exposure. *Journal of Personality and Social Psychology, 9*, 1–27.

Zanna, M. P., Kiesler, C. A. and Pilkonis, D. A. (1970). Positive and negative affect established by classical conditioning. *Journal of Personality and Social Psychology, 14*, 321–328.

Zebrowitz, L. A., Montepare, J. M. and Lee, H. K. (1993). They don't all look alike: Individuated impressions of other racial groups. *Journal of Personality and Social Psychology, 65*, 85–101.

Zebrowitz, L. A., Voinescu, L. and Collins, M. A. (1996). 'Wide-eyed' and 'crooked-faced': Determinants of perceived and real honesty across the life span. *Personality and Social Psychology Bulletin, 22*, 1258–1269.

Zelnik, M. (1969). Socioeconomic and seasonal variation in births: A replication. *Milbank Memorial Fund Quarterly, 57*, 159.

Zuckerman, M. and Driver, R. (1989). What sounds beautiful is good: The vocal attractiveness stereotype. *Journal of Nonverbal Behavior, 13*, 67–82.

Zuckerman, M., Hodgins, H. and Miyake, K. (1990). The vocal attractiveness stereotype: Replication and elaboration. *Journal of Nonverbal Behavior, 14*, 97–112.

Zuk, M. (1991). Parasites and bright birds: New data and a new prediction. In J. E. Loye and M. Zuk (Eds.), *Ecology, behaviour and evolution of bird-parasite interactions* (pp. 317–327). Oxford: Oxford University Press.

—— (1992). The role of parasites in sexual selection: Current evidence and future direction. *Advances in the Study of Behaviour*, *21*, 39–68.

Index

Note: **bold** page numbers denote references to Figures/Tables.